"The Yankees' famed 'Murderers' Row' era wasn't just about the power of Babe Ruth and Lou Gehrig. There were Hall of Fame–bound pitchers on that great team as well, none more prominent than the colorful local star Waite Hoyt, whose life story continues to fascinate students of the game's history."

—**Marty Appel**, Yankees historian and author of *Pinstripe Empire*

"Manners's skillfully edited and seamless narrative, compiled from Hall of Famer Waite Hoyt's lifetime of memories, is a real baseball treasure. Success, failure, doubts, and achievements, in baseball and Hoyt's personal life, are all here in his own words. This book will enhance Hoyt's status as a baseball star, as well as a man."

—**Alan D. Gaff**, author of *Lou Gehrig: The Lost Memoir*

"A great read! Manners makes the Waite Hoyt story—especially 'you-are-there' material about Babe Ruth and other Yankee legends—spring to life."

—**Rick Burton**, David B. Falk Professor
of Sport Management at Syracuse University

"An insider's view of Babe Ruth and Lou Gehrig, with intimate stories about Waite Hoyt's life as a fifteen-year-old pro, his grand times with the 1927 Yankees, his twenty-four seasons in the Cincinnati Reds radio booth, and most revealingly his showdown with alcohol. Full of honesty, intimacy, and hard-knocks inspiration. I couldn't put it down."

—**John Erardi**, author of *Tony Pérez: From Cuba to Cooperstown*

Schoolboy

Schoolboy

The Untold Journey of a Yankees Hero

Waite Hoyt with Tim Manners

Foreword by Bob Costas

University of Nebraska Press · Lincoln

The University of Nebraska Press is part of a land-grant
institution with campuses and programs on the past,
present, and future homelands of the Pawnee, Ponca,
Otoe-Missouria, Omaha, Dakota, Lakota, Kaw, Cheyenne,
and Arapaho Peoples, as well as those of the relocated
Ho-Chunk, Sac and Fox, and Iowa Peoples.

∞

Library of Congress Cataloging-in-Publication Data
Names: Hoyt, Waite, 1899–1984 author. | Manners, Tim,
author. | Costas, Bob, 1952– writer of foreword.
Title: Schoolboy : the untold journey of a Yankees hero /
Waite Hoyt with Tim Manners ; Foreword by Bob Costas.
Description: Lincoln : University of Nebraska Press,
[2024]
Identifiers: LCCN 2023044069
ISBN 9781496236791 (hardback)
ISBN 9781496238641 (epub)
ISBN 9781496238658 (pdf)
Subjects: LCSH: Hoyt, Waite, 1899–1984. | Baseball
players—United States—Biography. | Pitchers
(Baseball)—United States—Biography. | New York
Yankees (Baseball team)—History. | BISAC: BIOGRAPHY
& AUTOBIOGRAPHY / Personal Memoirs | SPORTS &
RECREATION / Baseball / History
Classification: LCC GV865.H69 A3 2024 | DDC
796.357/092 [B]—dc23/eng/20231005
LC record available at https://lccn.loc.gov/2023044069

Set in ITC New Baskerville by A. Shahan.

All photographs are courtesy of Chris Hoyt, unless
otherwise noted.
Frontispiece. The Power Trio: (*left to right*) Babe Ruth,
Lou Gehrig, Waite Hoyt.

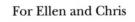

For Ellen and Chris

This memoir has been deduced from the way I have found life and the conditions of my chosen profession. They are individually mine. If somebody differs from me, why, that's all right. Let them have their opinions, but I will retain mine.

—Waite "Schoolboy" Hoyt

Contents

Part 3

Foreword

BOB COSTAS

UNTIL NOW, HERE'S WHAT I KNEW about Waite Hoyt: He was the pitching ace of the 1927 Murderers' Row Yankees. He wasn't Lefty Grove or Walter Johnson but was good enough to make the Hall of Fame.

He was a particularly close friend of Babe Ruth, wrote about that friendship in a book entitled *Babe Ruth as I Knew Him*, and, as the longtime radio voice of the Cincinnati Reds, enlivened his broadcasts with anecdotes featuring the Bambino. Those broadcasts were done in a unique past-tense style. The standard call would be "Pinson swings, and there's a fly ball to deep center. Willie Mays racing back, and he makes a running catch in front of the wall." In Hoyt's telling it became "Pinson hit a long fly ball to center, and Mays made the catch on the warning track"—almost as if he were doing a teletype re-creation. Okay, give him this—it was distinctive.

It turns out there was a whole lot more worth knowing. Hoyt had a life nearly as colorful and adventurous as the Babe's, a long life filled with one interesting episode after another. He was a vaudevillian, man about town, loser of several battles with the bottle, before getting clean and staying that way through the second half of his epic life. He played for John McGraw, Miller Huggins, and Connie Mack—and with three dozen teammates who later made the Hall of Fame themselves.

And all that is just the Cliff Notes. Read on.

Preface

TIM MANNERS

FOUR YEARS AGO, I WAS HAVING dinner with Waite "Schoolboy" Hoyt's son Chris and casually asked him why his Baseball Hall of Fame father, the ace pitcher of the legendary 1927 Yankees, had never published an autobiography. Before I knew it, eight banker's boxes of Waite Hoyt's notes, letters, interview transcripts, memoir attempts, and other recollections were sitting on my front porch.

As I began snapping the jigsaw pieces within those boxes into a narrative arc, it became clear that Waite Hoyt's significance was more than that of a formerly famous pitcher whose fastball was every bit as vital to the birth of the New York Yankees dynasty as Babe Ruth's and Lou Gehrig's home runs.

It was a reflection of an entire era, the heart of twentieth-century America, from a deeply introspective, complex, and conflicted hero who deserved to be better remembered than he was. Most important, it imparted what he learned and wanted to share with others about his life's choices and the paradox of his success.

Hoyt was in a knot over whether he should have done something else with his life—that is, something other than becoming the best pitcher on arguably the greatest baseball team of all time. Think about it: just 1 percent of Major League Baseball players are enshrined at Cooperstown, and yet Hoyt marked his induction into the National Baseball Hall of Fame by suggesting that he could have made a different career choice.

What was he thinking?

Hoyt's improbable journey began when the 1915 New York Giants signed him as a high school junior, for no pay and a five-dollar bonus. After nearly having both his hands amputated and cavorting with men twice his age in the tawdry, hardscrabble Minor Leagues, he somehow ended up as the ace pitcher of the legendary Yankees.

Over his twenty-three-year professional baseball career, Hoyt won 237 big league games across 3,845⅔ innings and one locker room brawl with Babe Ruth. He also became a vaudeville star who swapped dirty jokes with Mae West and drank champagne with Al Capone, a philosophizer who bonded with Lou Gehrig over the meaning of life, and a funeral director who left a body chilling in his trunk while pitching an afternoon game at Yankee Stadium.

Within these pages, Hoyt shares his thoughts on famous moments in baseball history, such as when he completed twenty-seven innings without allowing an earned run over three games of the 1921 World Series. He does not hold back in assessing legends like Ty Cobb, Stan Musial, Rogers Hornsby, and Pete Rose, not just as players but also as people.

He provides a window into three of the best-known baseball managers of all time: John McGraw, Miller Huggins, and Connie Mack. He waxes poetic over the art of pitching and how the game and its players changed—and didn't—over his lifetime. Indeed, most of Hoyt's insights remain applicable today.

After retiring from baseball at thirty-eight and coming to terms with his alcoholism, Hoyt found some happiness as a family man and a beloved, pioneering Cincinnati Reds radio sportscaster. To this day, he is fondly remembered in the Queen City, particularly for his fanboy tribute to Babe Ruth on the day the slugger died. Hoyt spoke on-air eloquently for more than an hour and a half, from the heart, without notes.

Hoyt was, in fact, one of the very first former professional athletes to cross over as a gameday announcer. Conventional thinking at the time was that players were too dumb and inarticulate to be on the radio. True to form, Hoyt, who had a Websterian vocabulary spiked with a Brooklyn accent, defied the odds and cut his own path.

Oh, and by the way, he also took up oil painting as a hobby and sold thirty-nine of his works, including several commissioned pieces. He said he was happier painting than he ever was pitching.

Reanimating Waite Hoyt's amazing, untold story was like stealing bases for me. As a genetically ordained editor, I never had so much fun as I did blue-penciling his journey.

I made a career of crafting and publishing profiles of high-profile marketing executives from companies including Procter & Gamble, Coca-Cola, and Disney by recording our conversations and then organizing their words to tell the story. It didn't feel right to filter, dilute, and potentially pollute their thoughts with mine. I used the same technique to ghostwrite hundreds of essays for executives of marketing thought leaders from Saatchi & Saatchi, J. Walter Thompson, and Ogilvy & Mather, including Chris Hoyt.

Naturally, I pieced together the boxed fragments of a remarkable, yet mostly buried, life in Waite Hoyt's own inimitable style. The man was nearly forty-years dead, but his voice was very much alive and well (and remarkably like Chris's). It was only right that someone revered as a master storyteller should be allowed to tell his own story as it had never been told before.

Being a ghostwriter took on a whole new meaning for me.

It wasn't clear, at first, whether these eight banker's boxes contained sufficient material to complete a book as first-person memoir. When I found a bright blue, three-inch plastic binder nestled in box number five, however, I knew I had something.

In it were the yellowed transcripts of interviews with the baseball legend, recorded by his niece for her own intended biography, some four years before Hoyt passed. Ellen Frell Levy graciously gave her permission to use these verbatim transcripts, which, with editing and arranging, provided the backbone of this book.

For the rest, I filled in with bits and pieces of Hoyt's own previous memoir attempts and the transcript of an epic speech he gave before Alcoholics Anonymous, along with snippets of various letters and notes, some of which provided critical guidance as to how he wanted his memoir to read and what he wanted to accomplish.

He envisioned his story as that not only of a baseball player but also of a man in conflict with himself. That conflict played out on multiple levels; Waite Hoyt was complicated. Athletic and aesthetic. Disciplined and delinquent. Refined and rough. Famous and forgotten.

I first met Chris Hoyt in 1982. I was just starting a public relations practice, found his name in a directory of local marketing consultants, and mailed him a form letter that opened with "Some guys get all the press." To this day, he insists the letter was mimeographed in blue ink and reeked of formaldehyde. Nevertheless, he called me.

Chris ranted about the broken, adversarial relationship between big brand manufacturers and retailers, which eventually developed into a breakthrough concept he developed called co-marketing (later evolving into shopper marketing) in which the two parties cooperated to improve the shopping experience for consumers.

We collaborated on opinion essays and speeches. I arranged media interviews. About twenty years in, Chris suggested I launch a business journal centered on the brand and retail experience. *The Hub* magazine, which featured interviews with high-profile retail and marketing executives, and at one time was displayed alongside *Forbes, Fortune,* and *Harvard Business Review* in Barnes & Noble stores, was also a platform for Chris and me to originate industry-standard research reports and white papers.

Thirty-five years later, I could trace 90 percent of my business, directly or indirectly, to Chris because he recommended me to anyone who would listen. He claims that I had the same effect on his consulting practice.

I had known Chris for at least two years before he first mentioned his father.

We were driving back to Connecticut from a meeting at Ogilvy & Mather some thirty years ago, and I think he was just bored and trying to make conversation. "My father was a Hall of Fame pitcher for the 1927 New York Yankees," he intoned out of nowhere, giving me a sideways glance and then waiting for my reaction.

I sat up straight and excitedly asked, "What was his name?" When he replied, "Waite Hoyt," I nearly said, "Who . . . What Hoyt?" I had no idea who he was. How was it possible that someone so accomplished and important to American popular culture and history was unknown to me?

As it turned out, I didn't know even one-tenth what made this man so fascinating.

When Waite Hoyt died in 1984, he left behind a legacy unlike that of any other American sports or pop-culture figure. He was practically the quintessential twentieth-century American: baseball, vaudeville, Prohibition, Coney Island—what says 1920s America more than those four things?

Perhaps most of all, he was a raconteur who punctuated his life story with awe-inspiring and jaw-dropping anecdotes, from jumping the gates at Ebbets Field as a kid to bottoming out as an aging alcoholic in a seedy Cincinnati bar.

Some of Hoyt's vignettes are funny, many are poignant, and others are tragic, but he never flinches from an unsparing account of his remarkable, and perplexingly paradoxical, eighty-four-year odyssey.

Schoolboy

Prologue

Brick by Brick

A CONFLUENCE OF SHORT, NARROW thoroughfares—Sullivan, Empire, Flatbush—formed the boundary of the famous home of the Brooklyn Dodgers, Ebbets Field. The street trio came to a point at the main entrance known in more glamorous days as the rotunda. It was marble-floored and domed with blinking stars in a painted sky, trimmed with small, caged windows, the ticket booths.

The almost-square block on which Ebbets Field stood had at one time been nothing more than a huge hole, some thirty feet deep, sheltering squads of squatters who had existed there like ground moles for years. Eviction notices were served and the hole filled in, and I watched Ebbets Field as it was built, brick by brick.

Ebbets was an edifice of charm to Brooklynites the day it opened, in 1913. I was only twelve years old at the time and had no idea of what was to come.

Twenty-five years later, May 16, 1938, to be exact, the place where I pulled on my first big league uniform was also where my jersey and socks came off for the very last time.

The dam broke, and my tears poured. I was engulfed by the terrible realization that it was all over. The life I had lived, loved, and believed would never end could not be revived. I just stared at Ebbets Field from outside its gates, thinking, stupidly, *Take me back—I'm not ready to quit. I want to go on.*

The saddest day for someone who has played professional baseball for twenty-three years has got to be the day he is dismissed forever—carrying inside him the gnawing, biting knowledge that it is over. Never again will he accept the challenge of the game or continue to perpetuate the dream he so fantastically pieced together as an impressionable youngster.

For me, the saddest day had arrived. It was over. Worse than that, it ended in tomb-like silence, steeped in bitter humiliation.

I had no quarrel with my release. I was thirty-eight years old. I had served my time. I expected the calamity. But when it came, it caught me unprepared, and to make a bad situation worse, none of the officials of the Brooklyn club, nor its manager, was gracious enough to say goodbye, or even offer an expression of good luck. Not even close. I arrived at Ebbets Field at about 12:30, and as I entered the clubhouse, I saw Heinie Manush and Roy Spencer standing by their lockers, still in their street clothes. I asked, "What's with you guys—a day off or something?" Manush didn't crack a smile. "You'll find out," he said, almost to himself.

My locker was the last one at the end of a line. When I reached my chair, a Western Union telegram was laying on the seat with other mail. I sensed what was to come, and there it was:

> Burleigh asked me to advise you he is giving you unconditional release today stop he will see you at clubhouse but we did not want you to read it in papers first and could not reach you on telephone.
>
> *John McDonald*

My arm was spent, my legs were gone, and my time was up. I was not the only one. The Dodgers, that year, were a shambles of a ballclub. Ebbets Field itself showed unmistakable signs of severe wear, tear, and neglect. It used to be a wonderful park, similar in atmosphere to Wrigley Field in Chicago, one of those small diamonds where everybody knew each other. You'd have box seats and wave across the field to somebody else on the other side. This was my initiation into big league baseball.

In right-center field, to the left of the scoreboard, was a big gate. It was only used for trucks that brought in provisions for the concession stands and things like that. It wasn't for the fans, but it featured two huge wooden, heavy oak doors, with cross beams to bolster them. If you were clever, you could put your foot on the lower beam, climb the gate, and get over it.

One day, when I was about fourteen, I scaled the fence out there in right-center field and dropped down inside. By George, Charlie Ebbets Jr., who was tall and lanky, happened to be there—not on the field but in a box out near the right-field fence—and he saw me. I was like a fellow late on making a double play. I didn't know which way to go. I stood there and hesitated, which gave Charlie his chance. He was a big, tall, mean son-of-a-gun and decided to take out after me.

I saw him running from the grandstand. He leaped over the box seats and started out toward the scoreboard along the right-field fence. I took off around the left-field fence and boy, I never ran so fast in my life. I slid around there with him after me. Then I got down to the box seats in left field, way over to the grandstand, and I leaped over the seats. He was gaining on me a little bit, and I took two steps at a time, up into the back of the grandstand. Spectators in the stands were cheering me on because nobody liked Charlie Ebbets Jr.

I skidded along the back of the grandstand, and I was afraid. I didn't know if I was going to get clouted or put in jail. Nevertheless, I ducked into the first door I saw, and what do you think it was? The ladies' room! I was afraid to go any further in, or to come out. I could hear the crowd yelling, and luckily the room was empty. A little while later, I peeked out, and everything seemed okay.

Charlie never did find me.

Yet there I was, nearly twenty-five years later, caught.

Everybody is, eventually.

It's so useless to tell any old ballplayer, "Well, you had your day." Listen, nobody can take away from me what I had in this game of baseball. For me, there were four episodes in particular. The first was being signed by the Giants at age fifteen as the youngest-ever big league recruit at the time. I was thrilled at being cast into the role of public figure. Next came August 1919, when I made my second appearance in a big league game, pitching for the Boston Red Sox versus Ty Cobb and the Detroit Tigers, winning 2–1, in twelve innings. I was walking on a cloud that night.

3

Then there was the second game of the 1921 World Series, pitching for the Yankees against the Giants and beating them 3–0, allowing only two hits. That was the series in which I pitched three full games, twenty-seven innings total, allowing just two runs, both unearned. The last was being notified of my election to the National Baseball Hall of Fame in 1969, along with Stan Musial, Roy Campanella, and Stan Coveleski.

Of some eleven thousand players who had participated in big league baseball at the time of my induction, fewer than 150 had been elected to the Hall of Fame. If there is a pinnacle of anything, that would be it. Very few people experience it. Nobody's going to take that away from me or any of the memories and the wonderful things I've thought of and done—the thrill of standing out there on the pitcher's mound, the exhilaration of winning and the disappointment of losing.

Even *losing* becomes, perversely, a very great feature. The intense disappointments that you suffer sometimes make you feel you're alive just as much as sticking a pin in you makes you jump out of a lethargy. Sometimes my heart goes out to the loser. I feel more quickly for the guy who's defeated in a tough one because there is no compensation for that. It's as if the bottom has dropped out of his world, like the kid who crashes his brand-new bicycle on Christmas morning. It is utterly devastating.

I lost two of the toughest games that ever were lost in a World Series. The first was the final game of the 1921 World Series when Roger Peckinpaugh made an error in the first inning. The ball came to rest behind him about fifteen feet in the outfield, and he couldn't find it. The runner for the Giants made it to home plate from second base. Neither side scored for the rest of the game. Then came the last game of the '26 Series, when Pete Alexander came in and struck out Tony Lazzeri. In that game there were three errors by our side. In both games, my pitching was not the problem.

It just carves you up, that's all.

A few personal effects had to be collected from my locker: gloves, shoes, sweatshirts, and other items of little importance. Then came the goodbyes—no great displays of emotion there. Professional players are inured to trades and other sudden changes in their careers. It was a simple "I'll be seein' you." I was then made to wait three hours for my final check to be prepared, but with that in hand, along with a feeling of complete desertion, I plodded slowly out of Ebbets Field.

The emotional impact was dulling, like that of a guy who had taken too many pain pills. As I stood outside, in the middle of Sullivan Street, looking up at the flapping pennants atop the roof, it seemed the whole history of my life—my career—rushed by in rapid review, yet clearly defined: accented scenes and events, cataloged in importance, underscored in influence, picturesque in degree and circumstance.

When I signed that Major League contract with the New York Giants at fifteen, I surrendered to temptation, just like my high-school English teacher, Miss Scoville, said I would. She called me in and told me, "Waite, I wish you would reconsider your decision. Professional baseball is a rugged game and not for a young man like you." She saw a very different future for me and wanted to help guide me there.

"If you finish your schooling here," she said, "I will tutor you through the school of journalism, and you'll become a writer." Then she took a long, serious look at me, shook her head ever so slightly and just about whispered: "But I suppose the glamour has got you."

She was right—the glamour did have me.

I have often thought about what would have happened had I taken Miss Scoville's advice and gone to a school of journalism. Lots of times, in lots of ways, I wondered if I wouldn't have been more at peace with myself had I chosen to go to art school. I was happier painting than I ever was pitching. I have an aesthetic side, and I do like, without reservation, the beautiful and gracious things of life, the wonders God has given us. I always believed in my innermost self that I was a person of two parts, the aesthetic and the athletic. Which was I really? I couldn't fathom my true destiny in life.

Miss Scoville's advice was on my mind when I was inducted into the National Baseball Hall of Fame, the greatest honor of my life. I was now recognized for achievement within the 1 percent of all-time great baseball players. It was a beautiful day in Cooperstown, and I was beyond humbled. Yet, I stood up on the dais next to Bowie Kuhn, the baseball commissioner, and after thanking everyone and saying all the usual things, I mused that "I could have chosen to become a journalist instead."

I could have forgiven the audience for thinking, *What the hell does this guy want?*

Well, I never really knew what I wanted; that's just the issue. I'm quick to confess it. When I review my life in its entirety, its escapades and the things I've done, it doesn't present a rhyme or reason. I always had a feeling that I should get on with it but didn't know what I should get on with. The word *confused* appears so often in my own detailed account of my life, and it strikes me that I've been baffled always, not knowing what was coming next or whether I was acting properly. I was introspective and found myself wanting a great number of times but somehow managed to bolster my ego with a self-sufficiency that carried me over the rough spots. I must say, fortune was with me when it mattered most.

My entrance into the big leagues certainly came through odd circumstances. I managed to stay there. I gave 100 percent, 110 percent. I wasn't a damn fool or kidding around with anybody. I led an exceptionally fine life, playing with the New York Yankees, the greatest team in the history of baseball. I gave it my best throughout my career, winning six World Series games, losing four, and establishing records broken only by Whitey Ford in the '61 Series with the Reds. Some say I was one of the best clutch pitchers in the business, and I had a very enviable reputation.

At the same time, my choices were scatterbrained. I was always an impulsive kind of fellow, and my life was a hodgepodge, a crisscross, the peaks and the pits of experiment and failure and success, wonder and puzzlement. A lot of ballplayers experience that, but I got into such peculiar situations and tried such odd activities.

Now, I don't consider myself such an unusual type as Babe Ruth or a lot of other fellows who played ball, but I do believe I got into certain spots that other ballplayers didn't. Ruth did, but in a different way. He was a little bit careless about certain moral codes and things of that kind. But it was all fun and exciting, and it was all, in a way, breathtaking. Babe played for a while in the Minor Leagues, for Providence, and of course he came out of St. Mary's Industrial School in Baltimore. I don't think Cobb played in the Minor Leagues at all. Neither of them experienced what I got myself into, at least in my early years. People are amazed when I tell them about it.

Why, I was only sixteen and playing for Lynn, Massachusetts, in the Minor Leagues, when I had one of my very first lessons in absolute debauchery. We had this pitcher, a big, strong southern guy named Carl Williams. In those days we didn't have any refrigeration, but there was a button on the wall you could push twice for ice water. Carl had a big washtub in his room, a huge room, almost a suite. He'd keep ringing for ice until that washtub was filled and then put bottles of Pabst Blue Ribbon in it. When he got back from the ball game, the ice would be pretty well melted and he'd ring for more.

The proprietor's wife, Jenny, would bring up ice in pitchers or buckets. After several trips, she said she wasn't going to bring any more. Carl got into an argument with her and threatened to spank her unless she complied. They continued to fight and then Carl actually did it. He took Jenny over his knees, belly down, pulled up her dresses and in front of five or six guys, he whacked her bare fanny. She screamed words I did not yet know the meaning of.

My eyes popped as big as half dollars watching this performance.

I thought, *This is baseball?*

It couldn't be. This was so far different from anything I learned as a child. I was brought up to come all cleaned, combed, and fully dressed in jacket and tie to the dinner table; to hurry home when my mother called; and to be off the streets when the clock struck ten. All the admonitions I had received from my parents were disrupted because they didn't hold true here. There were obscenities and violations of morals. I began to think that this was the real world.

What had my parents been talking about?

It was difficult to hold onto my respectability or my refinement. My mother always used to say, "That's not refined" or "People won't think much of you if you act that way. They won't think you came from a home of refinement." Lord knows the Minor Leagues in those days were anything but refined. They were just an education in disillusionment, and consequently I had a hard time justifying the path I had chosen.

I never wanted to consort with these unsavory characters when I was in the Minor Leagues. I was never accepted as one of them. I didn't know about poker or any of the card games. They didn't include me in those things because I was just a kid. I was too young to drink with them and never liked gambling. I was never a good card player or a craps shooter. I'm not a horse-racing enthusiast. Almost every morning for a couple years, while on the road, Babe Ruth came down to my room because my roommate, Joe Dugan, used to study racing forms. They'd call two of the finest handicappers in the country. Dugan and Ruth were doing very well with this; they were coming out ahead in 1928.

After either the '27 or '28 World Series, Joe went to Belmont Park, without the advice of the handicappers, and blew both his World Series check and his last paycheck of the regular season. That was quite a sum, and he lost it all in three days. I wasn't that kind of gambler. I would break the moral codes, or codes of normal behavior. When you're gambling with your existence, you're staying out at night when you shouldn't, participating in events you shouldn't, and leaving yourself open to criticism.

I would gamble with life, sure, but never with money.

I gambled wrongly in 1930 and as a result got myself traded from the Yankees to Detroit. I had been successful the way I had been going and didn't see any reason why I should change my philosophy or lifestyle just because my boss said so. I gambled with my place on the greatest baseball team of all time. I paid the piper for that. I can't point to a risk where I'd cross a railroad track with the train coming. But in ignoring or defying the moral codes of society, the conservative formula for proper behavior, I admittedly was not a rebel but the bad kid in the classroom.

And yet, for twenty-three years in professional baseball, I had this great dedication to pitching. I pitched in 687 big league baseball games, 3,845 ⅔ innings. I made eleven World Series starts and one in relief. My earned run average for those games was 1.83, and I allowed only 2 home runs over 82 ⅔ innings.

Then, it was over. Between thirty-five and forty is the average age at which they read you out of the game. I was thirty-eight. I was finished.

I took one last look at that glorious temple of bricks, Ebbets Field, on that day in May 1938 and began making my way toward the subway station. My mind was in a fog.

I knew full well that my final exit from baseball, however timely and inevitable it may have been, was of my own making. For the last time in my baseball career, I had set myself on yet another path to places unknown and uncertain.

As I continued along to the subway station, concession-stand proprietors, whom I knew more than somewhat, cast a sympathetic eye, as if to say, "Too bad! Knocked out of the box?" They hadn't yet heard that not only had I never been in the box that day but also that I would never again be knocked out of it, nor privileged to grace the little mound in center-diamond. A few of them yelled out, "Hello, Waite!" when it really was, "Goodbye, Waite!"

They had no idea that each step I took was a few more inches closer to my oblivion.

Part 1

1

The Family Web

THE ORIGINAL HOYTS WERE FROM MANCHESTER, Vermont. My father's mother's maiden name was Waite. It makes a strange first name for a child. It's not like John or Tom or Frank or Henry or Jim. When there's trouble and someone says, "Who did that?" there are lots of guys by the name of Jim. Which Jim was it? But when they say it was some guy with a strange name, it could only be me, Waite Hoyt.

When I was attending school at PS 90 in Brooklyn, we had a fire drill one day and lined up in the hall. I gave the kid ahead of me a shove, and he inadvertently pushed the kid ahead of him, which knocked down about twelve others. The principal called my mother and said I had knocked down twelve boys. How in the hell could one guy like me knock down twelve kids? I was lucky if I could knock down one, but they all fell down anyway.

I was a kid born to trouble, and being named Waite didn't do me much good.

I was born on Second Place in Brooklyn, but while I was still an infant, we moved out to Hawthorne Street in Flatbush. It was a beautiful place. The oak and chestnut trees were planted near the curb and, in full bloom, would reach over toward each other and sort of shake hands.

My earliest memory is when I was about four years old. The streets of Brooklyn in 1904 were not paved, and out in front of our house at 241 Hawthorne, the avenue was badly rutted. Vegetable hucksters came through with their carts and wagons, which completely tore up the streets.

My dad was such an enthusiastic baseball man. He and a neighbor named Herman Bank created a baseball diamond, Hawthorne Field, about three blocks down from us. It was quite an athletic field. Dad played third base on a team called the Hawthornes and was a pretty good ballplayer. Heinie Zimmerman, who at the time was playing with the Chicago Cubs, I believe, brought an exhibition team down there, and the Hawthornes beat them.

Dad would take me out and teach me how to catch a ball, field, and throw. We'd stand in the middle of the street, and the ball would bounce badly because of those ruts. Once in a while I'd get hit in the face, throat, or neck, and he would yell, "Keep your head down! Keep your head down!" If I cried, he'd shout, "Shame on you! Shame on you!"

Every good ballplayer keeps his head down on ground balls, and I had to learn this no matter how much it hurt because, as my father said, you have to accept the bad with the good. I was taught to scoop up the ball with a backward motion. Fielders don't shove their hand forward because that knocks the ball away.

My father would stand behind me, grab my wrists, bring my arms above and behind my head and then propel my right arm forward. He repeated this until I could do it by myself. Then a body turn was added, and finally, I was given an actual ball to throw. At first, we'd throw it back and forth on the lawn and then across the street, about fifty feet. I could just about reach him. Little by little I grew stronger and stronger. He would toss the ball high in the air, and I was supposed to catch it. Of course, I missed a lot. I had trouble finding it in the air.

I can still smell that baseball. It was made of horsehide and just had an aroma of its own: lovely, lovely—clean and burnished in a sacrificial aura, soon to be hit and scuffed. To a young disciple of the game, it was a thing of beauty to be petted, turned, and tossed with careful affection.

Actually, there were several kinds of baseballs. The nickel rocket was stuffed with old scraps of leather, and then there was the ten-cent ball; the twenty-five-cent lively bounder, which was rubber-centered and bounced like a golf ball; the fifty-cent ball; the seventy-five-cent ball; the dollar Junior League size, a big ball. Then of course there was the regular League ball, which cost a dollar and a quarter.

Gradually, the knack for throwing a baseball came to me, and oh, my father was so overjoyed. He told me that his grandfather (Walter Fowler Hoyt) invented the curveball. Others have made that claim, of course. In any case, I'm quite sure my great-grandfather's curveball was better than mine. I never did get the hang of that curveball.

My father was so wrapped up in my baseball activities. I'll never forget when I was playing on my grammar school baseball team, PS 89, and we were going to play PS 90, a school I had been asked to leave because of some obstreperous performances in class. I engaged in enough mischief to establish a reputation as the prime suspect in all aggravated cases.

PS 89 had baseball uniforms, but I didn't bother to put mine on because I didn't think enough of PS 90 to wear it. I was out there in my Eton collars with big silk bows and a Buster Brown jacket. In those days I was a second baseman, not a pitcher, and made three errors against my old school. We lost the game, and all of a sudden I heard this voice behind me, yelling, "Get home! Get home!" It was my father, who had taken the day off to watch me play, and boy, did I take it from him all the way home, six blocks from where the ballfield was.

Eventually I earned his approval, and when I entered the big leagues, he became my de facto publicity department. That was embarrassing. He'd say to anyone who would listen, "This is my son," and then he'd go into a dissertation about my pitching. At the '27 World Series, he told the guy sitting next to him that I was his son, and the fellow didn't believe him. He was hurt by that.

He wasn't very tall, my father—about 5 feet 6, I would say, and sort of rotund but not ungainly. He had a particular way of standing, with his right foot pointed out to the right, then he'd settle himself down on his left foot and nod his head. He often wore a gray suit with a vest and a watch chain across, as most men did. He usually wore a derby, or a straw hat in the summer, and he'd put on white pants in the summer with white shoes.

He grew up around Troy, New York, and had one sister, Alice, who was clever and very much a lady. She married a fellow named Marshall McDonald, who was a vice president of Swift & Company, the meat packers.

Professionally, my dad had a checkered career. He started with a firm called L. Heller and Son, which imported simulated pearls. He had a good position with the company and was doing very nicely, but there were four or five sons in the Heller family, and he could see no future in that, so he bowed out of there.

He used to make up little joke songs:

> Father's papering the parlor
> you can't see him for the paste
> dabbing it here
> dabbing it there
> dabbing it everywhere
> We can't find our piano
> it's broad and rather tall
> we believe it's behind the paper
> plastered on the wall.

That was supposed to be funny in those days.

He was a very good singer, too, and by the way, so were my mother and her sister Elizabeth. They sang duets. I can almost hear them now, singing, "Oh happy days, oh happy days."

My father used to coach the Masonic Temple in its yearly play, which would draw five hundred people or so every night for a week. He was very clever at that, directing and producing, writing songs and material for the program and show. He was so valuable that the Temple gave him a $5,000 bonus.

When he got that big bonus, he decided he wanted to go into vaudeville with an act called Ad Hoyt's Minstrels. (His first name was Addison, and it was shortened.) His was considered one of the better shows in vaudeville. He was one of the finest monologists I've ever heard. He was excellent. He could replicate any type of dialect and kept us in stitches all the time. Good grief, he could play a tambourine like nothing human. I loved him for those kinds of things. He always had a story or a joke. His life was beautiful to him, and me.

One time my father was playing a theatrical date over in New Jersey and brought me with him. We had to take a ferry boat to get there from Manhattan Island, and then another train or trolley to the theater. He sat me in the first row of the balcony, and he did very well, singing, telling stories, delivering a monologue, all quite successful. After a while, I looked at my watch because I knew the ferry boats stopped running at certain hours, and yelled out, "Hey, dad, hurry up, we'll miss that ferry!" I was just a kid, about eight years old at the time, but I'm pretty sure I got the best laugh of the evening.

Several years later, one of the actors fell sick suddenly, and my father couldn't find a replacement. Sometimes there is a stock of extras who are fill-ins, but this occurred so quickly that my father didn't know what to do. I was about fifteen at the time, and my father said, "Don't do anything, just sit with us in the circle." I tried to emulate the rhythmic antics, the choreography of the thing. It was so obvious that I was very young that the people down in front laughed at me.

In around 1912 my dad joined a theatrical union called the White Rats, which originally was a social-business theatrical society. At the time, conditions in and around the vaudeville stage were so poor that Samuel Gompers, the boss man of the American Federation of Labor, favored the Rats with a charter, and they began battling for more equitable contracts and better working conditions.

From 1912 to 1916 conditions did improve, and the White Rats enjoyed their new clubhouse on West Forty-Sixth Street. In 1916, with management sniping away at them, internal disorders, and clashes between trade papers, the situation became a mess. Management, led by Edward "E. F." Albee, started the National Vaudeville Artists (NVA), and performers, induced by better salaries and longer bookings, began jumping from the White Rats to the new and more glamorous NVA.

My dad stuck with the Rats. Management, through clever spy work and a system of informers, compiled a list of recalcitrants, one of whom was my dad. These rebels were blacklisted and eventually forced from the big time into a position of mean income, or retirement. My dad was unable to get profitable bookings and quit in 1918.

Subsequently, he joined my uncle Marshall at Swift & Company as a regional director between Detroit and the Atlantic Coast, where he worked for the last ten or fifteen years of his life.

When he made his last theatrical appearance in Chicago and came down stage to sing his final song, the audience was informed of his forced retirement. He sang the number "Smiles." The house manager later told him, "That was the first standing ovation I have ever seen in all my years here."

My mother wasn't so keen on my father's theatrical pursuits, but she tolerated them.

She was a beautiful woman, with a wonderful disposition. Born in New York City, up near the Bronx and Harlem, her birth name was Louise Benedum, but she called herself Lucia. She constantly pointed out that she was a Daughter of the American Revolution. My father, she complained, was eligible to be a Son of the American Revolution with lineage to an officer but never followed up on it. Way back in English history, one of my forebears was such a nut as to desire to do away with a faulty king and stood accused of regicide, whereupon the crest was knocked off the top of the family escutcheon.

So much about my mother was to be admired, but as much as I loved her, I never loved her like I loved my father. I'm afraid she was too much under the influence of my Aunt Elizabeth—and Uncle Joe—with whom I didn't entirely hit it off. Anto, as we called her, was a good soul, but she didn't have any children of her own, so she was always telling my mother how to raise hers. I think my mother listened to her and Uncle Joe too much.

With my father being away so often with Swift & Company, my mother dealt in private activities, one of which was reading philosophy and psychology. She passed along what she learned to me. She was very serious about raising her children according to her ideas of right and wrong. I'm rather awed today as I realize the context of the conversations between my mother and father. It was not just idle chatter or superficial theory. It amazes me, after all these years, that I'm still conscious of their serious considerations of life and its meaning—of cause and effect.

I used to see my mother writing. She was an excellent writer—I believe she wrote for *Harper's Bazaar*. I occasionally asked her about what she was writing, but her answers were never satisfactory because her subjects were too deep for my young mind. It was her own interpretations of life as she found it. She wrote about the meaning of character in a beautifully bound, but time-worn and now rather ragged, personal volume of collected expressions and verses called *Threads of Thought and Philosophical Echoes*, under her maiden name, Lucia Josephine Benedem: "Character is not of the intellect, nor is it of the physical, but of the disposition. Its qualities strike through to color the mind and the heart, and character is the joint product of nature and nurture. Character comes with the common places. Nature endows a man with the birth, material and environments, and man must mold these materials into qualities: industry, honor, truth and love."

Now, that passage is not necessarily anything brilliant. Some people might not agree with it or appreciate the literary execution of it. But it is, I believe, indicative of the serious intentions of my mother in the training of her children. It is definitely more rigid in determination than the sports-infected attitudes of my father and his hopes for me as a big leaguer, although he had a philosophical side too. More than anything else—baseball included—the atmosphere of my home was permeated with talk and pleasant reaction to the arts and classics. I am sure that both of my parents were more intellectually inclined than most. Without really knowing, I tend to believe that the first attractions of my mother and father to each other sprung from a mutual interest in philosophy.

Thinking back, it is most difficult to distinguish just how far beyond the normal my parents carried their cultural musings. Those were the days when adults sought self-occupation or had it forced upon them. There was no television or radio to consume their idle hours, and they were more disposed to keep diaries, write poetry, or attend public lectures.

In many respects my boyhood home on Hawthorne Street was the ladies' world. Most often home looked like a meeting of the PTA, for indeed the Ladies' Aid Society met at our house from time to time and helped whatever cause they chose between a few gossipy interludes. There were compensations for me. After the meetings, I was allowed to clean up the finger sandwiches and the little decorated cakes. That was a wonderful reward for having to listen to all that gibberish for a couple hours.

My German grandmother, who spoke with a dialect, was very much in love with me. She'd say, "Vaite, commen zie hein"—come here. She must have worn five flannel petticoats. She'd lift one or two of these petticoats, and underneath she had a big pocket in the red flannel petticoat where she had a big black purse, and she'd say, "Commen zie hein, I gif you a dollar." A dollar, in those days—boy, did I love my grandmother!

She gave me a two-toned bat for Christmas, black from the handle up to the thick end and very light down from one part of the handle to the knob. I couldn't wait to use that bat. Finally, springtime came around, and some kid, the first batter up in the game, borrowed it, took a swing, and snapped it right in half.

When I was about ten, I was playing in a ball game, and we lost. I went over to my grandmother's house, which was across the street. The family was so darn close-knit; we had to be because we lived like spiders in a web on Hawthorne Street—my uncle in one house, my aunt and the sisters in another. One afternoon, when she heard my team had played a baseball game that day, she said to my mother, "Mudder, the noos is good?"

My mother said, "No, his team lost."

So, my grandmother said, "Vasn't Vaite dere?"

She thought I could perform miracles.

I also had a sister, Margaret, or Peggy as we usually called her, who looked a little like me but was not sylphlike to any degree. She also grew up in my shadow. I was not exactly the model of decorum at school and had been called on the carpet several times. Peggy was singled out for something once and sent down to the disciplinarian at the head office who said, "Your name is Hoyt! You're not the sister of Waite Hoyt, are you? Well, that accounts for it!" Peggy was behind the eight ball before she even started.

Peggy was always a favorite of mine; we were very close. She was a lovely girl, but later in life she had a poor marriage to some guy up in Manchester, New Hampshire, and that turned out badly. She had a son, but nobody knows where he ended up.

She married a second time to a fellow named Bohan; they lived down in Clearwater, Florida. This didn't end well. She and Bohan were both seriously ill to begin with, and then they were in a terrible automobile accident. A taxicab ran a red light and crashed into their car. Peggy had nineteen broken bones, and both of her husband's arms were broken. She died soon after, and then her husband followed her almost exactly to the minute one week later.

Peggy had wanted to be an actress, but she really didn't have much talent. I realize now, but didn't fully appreciate then, that both of my parents, relatives, and most friends were disciples of stage, art, writing, and music. The Hoyts always lived on the fringe of show business. My cousins, Grace and Frances Hoyt, lived in the Dakota Apartments at Seventy-Second Street and Central Park West. They were social entertainers of the top strata. Back when salons were fashionable, their guests listened to monologues, the harp, and poetry. Visits to their home were excursions in culture. There was charm and talent—and something soulfully arresting beyond the playing of baseball—and lingering in its beauty.

I recall a definite suspicion that all was not well at home, which caused me to believe there was a breach between my mother and father. It was not a lessening of love and affection, for they could never have been accused of that. It was more because of the logic of my mother's contention—and very probably true conviction—that my father had chosen a whirl at the stage, which kept him away from home so many weeks of the year and forced her into a position of abject loneliness. Consequently, she felt a need to discipline and govern her household, a task for which she was not emotionally equipped.

This apparent wrongness in the situation at home tended to verify my eventual conclusion that there was no valid reason for seeking the security of home life.

2

There Goes Our Boy

WHEN I WAS TWELVE YEARS OLD, I contracted blood poisoning—
Streptococcus. Swinging from suspended ladders in the school gym, I
developed a fine cluster of blood blisters on both palms. I stuck them
with a pin, and both hands swelled to gigantic proportions. Then, right
around Christmas time I was roller skating, fell down, and slapped my
hands on the pavement, making them even worse.

Our doctor was Samuel Lazarus, one of the finest gentlemen and
best doctors I've ever known. He was a homeopathic doctor and said
an operation was necessary. After Christmas week passed, he said, "We
can't wait any longer, Mrs. Hoyt. We have to operate because it's getting
very serious."

He contacted a surgeon in Manhattan, who was supposed to come
over to our house and do the operation on New Year's Eve, but a
blizzard came up. It snowed so hard that the trolleys quit running. It
became very late in the evening, we could hear the whistles downtown
celebrating New Year's, and, oh, I was in terrible shape.

Dr. Lazarus said to my mother, "Mrs. Hoyt, the surgeon can't make
it." He said, "I've had some experience in surgery, and I'll give you a
choice. I can get a friend of mine, and between us we can cut Waite's
hands off and save his life. Or, we can operate and perhaps save his life
but it's going to be a dangerous, risky thing." My mother said, "Well,
he's certainly no good without any hands, so go ahead and operate."

They put me on the kitchen table and had this canister of ether.
They asked my cousin to hold the cone under my nose while they
poured the ether on it. The fumes got into his nose and he flopped on
the floor. So, they found someone else to administer the sedative and

finally operated on me. They made a hole in my right hand between the base of my middle and fourth fingers. You could almost see through my hand. Dr. Lazarus came every day to stick a big syringe up my arm, and my mother would hold a bucket. He'd squirt stuff up my arm and it would shoot out into the bucket. Oh, it was a fearful thing. I still have the scars.

Dr. Lazarus probably saved not only my life but also my hands, which I of course later used to make my living. Providence entered there, I believe. God was with me.

With my hands in good health, I played baseball in the Newspaper Leagues: the Brooklyn Times League, the Junior Eagle League and the Standard Union League. The Monday morning papers had four pages of printed box scores. They would run advertisements: "Game Wanted. Team ages 8–12." When the team showed up, the players were usually sixteen to eighteen, so I had to be careful about whom I was playing. We'd compete for a side bet of three or five dollars and the ball we used in the game.

One day I met this fellow who was talking about starting a team called the Wyandottes. I knew that if I could get on this team I would get a uniform, so I volunteered my services. He asked me, "What position do you play?" When I told him I played second base, he said, "Oh, we've got a second baseman and don't need any infielders." So, I asked him what he needed and he said, "We need pitchers." I had never pitched a game in my life up to that point but wanted a uniform, so I told him I could pitch.

That's how I became a pitcher, all just because I wanted a uniform. I joined the Wyandottes and became rather successful as a pitcher for them. We played on well-groomed diamonds at the Parade Ground, located at the south end of Prospect Park, and won the Junior Eagle League championship. I was now an established and recognized pitcher on a uniformed team, and it was a very happy experience for me. I also played for a team called the Albermarles, which won the Brooklyn Standard Union championship.

I pitched a lot before I entered high school and even more at Erasmus Hall High—the Old Gray School Forever, as one line of its song proclaimed. Erasmus Hall was a beautiful edifice of Gothic architecture. In the center of a huge quadrangle stood the "old school," a wooden memorial to the days of its inception, 1786. Erasmus Hall High was a very classical type of school and had a great dramatics club that turned out a number of people who were tops in their field: Clara Bow, Mae West, and Barbra Streisand among them.

Bill Sykes, the athletic coach, who was not a genius but a good man, had been a high school pitcher himself. Bill had suffered polio in his boyhood, so one of his legs was paralyzed, but he was remarkably adept at fielding despite the handicap. Sykes taught me the palmball, a change-of-pace pitch, which became a forte of mine in my professional career. The palmball is held with the little finger and the thumb, with the other fingers not contacting the ball. You throw it with a stiff wrist and kind of pull it back with a little jerk. After Sykes retired, Dick Elifie, one of the great scholastic coaches of New York City, came to Erasmus and taught me poise and control.

Baseball took such possession of me. Little else mattered. I was off to school with a ball in my back pocket, a glove under one arm, and books under the other. I had a catch with anyone interested enough to receive the ball and warmed up before the morning classes and again at gym period. We played baseball after school and had a Saturday-morning game, with one more in the afternoon and then a "skull session," in which we sat in a circle and talked of ways of improving our game.

Now, don't get the impression that I did nothing but play baseball, because there was plenty else to do. Through the age of fourteen, when I was a little fellow, we spent our summers away from Brooklyn, for two months. We went to a place called Red Hook, a few miles from Poughkeepsie, and we lived with people by the name of Picher, on a farm of sorts. They farmed, but it was not extensive, and they didn't live off their produce.

Red Hook had twin lakes, and we'd have roasts out there. The spits were carved from forked branches, with a metal rod crossing the branches so they wouldn't burn. We'd roast chickens on that thing, and they were wonderful. The water in those lakes was pure and clean. Those were wonderful days.

Then the Pichers died, and we stayed with another family, the Latins. This girl who lived in the house next door, oh, we hated each other. She was out riding her bicycle one day, so I fired an apple at her and hit her in the posterior. She took a Steve Brodie leap off the back of the bike.

It was a lousy thing for me to do, but it was the first evidence that I had good control.

That same year I was invited down to Washington Park, where the Brooklyn Tip-Tops played in the Federal League. A man from the league—I don't remember his name—had heard about my success as a high school pitcher and invited me to be looked over. The first big league catcher I ever pitched to was a fellow named Grover Land, if I'm not mistaken. He was very complimentary and told the bigwigs down at the Brooklyn Federal League about me. They wanted to send me to play Minor League baseball in the Colonial League, for a team in New Haven called the White Wings. When I went home and told my folks, my father was elated and my mother was kind of reticent, so they called a family meeting over at Uncle Joe's house.

Uncle Joe was the dominant character in the family, a big blowhard. He used to wear a diamond horseshoe, a stickpin, and all that sort of thing. He was the authoritative voice and said, "Why, can you imagine allowing a boy of his age to go out and play with those rough, rugged guys?" My uncle had a big, round, florid face, and I used to get mad just looking at him.

But he was doing the talking, and he said, "I would never condone sending a young boy like this to a professional baseball team. Look at him, only fourteen and just learning to shave himself. He's not only young but also uneducated, unworldly, and almost still a child. And you're asking whether to let him mingle with those tough, battle-scarred professional baseball players? I say no, positively no. It's not my decision to make, but you asked for it, and there it is." I waited for him to finish up by saying, "Bah, humbug!" But he didn't. As far as I was concerned, my uncle was the worst kind of scrooge.

The upshot was that I didn't go. Uncle Joe was right, but even he had no idea about the cast of carnival characters I would later encounter on the Minor League circuit.

About a year later, baseball players from Ebbets Field came looking around the neighborhood to rent a furnished house over the summer from a family, like ours, who went away. That's how I got to know fellows like Wheezer Dell, who played for the Brooklyn Robins, which of course later became known as the Dodgers. Dell was a big, 6-foot-4, right-handed pitcher. He had a very lovely wife who knew I had been pitching batting practice for the Federal League at Washington Park, and she arranged to have me invited up to pitch batting practice at Ebbets Field.

I brought my own uniform because I didn't know that the Dodgers would loan me a uniform or would even have one that would fit me. For years ever after, Casey Stengel would talk about that uniform. He'd say, "He appeared in a uniform his mother made for him!" That wasn't true, but it did look a little bit cheap alongside the Dodgers' uniform.

Stengel actually refused to go to bat against me at first. He was afraid that I'd hit him, but Nap Rucker, another pitcher, told him, "You don't have to be afraid of this kid. He can throw the ball over the plate." Stengel came around afterward and was generous with compliments. "Kid," he said, "Rucker was right. You're pretty good."

My father was a friend of Red Dooin, a catcher who was a coach for the New York Giants. As a youngster, I imagined that team's players must be great big fellas because of their name. When the Giants came over to play Brooklyn, my father asked Dooin if the team would give me a look-over. They did, and John McGraw, the manager of the Giants, asked if I would come to the Polo Grounds and pitch batting practice. I said, "Sure, I'd be glad to." From then on, every day, it took me two hours to get there: via trolley car, an elevated train over the bridge to Park Row, and a walk across Park Row to the Sixth Avenue El, which stopped every six blocks to the Polo Grounds at 157th Street. It was two hours up, two hours home, and boy, was I tired.

One day, in late August, I went to Mr. McGraw and told him, "I just can't do this anymore. Four hours a day of traveling is too much, and I am not pitching in regular games against boys my own age." What I didn't tell him was how nasty some of his players were. They were the meanest bunch of buggers I ever saw. The 1915 club wasn't so bad, but the 1916 club was awful. Guys like Benny Kauff—if I didn't pitch a low ball, he'd try to hit the ball right back at me. I wasn't learning anything as a pitcher that way.

McGraw said, "Young man, do you think you could have your father in my office Monday morning at 10:30?"

I said, "Well, I guess so."

He turned to John B. Foster, the secretary of the Giants, and said, "I want you to prepare a contract for this young fellow, an optional contract, not including any money. He doesn't get paid and can retain his status as an amateur, but if he should decide to play professional baseball, his services belong to the New York Giants."

When I went home that night and told my father, you'd think that we were ascending to heaven. We were there bright and early on Monday morning, and my father signed the contract because I wasn't of age. John B. Foster gave me five dollars just to make it legal. I got a big, long speech from John McGraw about my future and who I was going to become. John B. Foster congratulated me.

We got downstairs, and my father took my five dollars and said, "That's too much money for a boy your age." He bought himself a hat, and I coulda killed him.

In those days, a boy of fifteen was considered still a child, a youngster. I had no autonomy: "Don't speak unless you're spoken to. Take your elbows off the table. Children are to be seen and not heard." Yet, I was a national sensation, with my picture all over the papers: "Boy, 15, Signs with the Giants." I was a hero among my peers.

This did not mean I was a Major League ballplayer, exactly. My duties were limited to pitching batting practice for the Giants, and I would be required to sharpen my skills in the Minor Leagues before being called up to the Majors. I was still in high school, in my junior year, and pitching high school baseball, winning the city championship in 1915, by the way. My interest in school and whether Gaul was divided into three parts didn't excite me too much. Latin and the "xy over two equals so-and-so over five" didn't startle me to any degree.

Then a new Minor League formed in Pennsylvania, called the Pennsylvania State League. John McGraw called me and asked if I'd like to pitch in the Minors for a team in Lebanon, Pennsylvania.

I said yes.

Well, to tell you the truth, I couldn't say yes right away. First, there had to be a family conference on the second floor of our rather sedate, three-story house on Hawthorne Street. My nerves were on edge, as I sat on a straight-backed, cane-bottomed chair, saying nothing because I wasn't allowed a voice in the discussion.

Uncle Joe hadn't changed his opinion. "Don't let the boy go away at that age!" he persisted. My mother agreed with him. "Why take a young man whose character is still in the making and have it tarnished and jaded by contact with worldly things he doesn't understand? Who is going to look after him?" she argued. Nevertheless, my father was determined that I would become a professional baseball player and that was all that mattered at that point. I would go away to play ball.

A headline appeared: "Waite Hoyt to go South with the Giants." It was more like I was going south with the Runts in Minor League Lebanon, Pennsylvania, but it was my first step into professional baseball.

I'll always remember coming down the stairs, with my mother and father standing there, right by the newel post. We talked a little bit. I had my suitcase packed—I didn't have much but actually put on long pants to go away to play baseball. That was the first time I dressed like a man. Prior to that, I wore a jacket and knickers, black stockings, and shoes.

My father kissed me goodbye. My mother put her arm around me, kissed me, and turned away so sadly.

One of the things I prefer to remember about my father and my mother was their inner feelings, because I have the idea that if people were allowed to portray how they felt inside, the world would be that much better off. Sometimes we're afraid to disclose our emotions because we're worried somebody will think we're overly sentimental or mawkish.

My mother knew I would be spoiled by the world.

As I started away from her, she turned to my father and said, plaintively, "Ad . . . there goes our boy."

3

Odyssey of Oddities

IF YOU WANTED TO WATCH SHEER innocence enter a cage of lions, why, that was me, walking down the steps of my Brooklyn home, leaving my mother and father waving in the doorway.

Many others have headed into the great unknown, particularly those who have served in the military. But here I was, going into a profession not even knowing what professionalism meant. To a certain degree, I knew what it consisted of at the Polo Grounds and Ebbets Field, and in the big league clubhouses where I had pitched batting practice. But I didn't know, in terms of actual competition with peers, what that would be like.

As I rode along on that train to Lebanon, Pennsylvania, looking out the window, I realized that my refuge was behind me. I was on my own, with my own life to live, choices and success to make, and failures to endure. Here I was, a neophyte.

A lot of us are only grown children, of course. We retain a great deal of juvenile attitude. As time goes by, you begin to realize that all your life you were attracted to juvenile things, like amusement parks and merry-go-rounds, by illusions, mysteries, and fantasies. Movies and television shows are premised on hysterical and roguish themes. We must be juvenile in our minds to be attracted to those things. Illusions are wonderful, of course, and when you begin to destroy them, you start to erode mankind in a way.

People used to stand outside the Ziegfeld Theatre to wait for the stars of the stage to come out, to see Eddie Cantor or Al Jolson. Or, they'd stand outside a player's gate to watch athletes emerge. They'd conjure in their minds some fantasy that they would like to be like them. It gave them something to cling and aspire to.

I remember one time when I was pitching for the New York Yankees and had a fairly good reputation throughout the country. We had won a couple of pennants, like in '27 or '28, and I was on my way to Boston. I was riding in a parlor car, and opposite me was Helen Wills, the great tennis player. If there was anybody in the athletic universe I admired, it was Helen Wills.

I thought she was the pièce de résistance, and there she sat. She must have thought I was the freshest son-of-a-gun because I couldn't take my eyes off her. She was simply magnificent. I have as good a feeling about her today as I ever did, but part of that was an illusion. I had built up in my own mind what a great, magnetic personality she was and how amazing she was in the performance of her game, tennis. To destroy that illusion of your heroes is a terrible thing.

The thing I detest the most is when somebody says that if so-and-so hadn't been a baseball player, he'd have been a plumber. That's no knock against plumbing, but I believe he'd have been an artisan of some kind.

God loans us talent. When we die the talent departs from us and is injected into someone else. I wasn't given any talent; it was loaned to me by the heavens. It's the same with any athlete, entertainer, or scientist.

When I arrived in Lebanon, the oddities began. I took my little suitcase and walked up the streets from the station, unaware that I could have taken a taxi. I made my way to a certain hotel, as I had been instructed. It was one of those country hotels with a marble tile floor in the lobby and fellows sitting around in rocking chairs in the lobby, chewing tobacco with spittoons alongside them.

I walked up to the desk and asked the clerk, "Can I get a room here?"

He said, "Why, yes," and turned a register around on a swivel. There was a pen in a well with some ball bearings in it, and he said, "We have rooms from one dollar to three dollars. What would you like?"

Well, I didn't have any idea, so I shrugged and took a two-dollar room. On the way upstairs the fellow showing me the way said, "You should have taken the one-dollar deal because you'd have gotten the same room anyway."

I only stayed there two or three days before finding a family to live with. I forget their names, but they gave me a nice back room, including breakfast but no other meals. I ate lunch and dinner at a little restaurant across the street where they had home-cooked meals and a five-cent raisin pie—deep dish. How I loved that raisin pie. I ate so many of them that the fellows in the ballclub started calling me "Pie."

The Lebanon team told me to bring my own uniform, so we looked anything but uniform. The ballfield was at the fairgrounds; it was dilapidated. We each had to prepare our own positions, which meant I had to rake and groom the pitcher's mound myself and then pat it down with a tamper. The clubhouse was an improvised shack under the grandstand. The shower bath was an inverted bucket with holes punched in the bottom. I was almost dirtier after a shower than before. We had to buy our own towels, and for a quarter you couldn't get much of a towel. A kid like me didn't have many quarters, anyway.

There was a racetrack on the fairgrounds; we had to put on our uniforms and run twice around it for the equivalent of a mile. Shirking was not allowed. Our manager was Art Devlin, one of the toughest ball players ever, a great friend of John McGraw's. Devlin put us through our rigors. No matter how much we tried to groom the ballfield, it was in terrible condition, and the ball bounced badly. The groundskeepers tried to help us smooth it out and make it a decent place to play, but it was a fifth-rate diamond.

The town of Lebanon evidently didn't believe in our baseball prowess because they gave us a good lettin' alone. Nobody ever came to the games. We had about a hundred people on opening day, but from then on, we averaged about fifteen spectators. I don't know how the Pennsylvania State League made any money; somebody must have been backing it.

I once pitched nineteen innings in front of just six spectators. We lost, 2–1, in the nineteenth inning, against the team from Shamokin, Pennsylvania. That was still a feather in my cap because I received some national publicity for pitching that many innings in a single game. My arm was stiff the next day, and maybe two or three days after, so Devlin didn't pitch me again for about a week.

Not surprisingly, the league decided to give up the Lebanon franchise because nobody came to the games. We shifted to Mount Carmel, another little town in Pennsylvania. When we arrived at the hotel, we saw that someone had written on the sidewalks outside: "Shamokin Stinks! *To Hell with Shamokin!*"

I thought, *What kind of rivalry is this?* It only went downhill from there. We got to the ballpark, and it looked as if a chain gang had given it a working over. There was not a blade of grass in the whole field, just little pebbles. The outfield sloped downward, and from the player's bench you could only see the center fielder from the waist up. Stones and rocks were prevalent around there too.

Forty men with forty wheelbarrows could hardly have cleared this place in forty years. Little hillocks rose a few yards back from the third and first baselines, and on each stood a long, narrow, unpainted bench, beaten by the weather, splintery and worn by the seats of many trousers. These were the players' benches. Just behind them was a heavy wire screen—whether to keep us from the spectators or the spectators from us I wasn't sure.

Quite a good crowd showed up on opening day, a Sunday, and I said to a fellow sitting behind me, "Don't they ever clear this field of stones and rocks?"

The guy said, "Don't worry, buddy. When Shamokin comes here there won't be a rock left." I had no idea what he meant. He asked me my name; when I told him, he turned almost pleasant. "You're the kid who nearly beat Shamokin!" he exclaimed. "Well, all right! I hope you pitch next Sunday when they come here. We'll put the run on them for you. Won't take you nineteen innings either!"

I later found out that Harry Coveleski—the brother of Stanley Coveleski, with whom I was inducted into the National Baseball Hall of Fame in 1969—played in Shamokin at one time, years earlier. He was coming around third base to start for home and somebody hit him on the jaw with a rock and knocked him out cold. A brawl ensued, the game was never finished, and so nobody won. Luckily, when we played Shamokin, we won by a comfortable margin.

When we got back to the hotel that night, we found it had been overrun by flying insects—beetles or something. Devlin, his wife, and about six other guys, were beating on the walls, trying to kill them, with no success.

Luckily, a telegram arrived in Devlin's hands that the league had decided to disband and all players were to return home. Well, I didn't have enough money to get back to New York because I had not been paid a hot penny for the month that I played. Devlin wired John McGraw, and he sent just enough money for me and the other players from New York to return. I reported back to the Giants, feeling like a miserable failure and thinking that my mother was right that my experiment with professional baseball was a mistake.

Still, I soldiered on. Every day I took a trolley and subway, a ride of nearly an hour, to pitch batting practice for the Giants at the Polo Grounds. In the big leagues, I was no wonder boy—just a snot-nosed schoolboy who had no right to be on the diamond with grown men. I was cursed to my face or made fun of as if I were not even there, but I was McGraw's project and on that account was allowed to live.

McGraw himself was brusque and unfriendly. After fiddling around for a few days, he called me into his office and ordered me back to the minors in Hartford.

"Young man, I want to tell you something about Hartford," he said. "When you get there, a fellow named Jim Clarkin owns that club, and he's a tough cookie. I don't want you to sign any contract with him, okay? Don't sign anything."

McGraw knew I hadn't been paid for my time in Pennsylvania, and I hadn't the nerve to ask him for any money. He had assured me, and the other players, that he would take care of it. He never did.

In Hartford I was fortunate to meet Marty Neu, who, as long as I was in baseball, remained in my mind as one of the gentlest men I ever knew. Marty was no movie star, although he looked the part of a country ballplayer. He had a long, hook nose and a weather-reddened face. His hands and wrists seemed to protrude a yard past his sleeves.

Marty was one of those men who would "take over" a young fellow as if the Lord had put him on earth for that purpose. The day I arrived in Hartford, without anyone asking him, he brought me to his rooming house and shared a big, front double bedroom with me. He saw to it that I did my laundry and stayed with me in the evenings to make sure I got to bed on time. He even roused me out of my slumber to go to church each Sunday.

Marty was a great storyteller and loved baseball as a sailor loves the sea. It was not a business with him, or a chore from which he would hasten to escape when the last out was made. Baseball was his work, his play, and his dream of the future.

During my month in Hartford, it rained almost every day. I think I started only one game, pitched about three innings, and performed no miracles on the mound before it started raining and the game was called off.

Finally came payday. I went to get my check because I was flat broke. I didn't have enough money to eat. When I arrived at the club owner's office there was no envelope for me, and I was told to wait to talk to Mr. Clarkin, the owner, on a "confidential matter."

What could be confidential? It couldn't be a fine because I hadn't had any run-ins with umpires. Fines in the Minor Leagues were paid to the umpires in cash. I had several times seen men hand a five-dollar bill to the plate umpire before they were allowed to come to bat. I used to wonder whatever became of the money.

When I was summoned to Clarkin's office, he held my check in one hand, a contract in the other and said, "When you sign the contract, you will get your money." Clarkin was a massive, hard-muscled Irishman with a lean, sunburned face. He had been a maintenance man at the state prison in Connecticut after working as a policeman in Dublin. A story went that he had single-handedly disarmed and subdued a maddened inmate who had made himself a sword out of a piece of scrap metal.

My stomach was squirming as I stood before him, looking probably three years younger than my sixteen years. I knew I had to say something.

"Mr. McGraw told me not to sign anything," I breathed.

"You sign the contract, or you don't get your money!" he growled.

So here I was, with no money to eat. What was I supposed to do? I signed the contract, took the check, went right to the bank, cashed it, and got myself some steak and fries. I then called the Polo Grounds and told McGraw about the situation, and he roared at me until the receiver rattled. "You stupid kid! Get on the next train back to New York! Right now!"

Without even notifying Clarkin, I packed my stuff, boarded a train, reported back to McGraw at the Polo Grounds, and caught more hell from him. A few days later, he called me in and told me he was sending me to Lynn, Massachusetts, in the same league as Hartford. "Now, there will be some controversy about this because Clarkin will claim you belong to Hartford," McGraw said.

That's exactly what happened, but Clarkin didn't get anywhere with McGraw, and I finished the season pitching for Lynn.

The center-field fence in Lynn was adjacent to a beach, so it was a delightful place to play. After the game I would put on my bathing suit, walk through center field and out onto the beach. Oh, that was wonderful! But I had no social life. A kid my age didn't know anybody, and nobody invited me anywhere. The other fellows in the ballclub were much older than I was and were going out with people their own age. I was left pretty much alone, a lobby-sitter, you might say.

I did not win many games for Lynn that first season. Altogether, I pitched 71 innings, winning 4 games and losing 5. There were good teams as well as feeble ones in that league, and the competition was often bitter. Nearly every team had its share of street-corner roughnecks or small-town bullies from the farm country who were out to beat you any way they could.

Your own teammates could be as nasty and underhanded as the opposition. It was a dog-eat-dog world. Nobody ever felt sure of his job and hated on sight every new recruit who might be a threat to him or any opponent who might make him look bad. The first baseman might step on you as you hustled back to the bag, just because he could. An infielder might make a point of tripping anyone who rounded his position, or grab the runner's shirt to spin him off balance.

The manager in Lynn was Lou Pieper, a big, tall fellow, about 6 feet 6, who wore a beard but no uniform. He was slim as a clothes pole, with a rubbery face like a comedian's, and wore a plaid cap set straight on his head. His clothes draped on him like he was a coat hanger. Lou was very respected in the Eastern League, having been there quite a while, and had won a pennant or two.

Like Marty Neu, Lou felt a special urge to watch out for me, steering me into good playing habits. I'm embarrassed now as I think back to how I tried the poor man's patience. I was prompted by the best of motives but misread him and overstepped because of Lou's offhanded friendliness.

One day on the bench, Lou ordered a hit-and-run play. He had often shown us how the batter should try to punch the ball to the right, through the hole left vacant when the second baseman scurried to protect the bag against the man who had started down from first base.

I had seen John McGraw snarl his disgust at the way this maneuver often went awry and instead did just the opposite, a run and hit. That's where the runner takes off, like on a steal. If the pitch is in there, the batter hits it. If not, he takes it, and the runner is on his own. Sure enough, the hit-and-run blew up on Lou, with the batter missing the ball by a clear foot and the runner starting, stopping, and then getting hung up between first and second before being tagged out. Lou looked sadly back at the bench and shook his head.

I piped up and said, "The hit and run is a lousy play! Mr. McGraw doesn't do that anymore. He thinks it's dumb. He plays the run and hit."

Every man on the bench turned to stare at me as if I were a dog who had spoken the King's English. Lou took a deep breath, and I could see the slow anger surge up into his neck and turn his big ears flaming red. I knew at once I had done something stupid and expected to be set to running laps around the field right after the ball game.

Instead, Lou invited me to dinner and told me I should learn not to interfere that way, or it would get me into trouble—not necessarily with him, but in the big leagues, where I was surely headed—provided I could learn to handle myself.

4

In the Bag

WHEN THE MINOR LEAGUE SEASON ENDED in September, I returned to the big leagues to pitch batting practice once again with the Giants. John McGraw greeted me almost with affection. He knew every detail of my short career and even laughed about the argument I had with Lou Peiper over the hit and run. But when he sent me out to pitch to his crew of bandits, it was like I was a piece of red meat on the end of a stick turned loose into an arena of jungle cats who had gone unfed for a week.

They cursed me before I even threw and promised to ram the ball down my throat if the pitch did not suit them. If they fouled off a ball, or missed it, they raged at me and acted like they would let me have their bat across my face. They tried to drive the ball right back to the pitcher's mound, directly at me. Art Fletcher was especially adept at this and cursed grimly if I managed to skip out of the way of a hot ground ball, promising I would get it in the head next time. If I threw a high pitch at Benny Kauff, he would threaten to break my legs.

I did not own the right to talk back to these men. I just stuck in there, kept throwing the ball as best I could, jumping, dodging, skipping, and throwing my glove up in self-defense.

The Giants were in fourth place but on an extended winning streak that became sensational—thirteen, fourteen, fifteen, sixteen, seventeen games in a row—winning every day. After eighteen straight victories, McGraw began to offer cash bonuses to every winning pitcher. A spirit of elation and supreme confidence enveloped the whole squad. Sworn enemies were grinning at each other and rooting one another home.

I had no part in winning these games, except in one indirect way. You know the expression "it's in the bag"? We had this leather pouch, about eighteen inches deep, where we kept the extra baseballs, about four dozen of them. It had a little clasp and a lock on the top. John McGraw was superstitious, and in the eighth inning, if the Giants were ahead, he'd say to me, "Hoyt, run the bag into the clubhouse."

It was my duty to take the bag and sprint with it through center field, between the gates and into the clubhouse. The crowd would stand and cheer, because they knew this ritual meant that the game was in the bag.

We were playing the Chicago Cubs one day, and I ran with the bag through center field just as the Cubs came to bat in the ninth inning. I stopped to see what was happening, and the Cubs got a couple of hits. Then I disappeared into the clubhouse, and the Cubs scored a run or two but didn't quite catch up, so the Giants won the game.

Back in the clubhouse, I was feeling pretty good, but then I heard McGraw shouting, "Send that goddam kid in here!" He dressed me down, gave me Holy Ned. He cursed my impudence, my stupidity, my youth, and my appearance and insisted that I had damn near lost the game because I had paused for a moment to take in the action, just long enough apparently for the Cubs to endanger the winning streak.

But I was happy as a lark—oh, gee whiz—because I got a bawling out from John McGraw, just the way he yelled at his big league players. I felt I was important because he had singled me out as somebody of value since I carried the game in the bag. In my own way, I felt I was making a special contribution, apart from pitching batting practice. I thought I was truly part of a baseball miracle.

I have my own superstitions, just like McGraw did. All ballplayers have them—well, maybe not all of them, but generally speaking most of the ballplayers do.

I never stepped on a foul line, either going to or from the pitcher's box. In those days, you used to leave your glove on the field, and I always left my glove face down for good luck. We wore cotton undershirts under our overshirts, which were made of flannel. The uniforms were very heavy. If we won a few games with those shirts on, we wouldn't change them. Pitchers would take the same road to the stadium every day they were going to pitch. They always used the same glove. They had all sorts of quirks.

It was fatal to consider the game as won, or to say, "You only have six more batters to go." Nobody spoke about that. It was a rule of thumb that if a pitcher was throwing a no-hit game and it got up to the fifth or sixth inning, nobody called attention to the fact it was a no-hit game. When the broadcasters came on and thought they were obliged to give the public the facts, they broke the spell by saying, "Well, it's the sixth inning, and so-and-so hasn't allowed a hit." We wouldn't dare talk that way.

I think most people have superstitions or just believe in the power of certain things that have no real basis in fact. For instance, people have asked me, what is my mental approach before I pitch a game? Is there any way that I prepare my body? Is there any special routine? What about diet and those kinds of things?

Well, I'll point to a fellow like Lefty Gomez, who, when he was pitching with the Yankees, used to eat a 3½ pound steak at the Dutchman's, a famous restaurant behind Yankee Stadium, every night before he pitched. A lot of ballplayers used to eat there.

Back in those days, the players believed that if you ate steak there was a great deal of blood content in the red meat and iron that gave you strength. Nowadays, we know that red meat can be very hazardous for heart patients or people with bad circulation. I believe it must have had some deleterious effect on us back when we thought steak and beef were the right things to eat.

Years and years ago, certain people believed that any athlete who was going to participate in an athletic event should not engage in sexual activity the night before. Having sex was seen as a weakening influence on the physical self. To tell you the truth, we didn't think of it that way. I would like that understood because what's to follow becomes rather self-denying.

Even though some ball players believed in the weakening influence of sexual activity, it did not generally affect their behavior. This notion of enforced abstinence seemed limited to pitchers, because surely infielders, outfielders, catchers, and other fellows didn't restrain themselves. So, why should the pitchers? I certainly did not. However, I did refrain from any fond embrace when it came down to a decisive set of games, or the World Series. I played it on the safe side for the big games.

I'm hesitant to reveal this contradiction to the norm. It's wholly true that a pitcher or a player should be in full control of his body with a clear, unfettered, mind. It is desirable that any player perform his duties with a wholesome attitude. Yet, this is what confuses fellows at times and leads them to the wrong impression.

I experienced two situations myself. After a night of dissipation, I wasn't expected to play the next day, but one of the other hurlers had a bad arm, and so I was asked to pitch. I'd been out late at the Ivanhoe Club near Chicago and didn't get in until around three in the morning. I told the catcher not to bother with signals, that I'd just throw fastballs.

Luckily enough, I had good control and pitched by reflex. I did a heck of a job, and what do you think happened? The pitching and heat and one thing or another boiled whatever it was out of me. Of course, then we lost because of someone else's throwing error, but it had nothing to do with my late night out. Another time I went ten innings after a rather adventurous evening.

In some respects, my attitude in those situations was so relaxed, and I was so indifferent to results, that I took gambles that otherwise were taboo and got away with them. I'd say to myself, *What the hell.* If I didn't care what happened, the tension was taken out.

When I was having a bad middle of the season, I imagined that my situation might improve if only I could acquire a superrelaxed attitude. When a pitcher gets in a bad slump and isn't winning, he tightens up so badly that every time he starts a game his nerves take hold and the tension becomes so strong that he can't perform the way he normally would, or would like to. He finally gets around to not caring if he wins or loses, and he pitches a hell of a game.

The thing about that twenty-six-game Giants winning streak in 1916 was that it turned out to be all for naught. The team was in fourth place when the streak began but completely collapsed later in the season and ended up exactly where it began, in fourth place. The unheard of, and unduplicated, winning streak almost made up to McGraw, and the rest of us, for the loss of the pennant. But all the same, when the streak came to an end, there was a feeling of dismay.

Had I been an older man then, I might have found something portentous in the fact that, despite the glorious and uplifting string that welded the team into a beautifully invincible baseball machine, the season had ended in a grinding of gears.

I returned to Erasmus Hall High School that fall, feeling almost as out of place there as I had in Lebanon and Lynn. Having seen what I had seen, I just didn't envision myself as a high school student anymore. My friends who had been peers now looked like children to me, and I felt as awkward and out of place as a grown man trying to fit himself in a third-grade chair. I wasn't the oldest or biggest of my classmates, and yet I felt yards above them in sophistication and knowledge of the darker sides of life.

Their profanity and their "daring" stories, after the crude obscenities of the locker room, didn't impress me. I did use some of the experiences I had in baseball to show a little superiority and sophistication over these poor youngsters who were still going to school, which was wrong of course. My face still wore the rounded innocence of boyhood, but my heart and mind had grown more cynical and worldly-wise. My thoughts kept returning to baseball and the place I now felt I truly belonged.

I kind of dated a girl named Dorothy Pyle, whom I first met at a birthday party for another girl, Beatrice Dodge. My mother had forced me to go, and I ended up asking Dorothy for a date. Old man Pyle was a good sport, a well-dressed man and a little indulgent. He'd drive us down to Coney Island and knew I didn't have any money. So, he'd give me a five-dollar bill, tell us to have fun and meet back up with him in an hour. It was a nice little interlude.

At home, I was still the obedient son, with my chores to do and the family schedule to respect. But there was a delicate difference now in my status. My parents seemed to have acknowledged that I was no longer a child and treated me almost as an equal.

I wasn't very studious in school. I skipped classes. My teachers were very much discouraged about me. They talked about penalizing or disciplining me by suspending me for several weeks until I came to my senses but realized I was a lost cause. Skating on Prospect Park, now that freezing weather had arrived, took up much of my time, meanwhile, and helped me stay in shape for whatever would come next. What that would be, I had little idea.

Then, on a cold, January day, after cleaning the furnace at my boyhood home, a long envelope arrived in the mail. In the left-hand corner it was embossed: "National Exhibition Company"—the incorporated name of the New York Giants! It was an invitation, signed by John McGraw, to go to spring training with the Giants in Marlin, Texas. I rushed upstairs to tell my mother, and she said I had to get my father's permission, as if there would be any question about that. I began to prepare for my next adventure, this time in the big leagues.

Every morning, while the dawn was still gray, I jogged earnestly around Prospect Park dressed in a heavy sweater, flannel pants and tennis shoes. It was a three-and-a-half-mile run, past leafless trees and lampposts. I was not a good runner, and the exercise tortured my legs and wind. But I stuck to it, grimly. The burning desire to play professional base-ball and to win the approval of John McGraw would not be defeated by my aching muscles or winded lungs. Spurred by my hopes, I could have run forever.

I was off to Texas, in the bag with the Giants, never to return to Erasmus Hall.

5

Great Big Fellas

WE TRAVELED BY TRAIN TO TEXAS—I think it was called the Sunshine Special. The trip took three days and four nights, with a six-hour stopover in Saint Louis. We wandered around uptown for a while, and when we returned to the train station, coming through the gate was this trio of men, their voices raised in what could only be an Irish song. Down the platform I made out the singers, who were causing everyone nearby to stop and stare.

Two stocky gentlemen, with their arms around each other's shoulders, brayed out the syllables in faulty unison, halting now and then to cackle happily and slap each other's backs in drunken affection. A husky young man carrying a bursting dress suitcase walked glumly by their side.

I could not believe it at first that one of the men was John McGraw. The younger fellow turned out to be Mickey O'Neil, the older man's son, who later was quite a catcher for the Braves and finished his career with the Giants.

It seems they had been at the O'Neil house drinking beer for most of the six-hour layover, and old man O'Neil had persuaded McGraw to give Mickey, who was seventeen at the time, a chance in the big leagues. O'Neil had a brogue you could cut with a knife and was saying, "You take care o' me boy, Mickey. He'll be a fine boy for you, Mack, Johnny me boy." He was chummy enough to call McGraw "Mack" or "Johnny" but lucky for him he didn't try to call Mr. McGraw "Little Napoleon" because if there was anything he hated it was that nickname. He'd kill you for that, even though it suited him.

When the Giants were at batting practice before each game, McGraw would open the gate from the clubhouse and march across the center field, as if he were a general taking command of his troops. His cadence was a strut, as measured as a military step. Fully decked out in his neat uniform and cap, his chest was out, head high, and countenance beaming with pride.

The applause would begin as soon as his stocky figure appeared at the gate, and it would swell to a roar as he marched into the outfield. Then it would pour down upon him, wave after wave, as men, women, and children stood up to scream, wave, and howl their approval. He would acknowledge the applause with the graciousness of an emperor, lifting his cap and waving it to either side, smiling and nodding regally to the bleachers, the grandstand, and the press.

This was a glorious era in New York, and especially at the Polo Grounds, when flags flew every day as if from the battlements of a mighty fortress. All the famous men and women of stage and sport appeared in the field boxes to cheer on Little Napoleon. Ethel Barrymore was there in her enormous, feathered hat. George M. Cohan, who could tell you the batting averages of every player in the big leagues, past or present, made his presence felt. Before the games began, fans could revel in the reflected glory of such fame and beauty. But the truly great doings were taking place on the ballfield.

John McGraw was the most powerful figure in baseball at that time, leader of the greatest team of the day, and absolute dictator of his domain. His one-man parade would lead him directly to home plate, where he would pick up a bat, take his batting stance, and motion the pitcher to start firing them in. He would punch a hit to left and to right and then drive one through the middle, to demonstrate once more how he and his mates used to do it when he led the Baltimore Orioles as a player in the 1890s.

We were now a safe distance from McGraw's glory days in Baltimore, not to mention the Polo Grounds. Marlin sat in the middle of the wilds of Texas. We lived in the Arlington Hotel, this old, decaying, sandstone building. The rooms were large and high-ceilinged, with a vast, marble-floored lobby featuring a chandelier that must have weighed a ton. Dusty light fixtures with cut-glass pendants decorated all the rooms. The plumbing, chastely enclosed in brown wainscoting, was often stopped up.

Our training program entailed running out to the ballpark along the railroad tracks. We tried to make our overlong strides match the spacing of the ties, which was harder than it sounds. We had to run a mile and a half out to the park and three times around it. Then we engaged in practice for an hour-and-a-half, ran around the park twice again, and then went back to the hotel. I would have a sandwich or a glass of milk and then run out again, jog around the park, practice again, go around the park again, and then return for more drills.

McGraw used to keep me out there even longer because he had a handball court and wanted to play. "You can take it," he said. "You're a young guy." I had to stay out and play handball with him after all this practice. That was some grind. McGraw did not neglect my future as a pitcher, however. Every day I pitched to the batters, and every day they belted my best pitches hard and far. One afternoon, McGraw called me aside and told me to join him on the pitcher's mound. "I want to show you something about your pitching motion," he said.

My motion! If there was one thing I knew I was good at, it was my motion. I was proud of the smooth, slick delivery I had developed and had often been praised for it. This was the first time McGraw had ever offered me a word of advice about my pitching, though, and I was not about to ignore it.

"Your motion is *too* smooth," he told me. "It's almost pretty. You wind your arm a couple of times over your head. You pivot, turn, and throw in a perfect cadence: One. Two. Three. Four. Now, the batter gets that count into his head. He may not even know it himself, but he subconsciously times your pitch, and then *bang*!"

McGraw continued. "You probably wonder why you're being hit so hard," he said. "You have to learn to break up the unconscious timing. Vary your windup. Vary your stride. Keep him off balance. That's what the pitching effort is basically—an attempt to make the batter swing off balance, so he strides and swings either too soon or too late."

That was my very first Major League lesson, and it thrilled me as much as signing the contract with McGraw nearly two years before. It was, however, somewhat tempered by what went on off the field, in and around the Arlington Hotel.

The Arlington was surrounded by a huge lawn, and in the front yard were electric poles with big milk globes on top of them. The hotel was run by this old woman, and the food was terrible—overcooked and tasteless. It was so awful, I could hardly eat it. But I was there with fellows like Heinie Zimmerman, Benny Kauff, Art Fletcher, Buck Herzog, Davy Robertson, George Burns, and Christy Mathewson—heady company, indeed.

Except for Mathewson, this could be an unruly bunch of characters. We sat out on the lawn at night, which was the only thing you could do—there wasn't even a moving picture in town—no girls, no music, no shows, no fun. I could go to the drugstore and get a malted milk, and that would be the big excitement for the evening.

One night a kid came along with a BB gun. Heinie Zimmerman gave him a couple bucks to borrow it and shot out every one of the milk globes surrounding the hotel. The hotel owner was livid, and so was McGraw. Zim paid for the damage but claimed it was worth it for the entertainment value.

Then there was Bill Morrisette, who was a good pitcher but also a nut. He was a really handsome guy who was addicted a little bit to the ladies, latching himself onto a couple of the town beauties. One day we were running along those railroad tracks, and along came this horse-drawn farm wagon with two pretty women driving it. Bill Morrisette, in uniform, his spiked shoes hanging around his neck, was sitting on the tailgate, waving to us. McGraw was seething and gave him hell. When McGraw gave you hell, it was filled with obscenities in a voice and manner of delivery I hadn't heard before or since. He reduced you to humble ashes.

One night Morrisette ordered one of the Arlington Hotel's case-hardened, weathered steaks and then extracted from his pocket a length of rope, which he tied on the tail end of the inedible slab. Then he dragged it along the dining room floor, in and out among the tables, yanking the rope to make the steak hop after him, while yipping and barking like a dog. "Come along now, Fido!"

Two days later, he was dispatched to Baltimore and never found success in the big leagues, even though he had skill enough to be one of the best. The last I heard of Bill was that he rode a horse into the lobby of a small-town hotel.

Ballplayers lived under a stigma and never were treated well in hotel dining rooms.

One time we were in a hotel in Mobile, Alabama, and ordered steak. The waiter swung open the kitchen door and yelled, "Steak for the ballplayers." We were almost always given the worst food because baseball players didn't deserve anything better.

Ballplayers were a peculiar breed, sort of like circus people in a way. Charley "Boss" Schmidt, a catcher who later played for the Detroit Tigers, was a big, solid, rugged man. He came from Arkansas and was one of the strongest guys I'd ever seen. At one time, he was manager of the Mobile Bears, which had a big bear for a mascot. Charlie would take the bear to a local saloon and fill a cuspidor with beer, and the bear would lick it up. One of the attractions was to see Schmidt wrestle the bear at home plate. Everybody loved to see Charlie and the bear because they rather resembled each other.

Some of these fellows were just born entertainers. Benny Kauff was a dandified little guy, brash and handsome. He stood only about 5 feet 8 but was unbelievably cocky. He owned 75 suits and 125 silk shirts. He would change his clothes three times a day and always looked as if he were getting ready to walk onstage. When he joined the Giants, he swaggered about the Polo Grounds like he had just signed a lease on it. He had led the Federal League—an outlaw league—in batting and spoke scornfully of what he would do to National League pitchers.

Then there was Davy Robertson, from the Deep South, a soft-spoken and friendly fellow. He was a highly educated college man from down around the Carolinas someplace and imbued with Southern ideological practices. One night, a gang of about five or six of the Giants paraded up and down outside of his door singing "Marching through Georgia," which they knew he hated. Suddenly, the door flew open, and there stood Davy, hair rumpled, eyes wild, suspenders dangling, feet bare, with a long revolver in his hand.

The parade broke up in a mad scramble for cover, and Davy let go with two shots toward the ceiling. The players were cringing in doorways or huddled behind potted palms, not too sure about what he might do next. Davy trotted out into the hall with his revolver tucked into his pants and used both hands to unwind the long, flat fire hose. He twisted the wheel, and the water started to hiss. Then he took careful aim at the potted plants and sent them tumbling before a cannon stream from the hose.

47

The players, left shelterless, scrambled for the spiral staircase that led down to the lobby. Davy tried to turn off the water, but the wheel was rusted and would not yield. So, it poured on, flooding the hall and cascading down the staircase and into the lobby, covering it almost an inch deep.

Oh, the shenanigans that went on.

Baseball, to my teenage self, seemed to continue forever. Of course, I knew that it would end for me someday and that it did not hold a future like being a businessman would—earning a position through years of effort and to be held for life. It was like starting on a voyage around the world. There would be an eventual homecoming when I would have to think of fretful things again. For now, all I could see was the voyage itself, stretching out before me.

I had not really grown up in one sense, for I was still playing a boy's game. Playing it for a living did not make it a wholly serious business and only insulated me from the realities that many young men my age had begun to cope with—preparations for a profession, or a trade, and serious studies to ready myself for taking up the cares of adult life.

At the end of spring training in 1917, I knew it was nearly time for the rookies to be cut from the squad and that within a few days I'd be on my way back to a Minor League club. I decided that if I wanted to make my dreams come true, I needed to put my aspirations directly to John McGraw. So, I went to him after practice and asked for two things: first, to let me pitch for the Giants in a spring-training game and, second, to tell me which Minor League team I would be reporting to. McGraw stared at me in mild disbelief and then smiled a little.

"Sure," he said. "You can start for us on Sunday against Waco."

I beat Waco with the Giants behind me, and then McGraw sent me back to the Minors, playing for the Memphis Chickasaws. McGraw forewarned me, saying, "When you go to Memphis, you're going to be pitching under Mike Donlin, one of the toughest operators in the big leagues."

6

When Schoolboys Cry

I REPORTED TO MEMPHIS, AND MIKE DONLIN immediately took an interest in me because I came from the Giants. I had to feel my way around town and wound up living in a very pleasant room over a restaurant called The Yellow Dog, where a big yellow dog grinned down from a wooden signboard. Mine was an ancient chamber with a lazy ceiling fan that kept the flies awake.

What appealed to me was the meal ticket I got there because it cost only five dollars a week. There were big, white bowls of oatmeal in the morning, yellow cream and baked apples larger than my fist, all crusted with sugar and topped with cream. No matter how much I ate—cereal, buckwheat cakes, eggs, hominy grits, ham, baked apple—the price was just thirty-five cents. Eventually, I located a family, the Dillons, who had an extra room, and I moved out of the Yellow Dog.

One day, I was knocked out of the box at Memphis Park. I walked back to my apartment and took a seat in the front room to read a book. Through the parlor window, I noticed Mr. LaToura, known around town as the hot tamale king, pushing his cart. He had this sing-song chant, "Hot tamales, hot tamales, hot tamales."

Now, LaToura was more than the hot tamale king. He was very much tied in with the gambling set. He was a know-it-all, and a wise guy of the—almost the underworld. A shot rang out, and LaToura slumped to the ground, dead.

This was my first exposure to the mob but would not be my last.

Memphis was very difficult for me, just like all the other towns. It was hard for me to find associates of my own because boys and girls weren't free to peregrinate. The fellows were much older than me and went

49

with their own crowd. I was always belittled in front of them because I was young and also so naive.

I did strike up a relationship with Mike Donlin's wife's sister. She was a couple years older than me and far more sophisticated. We went out together, the four of us, for a while. I also met a girl, Marie Laurenson, who used to come to the games. She and I became fast friends, and she was lovely, a very nice girl. It was an innocent relationship. She was just a schoolgirl.

On an off day, Marie and I took a walk in the park downtown. It was not a big park, more of a central square. On this particular day, the warm air was just as sweet as honey, and there was a delicate flavor of honeysuckle surrounding us. The boat whistles on the Mississippi reached us occasionally.

Marie and I were sitting together on a bench, holding hands, and she slipped something into my hand. It was a tie clasp with my initials on it. She said, "I don't know what's ever going to become of us in the future, but I would like you to have this and just remember Marie Laurenson down in Memphis."

It was a lovely moment and a reminder of what a normal, teenage relationship might be like.

All in all, Memphis was a trial of embarrassment for me both socially and in terms of baseball. I hated going to the ballpark because we were losing, and I wasn't fulfilling my ambition. I wasn't justifying the confidence McGraw put in me when he sent me to Memphis. I thought of my father and mother, the way I was brought up and how it clashed with the indifference of my teammates to the norms of society. It only got worse from there.

One Sunday, during an afternoon game, it was raining like sin. The spectators fled. The Chickasaws, or the Chicks, as we were called, were leading for once, but the umpires wouldn't call the game. A called game would have been a rare victory for us. Mike Donlin raged at the umpires, but they stood fast.

The mud in the infield grew so deep, gee whiz, it was ankle deep. Even the pitcher was sloshing about out there in his position and in danger of slipping on the rubber and falling. No pitcher would dare execute a full throw on footing like that. So Donlin took his pitcher out, promising that he would make a mockery of the game. He said, "If the umpires are gonna burlesque the game, I will too."

Donlin went to the pitcher's box and turned the full force of his invective, using obscenities I'd never heard in my life before, shouted out loud in public. The few spectators who were left were horrified. The club owners were later waited on by indignant churchgoers who resented this desecration of the Sabbath, regardless of how apt or beautifully foraging the language was. Donlin couldn't pitch at all, and the opposing team scored about 15 runs off him.

That night he was fired. The next evening, we were scheduled to leave for Mobile, where we had a series coming up. It seemed strange to be gathering on the platform without Mike Donlin, who was supposed to be sort of a parental guide to me.

There we stood, the Memphis Chickasaws, with our baggage at our feet, conscious of the fans around us. I was trying to act nonchalant, as if they were not there at all. When the train whistled from way down the crossing, the road secretary seemed to notice me for the first time. He walked over, and right in front of me, my teammates, and the fans, broke the news.

"Waite, I'm sorry to tell you but you're not going with us," he said as he handed me a note. "We're sending you back to the Giants."

Like a child who is suddenly denied something, who is told he must stay home from a picnic, I stood staring wordlessly at the secretary. I began to choke up and everything began to gather in my throat. Not going? Fired? I had never been fired. *If I couldn't play baseball . . .*

I accepted handshakes and parted in a daze. I tried to act like a man, but the tears just spilled out of my eyes. I could feel my face contorting as the sobs forced their way out. Not going? How could I go back? By now the team was on the train, and I was conscious of a few hands starting to wave from the windows. I picked up my bag and turned away just as the train wheels began to roll.

Then I really cried. Believe me, the sobs rocked my throat and chest. The bitter tears just rolled like rainwater down my hot cheeks and dripped from my chin. I bit my lip and wiped them with my sleeve as I walked in a semitrance back toward the apartment.

So, this was what all the practice and dreaming and coaching and the illusions had come to. This was how my baseball career was going to end? I wanted to stop someone and explain that it wasn't my fault. I pitched well; it was all the errors by others that lost all those games. But there was no one in the world I could say that to. I had to go back to my room and the next morning go over to the office, collect my check, and return to the New York Giants in humiliation.

It really was heartbreaking. It was the first rejection that I ever experienced, and I was at a loss to know how to take it. I was still a kid. The fellows in that club, after I had been beaten, used to tell me that I had to learn how to lose because I wasn't going to win every game. By the same token, I had to learn how to win. Both were essential, but I didn't realize this. I just knew that somebody had found me wanting.

I wondered what John McGraw would say, what people in my hometown, in Brooklyn, would say. What would my father and my mother say? It was my first real failure, and it was traumatic. It dug down deep in my heart, but you know, as they say, you win by losing sometimes. It did teach me a lesson, and it was all part of growing up, a little more cement added to the structure that forms character.

I went back to the Giants, met up with them in Chicago, and McGraw was very nice to me. "I hear you had some tough luck down there," he said.

Well, I did have some tough luck. There was this one game where I had the other team beaten. I struck out the final batter, but the catcher allowed the ball to get away from him. The fellow reached first and eventually scored. It wasn't my fault.

Luckily, youth has a way of easily dismissing disappointments because other things bob up to free the mind. I was seeing new things, experiencing new episodes. Everything was new to me. Bitterness, joy, elation—all the sentiments I could include in my repertoire, I learned one by one, very quickly, and sadly in some respects.

McGraw sent me back to the Minor Leagues—this time in Montreal.

7

The Joy Clubs

WHEN I JOINED THE MONTREAL CLUB in 1917, I took a taxicab to this hotel, and as I was walking to the front desk to register, I was virtually run out of the way by a girl flying out of the dining room with blood coming out of her mouth and some guy chasing her. Here we go again, I thought.

I had gone in there to try to find Dan Howley, the Montreal manager, who proceeded to take me out for a walk and describe his family to me, how they had wonderful teeth.

I mean, Howley did have wonderful teeth, but otherwise he was kind of ratty. The whole team was ratty.

As we'd travel from town to town, the fellow who was going to pitch the next day would get the lower berth, but all the other pitchers got the upper berth. Sometimes we didn't have any berths at all. When we traveled from Richmond to Montreal, we stayed at the Imperial Hotel in New York along the way. When we got there late at night, the hotel only had three available rooms with two beds in them. You either pitched yourself across a bed or slept on the floor. The rest of the fellows played poker all night.

Howley told us to be at Grand Central early because the train would be crowded, and if we didn't get there at the crack of dawn there wouldn't be any seats. All of us were there on time and waited at the gate because Howley had the tickets. When did Howley show up? He was talking to some people, some friends of his, and forgot all about us. So, we ended up standing all the way to Albany before changing trains to Montreal. This was some ballclub.

In Montreal the ballpark was this huge affair built next to a convent. It was rectangular and had a small grandstand. The clubhouse floor slanted down and had a hole in the middle of it. It was the dirtiest place. When it rained in Montreal, it came down hard. If a sun shower sprang up, the bench would fill up with water, and we had to sit on other benches out in right field. They used to let the grass grow at four hundred feet behind right field because nobody could ever hit a ball that far anyway. It was like a hay field out there.

The bleachers held about ten thousand people, but nobody came to the ballpark except about four hundred returnees from World War I, which was still on at the time. They got in for free; paid spectators amounted to only about a dozen people. There was this one guy—the *only* one—in the bleachers, every day. He'd stretch out, cross his arms, and watch the game.

The Montreal club was owned by a fellow named Sammy Lichtenstein, who made millions supplying rags for the hot boxes of Canadian Railroad trains. Can you imagine that? He used to sit behind home plate and had this silver-tipped cane. When he pressed a button, a cigarette would pop out of the top. Then he had a contraption with a cord that ran through this wire netting, and it had a little tube in the bottom. He would write messages on a little pad about who to take out or put into the game and send them to the manager.

We were the last-place team. We sometimes had six straight doubleheaders but only four pitchers. If I got knocked out in the first game, I started the second. We had to wake up Eddie Zimmerman, the third baseman, between innings. He'd go to sleep on the bench. If a ball was hit hard to him, he'd just raise his leg and let it go into left field. He wouldn't even try to field it. Tommy Madden, one of our catchers, had fingers that pointed in multiple directions from being hit in his hand too many times.

I remember playing down on Long Island, in Riverhead, a night game. In those days a night game was unheard of. It was by torchlight. They had these huge flames out in the field, but you couldn't see very well. I was sure that this idea of playing games at night would never catch on.

The 1917 season in Montreal was very bad. I forget how many games I won, certainly not more than 3 or 4. On the last day of the season, we moved out of last place to finish seventh. Tommy Madden stood up on a chair and made an impassioned speech about what ingrates we were because all season long we had behaved ourselves and rested comfortably in last place, and then had to ruin it all by winning the last game of the season.

The year 1918, however, turned out to be one of the most eventful transitory years of my entire career. I went south again with the New York Giants for spring training. Same place—Marlin, Texas—and then McGraw sent me down to yet another Minor League team, this time in Tennessee, to the Nashville Volunteers, or the Vols, as they were known. A fellow named Roy Ellam was the manager.

We played in what is widely known as Sulphur Dell, which had no grass in the infield. It was all dirt, and groundskeepers used to keep the dust down by spraying it with oil. As a consequence, I had a hard time keeping my fingers clean. Right field was very short and went almost straight up, so the right fielder played high up, on a hill.

I got a room across the river in a boarding house and paid seven dollars a week. That included breakfast of ham and eggs, fried potatoes, pancakes, waffles, sausage, cereal, grits—it had everything you could think of, and I could eat as much as I wanted. At night, for seventy-five cents, we went to an eating establishment that passed the food, homestyle. Nashville had the best ice cream. It was sold in a cigar store, believe it or not. As in all those Southern towns, there was nothing to do at night, so we palled around with fellows who hung around the cigar store.

I was rooming with a fellow named Gus Helfrich. We looked a little bit like each other. Two sisters, Effie and Flo, used to come to the ballpark every day. They were what we called "Baseball Sadies." They followed baseball very closely. I became attached to Flo, and we had some romantic entanglements. It was a very pleasant setup while it lasted.

One day Gus said to me, "Are you running with that Flo?"

I said, "Yeah, why? What's the matter?"

He said, "For God's sake, do you know what you are doing? That's Roy Ellam's girl! You really want an early demise around here, don't you?" Just because she was the manager's girl, well, that didn't exactly stop me from going with Flo, but it did shorten the union somewhat.

With all the roaming and jumping around in professional baseball, where I went from town to town, I was exposed to all sorts of temp-

55

tations. I didn't wind up in every town staying with a lovely family. I was out in the world, and it was not sparing. The ballplayers did teach me how to protect myself from contracting a social disease. They had experience with women and some of the seamy sides of life. It was as if destiny had taken me by the hand and guided me in these different areas of experimentation, of trial and failure. Although I was still young in terms of worldly experience, I'd had a lot of it.

One night, I was rooming with Gus at the DeSoto Hotel in New Orleans. At around nine Gus said, "What do you say we go over to the French market and buy a couple of cantaloupes?"

I said, "Well, that'd be refreshing, but how are we going to cool them?"

Gus said, "We'll just order a couple of buckets of ice from downstairs, pour it in the basin and put them in there. By about eleven o'clock we'll have some nice cantaloupe."

We walked over to the French market, bought the cantaloupes, brought them back to the hotel, ordered the ice, and put them in the bathroom basin. We waited a couple of hours, but they turned out to be hard as rocks, and not fit to eat at all.

We had these big, wide windows in the DeSoto Hotel, with screens. So, Gus and I opened a screen and threw half a cantaloupe out the window. Two fellows were walking along the street below, one in a white silk suit, and it landed near him. He and his pal walked out into the middle of the street, looking up to see who was throwing things at them.

I said to Gus, "Jeez, I've got better control than you have." I took the other half of the cantaloupe and threw it out the window and it hit the other guy on the side of his straw hat. He was a big, fat guy, and it broke the rim off his hat. Then it hit him on the shoulder, sending the seeds and juice running down his suit. Gus and I went to shut the screen, and it fell out of the window, dropping about eleven floors. We scurried back to bed and turned the lights out.

Well, all they had to do was look for the window without a screen, and it wasn't fifteen minutes before there was a *knock, knock, knock* on the door and "open up, open up, police!" Gus opened the door. I made believe that I was in bed asleep, but my hair wasn't even mussed. I looked like I was ready to go to a party.

The police started to inspect the place and noticed cantaloupe seeds trailing over to the window. They told us to get dressed and escorted us to the courthouse and jail about five or six blocks away. We were thrown in the jug with a couple of boys dressed in girls' ballet costumes. They said they had been headed for a masquerade party, stopped at a local bistro, got plastered and arrested, and never made it to the party.

The police woke up Roy Ellam, and he had to come down to the court too. I was first up before the judge. The big, fat guy starts yelling, "He's a juvenile delinquent! He ought to be in reform school! The boy's crazy!" I was really scared. They read the charges: this, that, and the other, throwing refuse in the street, causing whatever. I stood accused, and the judge asked me for a statement.

I said, "Well, you see, judge, we did go over to the French market, bought the cantaloupes, iced them as much as we could, but they weren't fit to eat. We were afraid if we left the refuse around that it would attract bugs, so we threw the cantaloupes out the window, and one of them unfortunately hit this gentleman on the shoulder. Naturally, we were apprehensive about it."

The judge listened and then said, "Are you the fellow who pitched earlier today against the Pelicans?" In fact, I had been beaten by New Orleans, 1–0, that afternoon.

"I'm going to give you a suspended sentence," the judge said, "but you will have to meet the cost of cleaning this gentleman's suit and buy him a new hat." I yes'd him, "Yessir, yessir," all the way through it. What else was I going to do? Roy Ellam, for good measure, fined me twenty-five bucks. Nevertheless, I was proud of my control because I actually took a good shot at the guy.

My on-field behavior wasn't exactly one of refinement either. One afternoon the Vols were playing the Birmingham Barons. Ray, our shortstop, came in from his position to tell me to pitch a certain way to Jesse Altenburg, who could run like the wind. The first ball I threw to Jesse was right at his head. That wasn't Ray's instruction—it just got away from me, and I didn't mean it.

Jesse thought I did mean it; he dropped his bat and was halfway out to the mound to meet me. I dropped the glove off my hand and just stood there. I didn't advance to meet him, but he charged at me, which left him wide open, so I hit him on the jaw and knocked him down. We had a scuffle out there in the pitcher's box. Well, that got settled, and there were explanations and apologies. Jesse later on became a good friend of mine.

It was hot as sin down South. At night we'd take our chairs to the hotel roof so we could get a little air. Then we'd go back down to our room and turn on a tub of what was supposed to be cold water, but it wasn't even cool. We'd just get damp and turn on the ceiling fan over the bed. We would just lie down on the bed, damp and nude, letting the fan blow on us to try to cool off.

When we traveled, they'd wake us up at three in the morning and load us on a train with the windows open. You slept on your elbow. They used to call it "traveling Ted Sullivan." They didn't supply any berths or sleeping quarters. You just rested your arm on the windowsill of the train with the windows open and rode all night from three until about eight in the morning. When you got there your face was dirty from soot. It was awful.

On June 30, 1918, the league broke up for lack of attendance, and I was sent back to the Giants in New York, resuming my duties as a batting-practice pitcher. While at the Polo Grounds one day, with the Giants leading the Cardinals in the eighth inning, McGraw suddenly leaned forward and caught my eye. "Hoyt!" he said, "Go down to the bullpen!" Would McGraw actually put me in the game? Me? Pitch for the Giants? I stood up and headed over to right field in a bit of a fog.

In the bullpen I warmed up, barely conscious of throwing the ball but fully aware that a gaggle of fans was hanging over the bleacher wall, encouraging me. "Go get 'em, Schoolboy!" Then the moment arrived when I was called to the mound. "Just get the ball over the plate," the bullpen coach hollered. "They can't hit you!"

He knew something I didn't. I struck out the first batter on three pitches. Next was the Cardinals pitcher. Another three pitches, and he was back on the bench. Then came the lead-off man. He jumped on my first pitch and popped it into the air for an infield out. Seven pitches, and three outs! I heard the cheers pouring down from all sides, for me. I really was a big leaguer now.

McGraw called me into his office and told me I had done a remarkable job. "Someday," he said, "you will be a fine pitcher." *Someday.* My heart sank because I knew exactly what that meant. "I have a chance to take the pennant this year, or else I'd keep you," McGraw explained, his face friendly but intent. "But I have a chance to get Fred Toney from Cincinnati, and I have to make room for him."

I was sent back down into the Minors, to Newark, for my third season.

The manager of the Newark club, Arthur Irwin, did not take a liking to me. I thought he was despicable. He seemed to make a career out of being sarcastic, answering simple questions with questions. If I asked him for a baseball, he'd say, "Now where would I get a baseball?" I hated his whining profane voice and bristly mustache, his potbelly and the cocky way he carried himself. I thought he lacked John McGraw's brains, sense of fun, basic kindness and generosity, and, most of all, integrity.

Irwin's team was in such bad shape that he gave me an old jersey with "Montreal" ripped off the front and a pair of baseball trousers that didn't match the shirt. The trousers were missing two crucial buttons that I had to replace with a twist of heavy wire. I was issued a Newark cap and stockings, but the stockings didn't match those that some of the other fellows were wearing.

While I played for Newark, I lived at home in my comfortable bedroom, where I slept better than I had in all those third-rate hotels. Baseball in Newark was hopeless, however, just as it had been everywhere else for me in the Minor Leagues. The Newark franchise was so dilapidated and deteriorated that it was moved to Hamilton, Ontario, where we played on a cricket field until the end of the season.

Just before the season closed, Irwin cut the squad down to little more than a full team and a couple pitchers. I was turned loose and told to collect my pay from John McGraw, who insisted that Newark owed me the money, not him. The argument was settled when neither one of them paid me. There was no player's representative in those days, nor any commissioner to appeal to. A player who lost his pay was invited to whistle for it or get out of baseball if he didn't like it.

That's not to say that Irwin hesitated to impose fines for various infractions. Early in my career with Newark, when I was to get up at six to meet the club at Manhattan Transfer and travel to Baltimore, my alarm clock failed, and I missed the train. I promptly wired Irwin for instructions and just as promptly received his response: "Stay home. You are fined $50." That was almost a full week's pay.

With some irony, I used to refer to Montreal, Nashville, and Newark as "joy" clubs because the teams were so terrible and the compensation so tenuous that we could only be playing for fun. It certainly wasn't for the money, and I still hadn't improved as a pitcher.

By the way, McGraw's Giants did not win the pennant that year either.

8

Miss Scoville's Advice

MOST PEOPLE WERE IMMENSELY PATRIOTIC DURING World War I, especially at the beginning. Some thought it unpatriotic to play baseball at that time. In fact, in 1918 the big league ended the season early, on Labor Day, because enough people thought it an infringement for ballfields and battlefields to coexist.

This was the first time America had been in a war of that kind. It was a cruel and vicious thing. Everyone was conscious of soldiers returning disabled. Everything was dedicated to the war effort, and a great change in the personality and philosophy of the country ran through business, sport, and life itself. I thought it might be a matter of weeks before I was out of baseball and wearing an army uniform myself.

I welcomed going home to Brooklyn in the early fall of 1918 for the off-season because everyone was warm and receptive. I had a reunion with the guys I knew from high school and felt like I was back with my own group. I met up with Ed Moran, who had been our third baseman at Erasmus Hall. He was attending Middlebury College in Vermont and doing well there.

Ed said to me, "Waite, what are you going to do this winter?"

I told him I didn't know.

"You're eighteen years old, aren't you?"

I was.

He said, "Well, you know you're subject to the draft, so why don't you come up with me to Middlebury and join the Student Army Training Corps? If you enter the army under the SATC, you will be admitted to the college."

The problem was, I had left high school during my junior year and had only ten Regents credits. To graduate high school in New York and go to college, at least twelve credits were required, which were earned by passing Regents examinations given by the state.

Undaunted, Ed pressed on. "You'll get in," he said. "You're only short a couple of credits, and they'll let you make it up. The war is on, and they need people."

So, I took a train with Ed up to Middlebury College and arrived at dusk. It was so delightful, a beautiful little town. The leaves were changing, with the smell of fall in the air. Oh, it was a lovely place—wonderful. It was so still and yet alive, with lights in all the windows, a faint whiff of fireplaces, and dim figures of men and women out for a stroll.

Ed had reserved a room for us in a big, old-fashioned house, where a smiling, older woman made us feel welcome and showed us to the large, second-floor bedroom. It was a typical middle-class home of that day: warm and filled with the aroma of polished wood. There were old rockers and a Morris chair, a carpet with flowers on it, two enameled iron beds, and a white washstand with a big iron-stone pitcher full of clean, tepid water standing in a white basin. Neat little towels, stiffly ironed, hung in a row, and a fat cake of soap sat in a small porcelain dish.

We went to bed early, and Ed fell asleep right away. I lay awake, thinking about the wild chance I had taken. Could I turn myself into a college man after all those ugly years among hard-bitten men who would cripple me to take my job away? The drinking, fighting and filth—if I could get to the top of that heap, I could do anything. But if I missed, what then? I had to find a way to make college work.

Ed and I arose at dawn to a smoking New England breakfast. Then we had to hustle to the college, which was a mile or so away. We trotted through town in the crisp, morning air, past the harness shop already open and bustling, the country drug store with jars of horehound drops in the window, the hardware store with windows as wide as barn doors.

As we reached the edge of town, we saw the college spread out before us on a green hillside. Its buildings formed an enormous rectangle on an easy slope. Far up the rise stood the main dormitory, made of brick. Beside it rose a white-spired chapel, beautifully etched against the green hills. An almost wordless longing began to rise in my throat. *This is where I really belong*, I thought.

First, I had to join a long line outside the induction office where students became soldiers. Once inside, I filled out a lengthy questionnaire and stripped down for my physical. That was the easy part, because next I had to talk to the dean of admissions, who right away asked me about my credits. I told him I had twelve.

He said, "Do you have your Regents card with you?"

I told him I neglected to bring it and didn't know where it was.

"Well," he said, "I can't admit you without a Regents card, so you better write to Albany and get one."

I had never seen a Regents card and figured this was a good opportunity to see what one looked like. Sure enough, Albany sent me a Regents card with . . . ten credits. I did a very artistic job dissecting it before dropping it into a wastebasket. I needed a new plan, which came to me rather easily as I gazed out at the dean's office from my dormitory window.

The executive buildings at Middlebury College, along with some of the student halls and classrooms, were located on the ridge of a sort of bowl. The campus ran down into the bowl, and crosswalks from all the buildings intersected in the center.

I sat at my window and waited until I saw the dean leave his office and start toward the classrooms. I sprinted down the pathway toward him, affecting a panting sound as I ran, and caught up with him.

"Oh, Dean," I huffed, "I was just on my way to your office to see you! My Regents card came this morning!"

I started digging through my pockets, turning each one inside out.

I looked behind me, as if it had dropped on the ground somewhere.

"Where's the card?" I exclaimed. "It was right here!"

The dean looked concerned and began to help me look for a white card somewhere along the walk. I didn't let up. "I had it a minute ago! Don't tell me I lost the card! Where could it have gone?"

Finally, the dean said, "Maybe somebody will find it. There were twelve credits on it?"

I said, "Yes, yes, twelve credits."

He said, "Well, all right, then. Just keep looking and bring it to my office when you find it."

I was admitted to Middlebury College and the army, too, getting paid $30 a month, along with the other SATCs. The life we led had a special quality. We were told when to get up, what to wear, what to eat, and when to go to bed. All our basic needs were provided for. It was come day, go day, and who knew what Sunday would bring? Who knew indeed how long before the army would reach out and ship us away?

Yet it was not the real army, in that we did not feel the rigid pressure of discipline nor the harsh restrictions of the army system. The army part of our lives was reveille, brief guard duty, then the study of military tactics and regulations. It took up perhaps half our days. Besides that, there were standard college studies, in which a bare passing grade was all that was required. If you remember, I was not exactly a model student. At Erasmus Hall, I got a big fat zero in Latin. In mathematics, I was almost as bad. Being a baseball player, I could count up to three balls and two strikes—and three plus two is five—but that's about as much as I knew about addition.

What do you think they did with me at Middlebury? My first class of the day was mathematics. I forget whether it was calculus or advanced geometry, but in this class it was Y over 2 equals X over 6 or something or other, minus Z over 4. I didn't know what the heck they were talking about.

The professor called on us in alphabetical order: Harrison, Heyworth . . . Hoyt. I always just said, "I'm sorry, but I don't know the answer." One day, I walked into the classroom, and on the blackboard were problems, one of which had my name on it. Of course, I didn't know ABC about the darn thing and just stood by the blackboard. The professor asked me why I wasn't doing my problem. I replied, "Because I don't know the answer."

He said, "Everybody sit down but Hoyt" and then ordered me to stand alongside his desk. "Now, gentlemen," he began, "you have before you a living example of the wastefulness of youth. Not just wastefulness, but a wastrel, who is occupying the desk of a very deserving young man who could be improving his mind and education by sitting in this class and paying attention to his work. The man you see before you is indifferent to all the curriculum of this school and class. He is nothing but a lazy, indolent, no-good—" He didn't say "bum," but he meant it, whatever he said.

"He will go nowhere in life," he continued. "By the time he is twenty-one, I predict he will be this, that, and the other." He didn't say I would be lying in a gutter, but he did say something almost that bad. "Never will he amount to anything. He is an utter disgrace to this school, this class, and the peers of his generation."

"Before you sit down," he continued, "I would like to know what you intend to be when you grow up." I thought for a moment and almost wisecracked that I wanted to be a mathematics teacher. Instead, I just told the truth, which was that I did not know.

Fortunately, there was plenty of time for sports and social life. The sport was football. Ordinarily, I would have been barred from participation because I was a professional, but during wartime there were no restrictions against professionalism, and I became part of our rather mediocre team. I was a halfback on offense and a tackle on defense. Every moment of it was fun. We had no frantic manager to dress us down with profanities. Coach Brown was friendly, helpful, and encouraging. The locker room was warm and comfortable; the whole atmosphere was one of gaiety.

As it happened, our schedule was cut short by the influenza epidemic, which seemed to be killing far more soldiers than was enemy action. Men and women began to wear charms to ward off the dread infection, and large gatherings were discouraged lest the disease spread faster. Our games against Williams, Amherst, and Tufts never took place.

We felt no special fear of the disease despite the stories that reached us of the decimation of distant army camps, and the pictures of the temporary hospitals that had been thrown up near the larger cities, with nurses and doctors wearing gauze masks to filter out the wicked microbes. Influenza, like death, was something that happened to other people. Our main concern was the fraternity dances and the opportunity to meet up with the coeds and the free time to think up ways to celebrate being young.

The SATCs did not eat with the rest of the students at the main hall; we ate afterward. We had to maintain rigid silence while dining at a long, wooden table on hard benches. There were plates of food, butter and bread, generally within easy reach. One night, the butter was way down at the other end, so I yelled, "Slide down the butter!"

All of a sudden, there was a tap on my shoulder, and this big, fat mess sergeant said, "You have broken a regulation. You are supposed to maintain silence." He said, "Private Hoyt, you can either leave the table now and not be reported or finish your meal and I'll put you on report."

I was hungry, so I finished my meal.

He waited for me and then took charge as if I were under arrest. As I started through the doorway, he gave me a shove between my shoulder blades. I turned and dealt him a short, solid right to his chin. This was the worst thing I could have done, of course, because it meant I would be court-martialed. I could be sentenced to Camp Devons or Camp Dixon and possible death by influenza.

The next morning, I was summoned to the headquarters of Lieutenant Van Alstyne, the commander. I explained my side of the story, and he was inclined to sympathize because he relied on me to run errands for him in the village. He quickly decided on a not-guilty verdict and later that day hoisted me out of harm's way by making me a sergeant too. I was court-martialed in the morning and a sergeant by evening!

This had further repercussions, however, because a few days later Lieutenant Van Alstyne called me in and ordered me to direct a military funeral.

He said, "A young soldier, a citizen of Middlebury, has been returned from a training camp. He died and is going to have a military funeral. You're to pick a squad of eight men. You will precede the caisson, which will be draped in an American flag, to the cemetery, which is about two miles from the center of town. Read the military manual on burials for further instructions."

I had no time to read the manual, much less memorize it, but I was obsessed with making sure to uphold the dignity and solemnity of the occasion. The day dawned when the funeral was to take place; it was sleety and snowy, mixed with half rain. We sloshed our way through two miles to the cemetery. Marching as a guard of honor with the hearse was a fairly simple task, but we probably did it all wrong, albeit seriously and with military bearing.

The soldier's family lined up on one side of the grave, and the squad was on the other. The casket was placed on the rollers and bars over the open grave. The minister read the commitment, and then I was supposed to give orders for the rifle salute to the soldier.

I didn't know what to say. So, I yelled, "Ready. . . . Aim. . . ." and I'm thinking, *How do I give the order to aim at the sky?* I just hoped they would know what to do.

As I was about to give the order to fire, I saw to my horror that the rifles were aimed directly at the mourning family. Now, the guns were loaded with blanks, but this was not good. "Up!" I screamed. "Raise 'em!" The boys raggedly lifted the guns until they pointed skyward. "Fire!"

When the salute ended, the undertaker gave me a bewildered look. What came next? I couldn't remember what to say about lowering the casket into the grave, so I just said, "Lower away!" And they buried the poor guy. I hate to say this, because it sounds funny now, but it was serious at the time because he was a military man and had been part of the war effort. I was awfully sorry about the whole procedure.

I didn't have many more opportunities after that to give orders as a sergeant. Come November 11, 1918, the war ended and so did my time at Middlebury College. Since the army wouldn't be needing me, Middlebury would no longer support me. I was discharged by Christmas and headed back home to Brooklyn.

I have never fully resolved this turn of events. I had so much fun at Middlebury. I loved the association and camaraderie I found there, sharing in the ambitions and perplexities of my peers. They were puzzled too. They didn't know where they were going in life or much of anything about its responsibilities.

It was as if I had found my youth again. Instead of banging about the country in the company of older men, I was among my own kind and was offered the opportunity to use my best days the way a young man should: part in study, part in play, and part in getting ready for the serious burdens ahead. Nothing about my time in baseball seemed to be worth trading away my boyhood. There was a special comfort, perhaps a feeling of security, in being accepted for who I was, with no need to keep my guard up lest someone see the nervous child behind the cocky mask.

I had almost dropped baseball out of my mind. That was not the life I really wanted. I wanted to remain in these lovely hills and stay nineteen a while longer. I wanted to concern myself with books and examinations, coeds, football, ice-cream sodas, sitting up late at night, and talking with boys my own age about the ambitions we shared and the things we might do together.

I loved college, and because I was happy at Middlebury, I have often thought of Miss Scoville and her recommendation that I take the literary course. I still find myself envying the youngsters who could live out their youth among girls and boys of their own age. When I was a kid, we used to go to football games at Yale, Harvard, and Princeton because they were within easy reach. They were marvelous atmospheres. I used to read books like *Stover at Yale.* Boy, did I read.

Many years later, in 1957, I took my gifted son Christopher to enroll at Princeton. When we arrived on campus, I really had a heartache. I still do. I had so often strolled up and down the tree-bordered walks there during my high school days, when I had a strong and secret desire to be a Princeton Tiger.

As I walked down to the athletic field, I recalled how, way back in 1915, the Erasmus Hall High School baseball team had been invited down for a practice game against Princeton. I recalled pitching that game, just across the road from where my son now had his room. It was not as an alumnus returning but as a guy who wished he had been. I was happy Christopher had made it but also wished myself a student there and mourned the youth I had never properly enjoyed.

For that moment, at least, I'd have given up my whole baseball career in exchange for having taken Miss Scoville's advice.

9

A Bath in Badness

HEADING INTO 1919, JOHN MCGRAW TRADED me to Rochester of the
International League. This meant I was through with the Giants and
had lost any chance of being in the Major Leagues on that team. There
was a rule that a Major League team was only allowed to own a player
for three years, and for three years McGraw had kept me in the Minors.
The three years were over, the Giants were not calling me up to the
big leagues, so they had no choice but to trade me to Rochester with
a lousy, Minor League contract.

I had been so sure I would be successful. When I was a young boy, I
attached all my illusions and fantasies to baseball. I believed I was going
to be a very impressive, successful man when I finally got around to
pitching in the big leagues.

On the day I signed with the Giants, I was a sensation. Everyone
expected I was on my way to the Major Leagues, especially me. All of
that exploded in my face. I never succeeded in the Minors. Everything
I had looked forward to had been an utter failure and disappointment.
I was at a very low ebb. My self-esteem was worn down to a frazzle.

I kept saying to John McGraw, "How can I win if I'm pitching for
poor teams all the time?" I never had a good year in the Minor Leagues.
When I started out in Lebanon, I won 5 and lost 1, but then the league
broke up. When I was sent to Hartford and Lynn in the Eastern League,
I won 4 and lost 5. The next year in Memphis I won 3 and lost 9 and
that same year in Montreal, 1917, I won 7 and lost 17. Can you imagine
losing 26 games in a season? The next year, in Nashville, I won 5 and
lost 10, and then in Newark I won 2 and lost 3.

McGraw said, "That's the way you learn. You learn more from your losses than you do by your victories."

I certainly could not recall any satisfactory conversations or sessions of advice given me by Minor League managers. If there was any, it was all technical, such as "get the first pitch over" and a recital of dos and don'ts, such as "never throw a .220 hitter a slow ball" or "never throw a slow ball with the count of three balls and no strikes."

A multitude of such rules seemed to be the established advice from coaches. But as to wisdom regarding psychological applications during pinches or crucial situations, I cannot recall receiving any in the Minor Leagues. In fact, my recollection provides very little of any worthwhile advice by so-called coaches even in the big leagues. What little I learned was absorbed through the very difficult medium of trial and error, or sheer experience. I did improve, naturally. This is what McGraw meant, I'm sure, when he said I'd learn more by losing.

There was a fellow down in Memphis, Vic Willis, who took me in hand and tried to teach me the ins and outs of pitching as practiced by big leaguers. But that didn't help when I got to places like Newark and Montreal; they were just abjectly putrid, terrible ballclubs. They didn't care. They might have had some talent, but the players didn't bother using it. You become infected with that, and the unsparing attitudes, bitterness, and jealousies rub off on you.

In Lebanon, Hartford, and Lynn, I was wise enough to realize I wasn't pressured to perform great feats, and any victory or outstanding performance would be considered unusual, while my failure was rather expected. But as each year unfolded, I assumed that McGraw was looking forward to a noticeable rate of improvement and progress.

In Memphis I excused myself because I pitched good baseball even when the team lost. In Montreal the team was disorganized and disgraceful. Nashville was another wretched experience, while Newark and Hamilton were merely a shambles. I didn't blame myself for my record, yet pitching was pitching, and others were winning. Why one of them wasn't me preyed considerably on my confidence.

Almost nothing about my experience in the Minor Leagues built my self-esteem. Quite the opposite—my teammates could not resist hazing a newcomer, especially one who looked like a schoolboy. They would yell obscenities at me, ridicule me endlessly from the coaching lines, and cook up crude practical jokes to make my time with the club as miserable as possible.

The hotel we all lived in when I played ball in Lynn had been home for the ball team for many seasons, and the players roamed it like it was their personal parlor. The place puzzled me. It was a shabby spot, patronized during the week by no one but ballplayers. Anyone with any sense either went on to Boston to stay in a real hotel there, lived in a beach boarding house, or stayed in one of the great hotels catering to the vacation trade down by the seashore.

On weekends, however, there was always an influx of patronage, all young couples, who seldom carried more luggage than a tiny hand-bag. In an idle moment, I stood by the desk and read the register, marveling at the number of times John Smith and his wife had stayed with us, along with all the Browns and Joneses who came there week after week. I mentioned this to one of my teammates and he couldn't stop laughing.

"My God," he said. "You *are* a kid!" In that moment, I learned what a one-night stand was and what the hotel was really in business for. I was stunned and confused about living amid the kind of sin that decent people only whispered about.

There was that night my roommate, Gus Helfrich, said to me, "Let's take a walk, I want to go see somebody." So, we went for a walk, and I assumed we were going to have a nice little visit with someone. Where do we wind up? In a—if you care to call it—a house of ill repute. I didn't want any part of it because I had been briefed by my parents that this was not just immoral but also downright obscene, degenerate, and dangerous.

The madam couldn't persuade me to visit any of the girls in the place. She knew I was just a kid, and she seemed like a nice person, in a way. She and I sat and talked while Gus was busy with whatever he was doing. Perhaps not so innocently, I asked her, "In the performance of the act, who gets more pleasure out of it, the man or the woman?"

"Well, Sonny," she said, "that's a disputed question. The best answer I can give you is, did your ear ever itch inside? Did you ever take your little finger and sort of push it in your ear and twist it around? Okay, so which feels better, your finger or your ear?"

The point is, I was exposed to that type of thing very early in life.

You wouldn't believe some of the things I saw—once in a single day. I was in Birmingham, at the Tutwiler Hotel, I think, on a warm day that started out very ugly. Gus and I came down in an elevator with a nicely dressed young man, in his thirties, who was carrying a small suitcase. Right outside the elevator was a young lady with an insignia on her cap for some sort of charity, asking for funds to help the war effort. We each gave a dollar, for which we received a button or some such thing. The young fellow with us gave even more than we did—two dollars, as I recall.

We all filed into the dining room, and the young man took a table on the opposite side of the dining room. Before long, we heard a commotion. A girl was hovering over the young man, demanding a contribution. He said, "Lady, I already gave one, out in the lobby, when I came down in the elevator." She said, "Where's your button?" Well, he couldn't find his button. She accused him of being a slacker and left the dining room in a great huff.

After breakfast, as was our wont, we sat in the chairs outside, and pretty soon we heard a commotion coming from down the street. People were bellowing and yelling. A group of ruffians had grabbed the poor young fellow from the dining room, tarred and feathered him, and were riding him out of town on a rail! A little while later, we looked across the street, and saw a man haul off and belt another. It wasn't a half-hour later that a man and a woman came along, and a fight started between them. She accused him of cheating on her, whipped out a knife and started slashing at him.

After dinner that night, a siren went off, and a rush of people came down the street toward a restaurant. Somebody had discovered that the eatery was serving sugar, which it was not supposed to do during the war. This mob broke in the windows of the restaurant and tore up the place. Then on the way to the station that evening, by George, if there wasn't another battle between two men, beating up on each other. As awful as all of that was, it was nothing next to the night I saw a mob of men bind a fellow to a log over a pit, douse him with kerosene and set him on fire. Later on, we heard he had been accused of rape but turned out to be innocent.

Nobody would ever believe me when I talked about what I had experienced because I was still a very young-looking kid.

It was not that I had been forced by overly ambitious parents into growing up too soon. It was *my* ambition that drove me to baseball, and my father had only encouraged and supported it. Still, if perhaps I had been made to stay home like most fifteen-year-olds of my day and had gotten all my schooling, I might have grown up more content with myself and confident about my future.

I had experienced enough of reality to be my own man in a way, and yet I wasn't fully developed. I had neither the wisdom nor experience to analyze myself properly. I didn't actually *know* myself. I had been through a whole lot in my professional experiences and my wintertime interludes, all of which had taken place during my boyhood. It seemed I never had any respite from adventure.

I had used baseball as a façade for a lack of adult reasoning, or wisdom. I knew I lacked experience in the realities of life, but I smeared it over by believing that being a professional ballplayer at such an early age, and gaining somewhat of a reputation, counterbalanced any of my weaknesses. I had vulnerabilities, which I should have realized. Nothing elevating ever seemed to happen to me in the Minor Leagues.

I managed to maintain a basic element of refinement, which rested in the well of my psyche. It was always present, but it wasn't flowing. It was dormant. It wasn't coursing through my veins, and I was substituting a sort of irritant for it but didn't realize exactly what was taking place.

McGraw kept telling me he was satisfied with my work, but that didn't prevent him from releasing me and sending me back down into the void, permanently.

Decades later, at a banquet in his honor, McGraw said, "In 1918 I had to trade Waite Hoyt to Rochester, and that is one of the things I have regretted all my life."

Small comfort. At the time, my life took on a somber aura. My future appeared decidedly bleak and uncertain. I was trying to take a personal inventory of myself but was in a state of confusion and not getting good advice from anybody. The change in my fortunes that now lay close by found me totally unready. Had I been a little older and more experienced, I might have read the signs, but I wasn't sophisticated enough to decipher just what was happening.

I look upon my life—or the thread of it—as a boy born of good, attentive, moral, middle-class parents who were guided by the moral codes of the day. I was brought up to embrace all the admonishments of culture, discipline, and correct behavior patterns. My big mistake was venturing into a world while still innocent, uninformed, naive. My character and personality were susceptible to temptation through association with uncivil, rugged, and abrasively sophisticated men.

I believe I was, by fact of birth and nature, good, and that refinement was a native virtue. I was not ready for the world as it was at that time, and by the time my Minor League career was done, I was inoculated with the wrong philosophies and practices. I learned more about life in the Minor Leagues than I did about pitching.

It was a bath in badness and things a fellow shouldn't know.

I didn't announce it to anyone but decided not to play baseball anymore.

Part 2

10

Industrial Strength

HERE I WAS, CUT LOOSE FROM the Giants, footloose and fancy free, not knowing what I was going to do with the rest of my life.

Out of nowhere, I was visited by a very fine gentleman from a rubber company that made automobile tires, somewhere in New England— Springfield, Massachusetts, or up in that area, as I recall. He came to my parents' home in Flatbush, sat down with my mother, my father, and me and offered me a job. I would be required to learn the trade but also play on the company baseball team in an industrial league. This would pay me more money than the average person, a very liberal sum, certainly more than if I had signed a contract with Rochester in the Minor Leagues.

I told the nice man I'd think about it.

Then, almost immediately after he left, I had another offer from the Baltimore Dry Docks and Shipbuilding Company in Maryland as a pitcher in the Shipyard League at a very handsome salary. I wouldn't have to work on ships while I was playing ball. My parents favored the rubber company because they thought it would ensure a future beyond baseball, but I didn't know whether I wanted to learn the rubber trade. Perhaps they were right. Looking back, I think it would have been a very advantageous thing because rubber was a promising industry.

With the war over, returning veterans found it difficult to obtain any type of worthwhile position. Office jobs were scarce, and it was a time of indecision for most everybody, and much more so for me because I had scant experience in the business world. It was impossible for me to apply to a company and receive an offer for something that would fit what little talent I had in business.

The family was greatly dismayed over whether I should continue playing baseball at all, for anybody, or whether I should turn myself and whatever ability I had to some other occupation. I was still only a teenager and could enter some kind of business. I felt rather compelled to accept a baseball job and decided to go with the Baltimore Dry Docks. I simply followed my inclinations and impulses, which for whatever reason were to go to Baltimore.

The Dry Docks were all former professional players, and we were a good team. I found myself in the company of fellows who knew what baseball was all about. Some were at the end of their careers, and others, like me, had quit in disgust. At least four Hall of Fame baseball players—Bucky Harris, Casey Stengel, Bill Terry, and me—either quit or said they were going to quit professional baseball at one time or another. That should prove something to youngsters who are sometimes discouraged with what they're doing, don't you think?

Baseball can teach us great lessons. A full game of baseball can incorporate frustrations, heartaches, elation, good luck, bad luck, errors, and accomplishments. You come from behind and win if you persevere. You're behind the eight ball at times, and yet you struggle, overcome adversity, and come out on top. It teaches you to stick in there, stay with it, and keep plugging away because you never know what's going to happen. Anything can happen in baseball and usually does.

It's the same in life, pretty much.

If you asked me why I went to Baltimore, I couldn't tell you. I was magnetically drawn to it. At the same time, I was seized with that vague premonition that baseball was not for me. I couldn't rid myself of that feeling. Perhaps fate was telling me something.

A certain content of nervous energy drives a great many people onward. It leads us into not only mistakes but also accomplishments. If we did not have that nervous energy, we would not experiment or take the initiative to attempt certain things or take chances. I look back and wonder why we are so imbued with this nervous energy or willfulness to experiment and get into trouble. Why don't we harness that energy and direct it into a constructive force?

I'm not talking about inventing something, like Thomas Edison did. I'm talking about the inspiration, drive, or ingenuity to get off your fanny and go at it, and the restlessness of not being able to sit still. I have a lot of it myself, I believe, and that led me into trouble sometimes. I wasn't smart enough to get out of it. Down south they call that ornery. He's an ornery so-and-so. I suppose that was me.

To be challenged and constantly clearing hurdles is part of life. I was always daunted by something. They say it's survival of the fittest, and it is competitive. Getting anywhere can mean gambling with your life and the lives of others.

Sometimes I had to make risky choices, as I did when I decided to go to Cincinnati in 1940 after my baseball career truly was over. I didn't know whether I was going to be successful when I went there to broadcast ball games. I brought my second wife, Ellen, and my three-and-a-half-year-old son Christopher. What if I didn't make the grade? I didn't know whether I'd last a month or six months. If I didn't last, it would be rough sailing. But I had to have confidence, a belief in myself, and a determination not to fail. That's the greatest thing in the world. That often doesn't hold true, either, but it bears out most of the time.

If you really determine and dedicate yourself to the task at hand and plunge into it with a fury, you'll come out on top. Now, it might be at the sacrifice of your family a little bit, but you cannot let your family disintegrate, starve, or decline either.

If you have any guts, you fight. I did that. If there was an obstacle, I would meet and drain it from every possible angle so that I knew I'd done my best. I learned that from pitching. When I got into a bad inning, with things looking bleak, I said to myself, *Dammit, I'll get out of this. I will get out of this.* Sometimes I didn't, but I had to give it my best shot. If that was good enough, I would get out of it. If not, I'd resolve to do better next time.

I figure that a good baseball team, a pennant winner, prevails around 60 percent of the time, sometimes 70 percent. So it is in life; if you can come out a little bit ahead, if you average 60 percent, you'll come out all right. If your personal character attains 60 or 70 percent of goodness, that should be considered good enough. We have a 30 to 40 percent margin for error. We're not perfect. We all make errors and do stupid things. We sin and are abrasive at times.

I don't know whether that's wisdom or foolishness, but it's a certain theory of mine.

• • •

I still think of my time in Baltimore with a great deal of affection. I didn't drink very much in those days. I wasn't a drinker at all, per se, until later in life. One day, the Dry Docks won a doubleheader. I pitched a heck of a good game, and someone gave me a bottle of champagne. I had never had any kind of alcoholic drink before. Another fellow and I took the bottle and went down to a canoe club at the Patapsco River, which runs into the ocean in Baltimore. I had never been in a canoe and didn't know anything about it.

We went out onto the water with these two girls, who were all gussied up. The other fellow and I were in bathing suits, drinking the champagne. We got to kidding around with the girls, and the canoe tipped over. This was all right with us because we had on bathing suits, but the girls had on these frocks and it was a disaster for them. They understandably decided that we were not fit for company!

I was more than fit for baseball in Baltimore, though, and competed against some pretty good clubs. I really came into my own down there. Having failed in the Minor Leagues, I just let nature take its course and perhaps inadvertently was following what destiny had in store for me. I blossomed as a pitcher because I was working against good teams, former pros. I became something of a sensation.

It seemed I had turned a corner, yet I didn't have any real expectation that Baltimore would lead me to the big leagues. I certainly was available. At the time, the American and National Leagues had a quarrel with the Minor Leagues. If a player had not signed a contract with a Minor League team, the big leagues could take him as a free agent. I had not signed with Rochester, so I was a free agent.

I shut out the Cincinnati Reds in an exhibition game, 1–0, which made a big impression on Tom Swope, a writer for the Cincinnati paper. He went to Pat Moran, manager of Cincinnati, and said, "Hey, there's one hell of a good-looking pitcher down in Baltimore, playing for the Dry Docks. He is a free agent. You could sign him." Pat Moran was playing poker or was a little bit stiff from drinking and couldn't be bothered, apparently.

Meanwhile, a fellow named Norman McNeil caught for me in Baltimore and, like me, had not signed a Minor League contract, so he was also a free agent. The deal we each had with the Dry Docks was not binding, and the Red Sox signed him. I was pitching beautifully, so Norm told Ed Barrow, the manager of the Red Sox at the time, about me.

I went over to pitch batting practice for the Sox when they were playing in Washington DC and about a week later got a telegram from Ed Barrow offering me a position with the team if I would have a chat with him. I caught a train for Boston and got off at South Station at 7:30 in the morning. I knew darn well the offices at Fenway Park didn't open until nine or ten, so I ate some breakfast and then took a nap on one of those benches they used to have in railroad stations. Once refreshed, I got directions to Fenway and walked out to the ballpark for a conference with Mr. Barrow, who promptly offered me $600 a month.

I was an impulsive kid, and that prompted me to say or do things without thinking. I was very impetuous and foolhardy in lots of ways. In baseball in those days so many people had direct authority over you, and it wasn't wise to jeopardize your position by arguing with them or countermanding their orders. This inequity lodged in my brain and fomented a resentment that didn't do me any good. I was always a little too quick to assert myself.

I said, "Mr. Barrow, I appreciate your offer, and I'd love to pitch for the Red Sox, but I'm not about to sit on the bench and then be shipped out to the Minor Leagues as I had been with the New York Giants." I told him he had to put in my contract that I would start a game within four days of reporting to the Sox.

Barrow just looked at me in disbelief. "Young man, you've got a lot of nerve!" he exclaimed. I didn't dispute that but reiterated my position: "I'm not going to waste my time sitting around, being passed from club to club." He paused for a moment, and then said, "I like your spirit. It might help around here." He put my stipulation into the contract. Of course, I still had to go back to Baltimore and clear everything with my employer there before I could sign anything. When I told the president of the Dry Docks about the offer, he graciously said, "Go ahead, and be a success."

It was only because of a technical quirk that I was back in the big leagues. Had I signed that contract with Rochester, the Red Sox never would have made me an offer because they would have been legally barred from doing so. I had determined my future by an impulsive decision, one that I wasn't sure about at the time. There was nothing wise or wonderfully smart about what I did, but I was on my way.

After signing with the Sox, I returned to Baltimore until Christmas. I lived with a family, the Biemillers, on the outskirts of Baltimore. Harry Biemiller was about my age, and it was a lovely family. He was a pitcher too. The strange thing is he only won 1 game in the big leagues, for Washington, and who do you think he beat? Me. He always liked to kid me about that.

I went home to Brooklyn for Christmas, and there was a period of inactivity until I was to report for spring training with the Red Sox in Hot Springs, Arkansas. Every morning, I got up at six o'clock and ran five miles around Prospect Park to keep in shape. In the afternoon, I'd go down to the YMCA in downtown Brooklyn. I had use of the gym there and would play basketball. There were a lot of pro players at the Y, but we didn't play any games. We just shot, hauled, pushed, shoved, and bumped. This went on for an hour or so without stopping. It kept me in shape. Then I went to Hot Springs to train. My world was now slowly starting to develop into some solidity.

My life, heading into 1919, was turning into what it was to become.

11

Red Sox Hop

THE FIRST DAY I JOINED THE Red Sox, I was introduced around. Some of the players were wisecrackers, but mostly everyone was cordial, receptive, and apparently glad I was there. Here were fellows who I had come to know through reports, like Everett Scott and the great Wally Schang. Then there was this homely but personable-looking guy, just peeling off his shirt, the fellow everybody was talking about in amazement and awe: Babe Ruth. Barrow led me over to the big guy and said, "This is Waite Hoyt."

Babe gave me a quick once-over and said, "Hiya, kid."

I didn't know then that Babe had not the slightest ability to remember names, nor was he particularly interested in newcomers until they became, for one reason or another, vital factors in his life. Years later, after playing ball with the Big Fellow on the Red Sox and then the Yankees for the better part of a decade, do you know what he said to me as I left the clubhouse for the last time in 1930? He said, "Take care, *Walter*."

My personal introduction to George H. Ruth in Boston on my first day with the Red Sox in 1919 was not the first time I had set eyes on him. I had seen Babe pitch three years earlier, when I was playing for Lou Pieper in Lynn, Massachusetts. With the Red Sox only a few miles away, I had taken the interurban trolley over to Fenway on an off day to enjoy a big league game.

I found my way to the pass gate, where the newspapermen and others went in for free. Back then, if you were a professional ballplayer, you were permitted to enter without a ticket. All you had to do was walk up to the gatekeeper and declare, "Recognize the profession!"

I did that, but the fellow at the gate just looked at me and said, "*What?*"
I said, "I'm a professional ballplayer."

He did a double take and said, "Get out of here kid, beat it! Beat it!"

I didn't have any proof other than an identification card, so I showed it to him, and when he recognized my name, he said, "Oh, you're the kid everybody talks about, from Lynn. You're John McGraw's schoolboy wonder." They brought me in, gave me a box seat, and made an announcement over the megaphone that I was there. I was king for the day.

The Red Sox were on their way to another pennant at the time, but they didn't look especially menacing to me. Ruth hardly seemed to take time to think between pitches, and I'll never forget watching the first Red Sox batter, Harry Hooper, drape the bat over his left shoulder. I thought, *What a peculiar batting style. Nobody in the National League would hit like that.* The Red Sox lost to the St. Louis Browns in a shutout, 3–0. I wasn't impressed and concluded that the American League wasn't very good.

I could not have imagined then that I would soon be playing in the American League as Babe Ruth's teammate on the Red Sox and then the Yankees, much less that he, Lou Gehrig, and I, along with Miller Huggins and our teammates, would make baseball history.

Or that Babe and I would one day come to blows.

Babe Ruth's feud with me first became apparent when Miller Huggins, the Yankees manager, let me return home to New York from a road trip before the rest of the team. I had pitched in the third game of four in Washington, and there really was no reason to keep me there. It was just a nice gesture on Hug's part to allow me to leave.

Well, after the rest of the team returned, Carl Mays, one of our other pitchers, told me that Babe was mad at me because I was given this privilege of an early return. Carl said that Ruth wanted me to know he wouldn't talk to me anymore. I guess in Babe Ruth's mind, nobody should have ever been ahead of him in anything.

Then again, it probably didn't help that Babe and I had been seeing the same showgirl (more on that later).

It was such a ridiculous thing. Right away, I approached Babe to talk about it, but he wouldn't budge. He said our relationship was over. This went on for months on end, and then about a year later, things got even worse. One afternoon when I was pitching, Babe missed what should have been an easy catch in right field. He short-legged it. It looked like he just couldn't be bothered.

I stood on the mound, hands on my hips, and glared at him. At the end of the inning, back on the bench, he cursed at me, but I didn't take the bait. The following inning, my game fell apart, and I was sent to the showers. When Babe and the rest of the team returned to the locker room after the game, I was sitting there in nothing but a towel. He immediately started in on me again, calling me names, yelling at me and threatening to punch me in the nose. I called him a fathead or some such, dared him to hit me, and the fists began to fly.

Miller Huggins tried to get in between us and got himself punched. Hug was only 5 feet 6 inches tall and weighed about 140 pounds. He walked with his feet pointed out. He was a little fellow who had Babe Ruth and a temperamental ballclub to manage. A couple of the other fellows broke it up, but Babe's feud with me was now worse than ever.

Another year or so passed. Then, one night, on a train from St. Louis, Babe brought in some bottles of beer and was giving them away. He did that sometimes. He offered me one, but I declined. He just looked at me with those eyes of his. "Forget about it," he said. "Take a beer, kid." So, I did. I was glad the feud was over.

It was impossible for me to dislike Babe Ruth. He was so misunderstood and misrepresented by so many. To begin with, he was not a carousing bum, nor was he fat, and he did *not* have pipestem legs. His legs were good-sized, at least as big around as mine. I saw Babe Ruth naked many times, and his chest was as thick as his stomach. He drank no more than an insurance agent—and less than many sportswriters during the prohibition era when everyone, it seemed, took advantage of an opportunity to indulge.

To know the Big Fellow was a privilege, and to play with him was an even greater honor. To sit on a player's bench in between innings of a game I was pitching and think to myself, *A couple of men on base; Ruth is going up to bat in a moment,* was as big a lift as I ever knew as a pitcher. For the rival pitchers it was a different matter, of course.

In any case, in Boston, I felt wanted. Everett Scott was particularly cordial. He asked me to dinner at a rather fancy restaurant one of my first nights there, which reminded me that I was in the big leagues. This doubtlessly strengthened my determination to stay there. When I joined the Red Sox, my confidence was restored, although it was with an element of fear. Fear was always with me—not physical fear, but rather the fear of humiliation, defeat, or failure. This made me a little more determined.

At times I resorted to asking God for help. I also lived a façade. I acted brash and careless so that people wouldn't know I was quaking inside. I used to say that the money I made playing baseball wouldn't do me any good. What prompted me to say a thing like that? I wasn't certain of myself or that I was going to finish well. Something instilled in me that uncertainty about my profession. One side was telling me I should be more of a model, affable, pleasant, wonderful kid, young man, or whatever. I envied some of the fellows in the club who seemed to live normal lives, who were retiring in nature and didn't project themselves.

I mean, people always knew when I was around. I don't think that was so good, looking back on it. It worked to my advantage in later years, but there was a time when I couldn't control it. I got myself into situations, some of my own making, others prompted by somebody else, that I wish hadn't taken place. I wasn't battling with any league heads or umpires, but in one way or another I was always thrust into the limelight.

In the life I led—not only in baseball, but a whirl on the stage in vaudeville, pro basketball, and other activities—I was always being featured. In some ways, the other side of my personality rejected that. I loved it on the one hand and spurned it on the other because it carried a great deal of responsibility, the need to conduct myself in the manner the public anticipated or expected. That's not easy, and it was contrary to the other side of me that didn't believe in that. I was sort of a schizophrenic, it seemed.

• • •

After the third day of the 1919 season, faithful to the contract, Ed Barrow told me, "Hoyt, you are pitching tomorrow." The nervousness didn't delay. Within two minutes I was worried and scared. Then came the headache: a beauty, a migraine that persisted all night long. The night was spent in bad dreams, thinking of how I would pitch in my first start, against the Detroit Tigers: Bobby Veach, Harry Heilmann,

Donie Bush, Eddie Ainsmith, George "Hooks" Dauss, and, most of all, the amazing and notorious Ty Cobb.

The Georgia Peach, as I was to learn over the course of my ensuing career, was almost a mathematical problem. As I stood on the mound watching him, I could almost see the tumblers of his mind calculating. I don't think Cobb ever approached a batter's box without a thought-out pattern evolved from reckoning. I don't believe he ever went to bat depending on sheer instinct alone.

His bluff bunts and half stabs, with his hands sliding up and down the bat, were products of his own design. His stalling—his words with the catcher or the umpire—were all calculated moves to keep a pitcher flustered, off balance, and puzzled. Cobb sought every advantage. He was a determined fellow without ethics or regard for his fellow man. Cobb's credo was simply the survival of the fittest, and if his competitors fell by the wayside, that was just too bad.

He researched the character, courage, and strength of his opponents. If a new man came into the league, Ty sidled up to the rookie, grabbed him by the bicep or gave him a healthy slap on the back. This was not a courtesy; Ty was feeling the man out, estimating his chances if occasion demanded a physical battle.

Part of Cobb's success was his preparation for the future. He always looked ahead to the day when he could reach down into his bag of resources and come up with some artifice he had laid away for just such an occasion.

He liked to soften opponents with psychology if he thought they were susceptible. He tried that stunt on me one day in New York. Detroit was playing the Yanks. It was 1925—the Yanks were in seventh place and having a bad season. Detroit was in fourth and still had a chance. Cobb wasn't in this ball game; he was coaching at third base. I was pitching for the Yanks and doing a credible job. After each inning, Cobb had to pass me on the way to the Detroit bench. After each Tiger turn at bat, he had a friendly, warm word for me: "You look good today. That was a nice inning."

About the sixth inning, with Detroit making no progress, he gave me the full treatment. He said to me as he went by, "I'll be making a deal for you next winter. I want you with me. What do you say? Okay?"

Ty was trying to soften me for the balance of that game. I told him, "Nothing outside a national calamity would get me to pitch for you if I didn't have to. I don't like you or your methods."

Cobb's methods certainly worked for him; his lifetime average of .366 is the highest ever rung up by a batter. Rogers Hornsby is second with .358. Although I concede I had my troubles with Cobb, I believe his average was not as high against me, but I have no figures to substantiate my contention. Cobb hit us all—and often. Whatever success I had against him may not be so much to my credit as to some circumstances not known to me. Perhaps it was Cobb's overeagerness on my change-of-pace pitch, which against most other pitchers was not a weakness of his.

Cobb understood baseball as few others did. He worked at it the way a scientist works on the most intricate of problems. He could not understand ballplayers who regarded their business as a summer pastime—a romp. He started with a big talent and built himself to the level of the greatest player in the national game.

But he was a competitive demon. He would grab the advantage, even if it meant belittling the opposition—team or man. He once made the mistake of picking on a fellow whom he thought was too nice to strike back: Wally Schang, our catcher.

Wally was bald. With his cap off, his head looked like a fortune-teller's crystal ball. It was a Sunday, with forty thousand people in attendance, a nice audience in front of whom Cobb could parade his talents and ego. A little misadventure in humiliation might add a nice touch, he must have thought.

When Cobb came up for the first time, Schang was standing idly by, his mask under his right arm, his glove on his left hand. Cobb reached out and with a great flourish removed Wally's cap and started to rub his head. The sight of Wally's naked dome did send fans into a state of hilarity. The usually cheerful Wally, with muscles like Atlas, was infuriated. He hunched his shoulders and uncoiled a vicious uppercut with his gloved hand, catching Cobb flush on the button. Cobb went down like a statue knocked off a pedestal.

Cobb's overaggressiveness brought troubles to himself, his club, and his players. With the certain talent he had for creating uncompromising situations, he managed to antagonize almost everyone in the American League.

As the years went by, it became apparent that Cobb thrived in an on-field atmosphere of high-velocity competition, of bitterness and recrimination. A melee in which he was recognized as a central figure seemed to compliment his ego. It gave credence to the ever-enlarging fable that he was a fierce and vicious rival, a man to be feared everywhere. It gave him, as he believed, his edge.

Another Sunday in Detroit—a never to be forgotten Sunday—brought together, once again, two slugging rivals: the hard-hitting, slashing Tigers and the powerful New York Yankees. Once again, it was Cobb versus Ruth, the Rapier versus the Club. Cobb sought his edge even before the series started by arranging for thirty or more risers of circus seats to be erected in left field, just short of the already close-in fence.

Ty announced they were there for the expected overflow Sunday crowd. This was reasonable in theory but inexplicable as to why they were put up on Friday, when no tremendous crowd was due. At the ground-rules meeting with the umpires before the game, Ty stipulated that a hit into the "circus seats" be scored as a triple, figuring of course that the Yanks could power the ball over the wall, whereas his hitters, while terrifically potent, were more the line-drive type than sluggers.

On Sunday there was indeed a crowd that not only surged beyond the limits of the grandstand but also swamped the temporary seats in left field. Spectators spilled around the outfield with ropes containing the overflow. Mounted police used the rumps of their horses to rein in the itinerant. It was a whooping, shouting, crowd—decidedly Detroit. The thousands didn't have much to shout about, however, because the Yanks jumped into the lead and stayed ahead by a comfortable margin past the middle of the game.

There was an early incident, involving only Yankees. Joe Bush and Freddy Hofmann had a run-in with the umpires following a bit of bench jockeying of Tigers runners. The umps thumbed Bush and Hofmann out of the game. The only exit was through one end of the Detroit bench. When Joe and Fred reached the Tiger dugout, they made an abrupt left turn and stopped at the waterspout to take a drink. It was a deliberate taunt. They then walked down the narrow aisle toward the exit and on their precarious journey managed to step on a few toes. There were a few curses—a few well-turned epithets—but no action.

The Yankees, in keeping with several other clubs in the league, suspected Cobb of deliberately ordering knockdown pitches. I say, "suspected" because we had no real proof except the evidence of our eyes. We believed that whenever Cobb, while playing center field, picked up blades or clumps of grass and chewed them, it was a direct signal to the catcher to order the pitcher to lower the boom on the batter.

As the game turned into its final stages, Cobb was seen to reach down for the grass.

He nibbled.

Bob Meusel was at bat. Bert Cole, a tall left-hander, was pitching. We'll never know whether it was just coincidental that the very next pitch was at Meusel's head. It may not have been a deliberate bean ball, though the Yankees thought so. Meusel charged Cole. The riot was on. Meusel and Cole exchanged phantom punches; no one was hit. They danced about like shadow boxers, but now here came the thousands of fans who had been penned behind the ropes.

We pictured mob violence and grabbed bats to ward off attackers. The crowd charged the pitcher's box and milled about, shouting. We plowed a path to Meusel, but the crowd had done an about-face. Mob psychology, I guess. Whereas they had been strictly Detroit sympathizers, they now believed Cobb to have incited the incident. They were yelling, "Get Cobb!"

We rushed Meusel to the clubhouse, although Bob was well able to take care of himself. We sat waiting. Outside, the shouting crowd continued to roam.

It was tedious for me, as I was the Yankee pitcher, and we held a comfortable lead at the time. Long waits sometimes are ruinous. Finally, the word came in: "The game is forfeited to the New York Yankees, 9–0." The Detroit management had failed to clear the field in the prescribed time set by the umpires.

The victory for the Yanks was acceptable but didn't help me any. I seemed to be on my way to a comfortable win, but in forfeited games there is no winning pitcher.

During another game, Cobb and Ruth nearly went at it. Earl Whitehill was pitching for Detroit against the Yanks in the Stadium. Detroit was winning, going away, 8– or 9–2. Gehrig came to bat. Earl broke off two good hooks, both of which Gehrig missed. Whitehill jammed him with an inside crossfire fastball. The pitch struck Gehrig on the back of the head. Lou, usually cool and calm, worked up a head of steam. He thought Whitehill had thrown at him, a rather foolish conclusion with the game almost at its end and the score lopsided in Detroit's favor. There was no logic in dusting off Larrupin' Lou.

Nonetheless, Lou let off some verbal steam at Whitehill. Earl was never known to back down. He called Gehrig a few unflattering names and told him he'd be ready for him.

In Yankee Stadium at that time, the visiting team had to pass through the Yankees bench to and from the field. After the final out of the game, Gehrig waited under the stands for Whitehill. Earl gave battle. There were blows, Whitehill charged, Gehrig backed up, and his head hit the down-slanting concrete understructure of the grandstand. Down he went, stunned, unconscious. Players were pushing, shoving, and swinging. Cobb emerged from the center of the group. Gehrig by this time was prostrate, head resting against a dirt incline. Cobb aimed a couple of kicks at him. Heilman intercepted the shots and shoved Cobb aside, then pushed him, struggling, away from Ruth, Tony Lazzeri, and that gang.

Ruth helped Gehrig to his feet, and Gehrig, stunned from his head hitting the stand, was half carried to the clubhouse. Ruth decided he'd challenge Cobb. Babe entered the Detroit clubhouse with Meusel and Lazzeri right behind him. There were threats by Ruth and counterthreats by Cobb, and finger-pointing, but when one started at the other, the players interceded. From that day until almost their days of retirement, they had little use for each other, although in later years they patched up their differences and laughed about their dustups.

• • •

Ty Cobb had been in the league fourteen years before I faced him, in 1919, on my first day as a starting pitcher in Boston. After all my rookie braggadocio in front of Ed Barrow, and my insistence on making my debut within four days of the start of the season, could I face the ruthless Ty Cobb and his gang? Would I flop? Sure, I had pitched that one inning for the New York Giants the season before, but this was my first real Major League game.

The next day at the ballpark, Barrow asked, "How do you feel?" and I said, "Fine." He said, "You look nervous. You're sure you want to go through with it?" Ed was right, I was scared, and the headache was still there, burning and pounding. I wasn't so sure about starting, but this was no time to weaken. I had a pretty good ballclub behind me: Babe Ruth was alternating between the pitcher's box and the outfield. On defense I had Stuffy McInnis, Red Shannon, Everett Scott, Harry Hooper, and Oscar "Ossie" Vitt, with Wally Schang catching. I threw the first ball warming up, and the headache disappeared.

Donie Bush was the first Detroit batter. Ty Cobb was the third. True to form, Cobb always did something special for rookies. The first time he appeared at bat, he ignored me. He stood on home plate with his back to me, talking excitedly to Wally Schang and the umpire, George Moriarty. The base umpire behind me said, "Don't pay any attention to him; he's only trying to get your goat."

Cobb turned about to face me in his famous crouch. So, I repaid the favor, turned my back on him, and stood talking to the umpire behind me for a moment, making Cobb wait. Then I threw him a breaking ball. He swung and missed it by a foot. The crowd roared, and I felt better. In the eighth inning, however, Cobb tripled and scored the tying run. The game rolled along, 1–1, until the twelfth inning.

Mike McNally, running for Everett Scott, reached second base with one out. The next batter grounded to the Tiger shortstop, who threw to first base while McNally, who had been on second, tried to score. Eddie Ainsmith, the catcher, and the third baseman got McNally in a rundown between third and home, but Mike scored.

I had won my first big league start, 2–1, in twelve innings.

Unhappy with the way the game ended, Harry Heilmann of the Tigers and his teammates rushed the umpires under the grandstand and wound up in a brawl. No one was hurt, but I thought, oh boy, Mother was right. I never should have walked into this sort of thing.

My father was another story. Every time I pitched, he tried to find out the scores like a youngster waiting for a birthday present. He went half nuts. In those days, we didn't have radio or television, and there was no way of knowing what happened other than to buy the evening paper, which might have only partial results. I didn't have the money to wire him or make long-distance calls, so he didn't know whether I had won or not until the next day.

After that first game, I walked on air and floated around Boston. I had made it. There were wires and messages and newspaper interviews. I had justified my belief that I could start and win, and yet, once again found myself involved in the bizarre and unique. As soon as Jules Heineman— owner of the Rochester Minor League team to which John McGraw had traded me—heard about my win, he wired the baseball big brass, demanding a large sum of money, claiming me as his legal property. The big league authorities pointed out to him that I had never signed with Rochester. I had refused to report after the Giants had traded me. So, I was free and clear to sign with the Red Sox.

Then I pitched and won a second game, beating Cleveland with Tris Speaker and that gang. Heineman's demands and indignation mounted. I beat St. Louis, for a third straight win, and the controversy became charged with vituperation. Barrow called me into his office and said, "Waite, we're in trouble. We hate to get into this violent dispute with the Minor Leagues, and Heineman wants $8,500 for you. I can't pay that kind of money, and we might have to let you go."

It looked like my Major League career might end just as soon as it had gotten started. Here I had won 3 games, lost none, and thought I was on my way, but Barrow was telling me I might have to go back to the Minor Leagues in New Orleans. Even though I never signed a contract or reported, Rochester had traded me to New Orleans for a fellow named Al Nixon. Well, Nixon never reported to New Orleans either. It was what they called a phantom trade. Barrow still thought he couldn't ignore Heineman because the Majors had to live with the Minors. He first offered $5,000 and then wired Heineman that he would pay the $8,500.

The thing was, Heineman had already wired Barrow that he would accept the $5,000. He had no more than left the telegraph office when the city was visited by a hurricane that blew down all the wires. Heineman's telegram, the one saying he would accept the $5,000, got through to Barrow, but Barrow's wire saying he would pay the $8,500 never reached Heineman. Barrow wasted no time filing the acceptance of Heineman's offer with the National Commission, and

I was Boston's property for $5,000. The next spring, we played in New Orleans, and when Heineman saw me, he said, "You know, you owe me $3,500!" When I told him about the wire that never arrived, he nearly fell over.

That first season with the Red Sox, in 1919, was the year Ruth hit 29 home runs for the Sox, breaking Gavvy Cravath's record. I pitched the game in which he tied the record. We were playing against the Yankees at the Polo Grounds. In the first inning, the Yankees scored one run against me, but I pitched eleven perfect innings after that with no one reaching base until the thirteenth inning, when Wally Pipp tripled and Del Pratt knocked him in with a sacrifice fly ball. So, I pitched eleven perfect innings, and Ruth tied the score in the eighth or ninth inning with the home run that tied the record.

The next day in the newspaper, the story was all about how Babe Ruth had tied the home run record. At the very end it said, "Hoyt pitched." Nothing at all about my eleven perfect innings!

The season ended with me winning 4 games and losing 6. I didn't like losing those games, but I was very much satisfied with my performance, and so was Ed Barrow. That fall, I returned to Baltimore to work in the shipyard and again lived with Harry Biemiller and his family. One morning, I picked up a newspaper with the big, blaring headline: "Babe Ruth Sold to the New York Yankees for $125,000." Harry Frazee, the owner of the Red Sox, needed money because he was a theatrical producer. He wanted to fund and produce a comedy called *My Lady Friends*. The fans in Boston went nuts.

Once *My Lady Friends* made it to the stage, Frazee invited the entire Red Sox team to see it. In the theater that night were these two ladies, and one kept looking at me. I looked back at her, but she was older than me, so I didn't think much about it. I was not very experienced in flirtations. The show ended, and it was delightful. Everybody loved it. After I went back to my room, there was a knock on the door. It was this bellboy in a red and gold outfit and a little skullcap. He handed me a note on a silver-plated tray.

I opened the envelope and it said, "I would be pleased to share with you a little midnight snack, and if you would care, please just tell the bellboy yes or no. If it's yes, meet me in a half hour or so." I was excited like a kid, so I said, "Yeah, sure!"

I got dressed and a half hour later knocked very timidly on her door. It was opened by this very lovely looking woman in a very astonishing negligee, the kind of which I had never seen before, and rather revealing in its aspects. Off on one side of the room was this little tray with hors d'oeuvres, some sweets, and a pot of coffee. We had a nice tête-à-tête and then followed an invitation, ah, to remain a while and perhaps discover the niceties of cohabitation.

I don't think she saw it—when I took off one shoe, my big toe was sticking out. I had a hole in my sock! I thought, *Oh, good God, if she ever sees this, the whole thing is off!* I stuffed my foot quickly back in my shoe.

It turned out to be a very nice contact for me. I don't know how she felt about it. I found out later she was a United States senator's wife, and the senator was a friend of Harry Frazee. I guess she was using me as a test case or something or another, for robbing the cradle, as it were.

I waited to go south with the Red Sox, to Hot Springs, Arkansas, and looked forward to the 1920 season. That turned out to be one of my worst seasons, but not because of poor pitching. I opened the season and shut out Babe Ruth and the Yankees, 6–0. I was riding the crest of the wave once more. We then went to Washington, I think, and came back to the Polo Grounds to play the Yankees again.

This long, electrical cable was hanging from the locker-room ceiling with a bulb on the end of it, almost seven feet off the floor. We played this game called hitch-kicking, where you kick with one leg and then kick higher with the other. A lot of the fellows were doing this, and so I tried it. Suddenly, I got an awful pain in my groin. I wound up in Boston Hospital for thirteen weeks with a double hernia. Following an operation, I fell on my crutches and ripped myself a second time. My season was ruined.

I can't say I was disappointed in the hospital. It was a period of service and attention I had never known, and I had a swell time. I hated to leave. When I did, I failed to recover any degree of health or stamina for the balance of the season. I finally did get out of the hospital and joined the Red Sox on the road. When we got to Chicago, my upper lip began to swell. It was so fat, and, oh, it was terrible looking. It hung down over my lower lip. I had a very serious infection and wound up in Mercy Hospital in Chicago for two weeks. In the latter part of the season, I tried to pitch batting practice and couldn't reach home plate.

My arm didn't hurt; it was just very weak. Ed Barrow was tolerant and understanding.

Barrow had more on his mind than his indisposed rookie pitcher. We met downtown one day, and he asked me to ride to the ballpark with him. It turned into a trolley ride I will never forget. He talked to me at length, and seriously, in words vague and troubled. "You and I may not have a profession next season," he said. "This may be our last." For a moment I thought he was speaking about my poor physical condition, but he cleared that up, saying, "It hasn't anything to do with you or me personally—it's a vast and terrible thing, and you'll read about it soon. But remember, son, that all people in all professions cannot be good, nor can they be wholly honest at times."

He began an extended monologue. "All professions have their doubtful angles and characters who are not wholesome, good people," he said. "Baseball is no different. It's a rugged, earthy game, and we never get around to examining the characters of players much before we take them. We ask very few questions, and I wouldn't invite some of them into my home. We also have some good men. But whatever happens, keep your faith. If the end doesn't come in a couple of weeks, if baseball survives as I hope it will, it will be a fine career for you that won't let you down if you don't let it down."

It sounded like a fine preachment to me but said so seriously and regretfully by a man for whom I had great respect that I wondered why he felt compelled to unburden himself on me. He continued briefly, saying, "I stand to lose a lot of money, not to mention the energy and work I have invested in this business. You haven't started yet, but try not to judge bitterly. Perhaps it will all come out all right."

Within two weeks I understood what he was talking about. Baseball rocked on its foundation when it was disclosed that the Chicago White Sox had thrown the 1919 World Series. Men were guilty of dishonesty, fraud, and, by their own admission, the most unpardonable sin in sport—the breach of faith with the public.

A second blow came the following season when Carl Mays, the submarine-ball pitcher of the Yankees, let go of a ball at bullet speed that slammed Ray Chapman of the Cleveland Indians in the temple. Chapman got to his feet eventually and walked slowly to first. Once on the bag, he tottered and was forced to leave the game, assisted through center field by teammates. Early the next morning, after having seemingly recovered from an operation, Chapman died.

Ray Chapman was a splendid man, well regarded in Cleveland, a fine ball player.

Carl Mays was a tough player with an unenviable reputation for knocking batters on their pants. He was accused of deliberately taking aim at Chapman, and the Cleveland players wanted him barred from baseball. Rumors circulated about Cleveland tough guys plotting to capture Mays and cut off his pitching fingers if he ever made an appearance in Cleveland. Mrs. Chapman sensibly advised against repercussions of any sort.

A year later, I would be Mays's roommate. We never spoke seriously or at length about Chapman, but I believed Mays when he told me he was not trying to hit the man. Despite a long series of accusations that he threw at batters, perhaps most of them true, I believe Carl Mays was wrongly accused when he hit Ray Chapman.

The Black Sox scandal meanwhile resulted in a rush to set the official house in order. Judge Kenesaw Mountain Landis, after much persuasion and his demand for absolute and unquestioned authority, accepted an appointment as baseball's first commissioner. Ed Barrow's dire prediction did not come to pass. Baseball survived because of the public's faith in Judge Landis, not to mention the potent bat—and personality—of Babe Ruth.

12

Me and the Babe

THAT WINTER I WAS BACK HOME in Brooklyn. Once again, I took to running as often as possible, along with workouts in Brooklyn's YMCA. My father and I would go out every Saturday and Sunday and throw, all winter long. On the coldest of days, the temperature near zero, we went together to whatever field we could find, and for half an hour, he caught while I pitched. Passersby must have thought we were nuts.

My father had always given me moral support. Being a father, and I imagine parentally tactful in pointing out mistakes, he never undertook a character reading, but he was the one person who seemed able to get me back on track after derailment.

Those close to a person or situation, because of long and intimate association and the opportunity to estimate and study, or because of a steadfast regard, can instinctively offer constructive advice. In 1950 the baseball world snickered when it learned of the administrations of a hometown friend—and, as it happens, a mortician—to the pitching ills of Jim Konstanty, a right-hander who was blazing a trail to the pennant for the Philadelphia Phillies "Whiz Kids." Their coaching relationship wasn't as much of an absurdity as it appeared to be; Konstanty's mortician friend knew things about him that others just couldn't know.

It was the same way between my father and me. My dad understood none of the intricacies of pitching, but he did know his son. He had watched me from early childhood, studied my style and delivery. The image of his boy throwing a baseball was indelibly etched upon his mind. When I was having trouble, I'd ask him to a game. The advice was never long in coming, perhaps this:

"You're not reaching back far enough. Reach back, extend that arm full length. Make believe you are trying to remove a ball from a table behind you, just out of reach. Pivot on that right foot, loosen your wrist, and let fly."

As my fastball remained my Sunday pitch, his advice was always most welcome and usually helpful.

I was no longer his little boy, but he was still there to encourage and also caution me against pressing. Little by little, my strength was returning. The days and weeks were given to just this and nothing more. Baseball was my business, and now, instead of just a game, it became a challenge to accept and whip. My father kept asking, "How strong do you feel?" I couldn't give a concise answer about something that required the supreme test, pitching under strain to batters in a pinch. I just told him what I knew and how I felt, but his repeated question made me uneasy.

One morning he said, "You're gonna get a great Christmas present, I believe." He looked strangely wise and self-satisfied. He kept repeating this cryptic message. "Wait and see," he'd say. "Boy, will you love this Christmas present!"

I thought, "What the hell's going on here?" He was going overboard repeating it and started to annoy me. "I heard more about that Christmas present," he'd say, with a big grin. I was beginning to question his sanity, and he definitely was toying with mine. I thought to myself that the only worthwhile gift I could receive would be a new pitching arm, although those throwing sessions were beginning to produce satisfying results.

The morning of December 15 at 7:30 a.m.—I'm quite sure that was the date and time—I felt somebody shaking me on the shoulder, roughly. It was my father. He woke me up, shouting, "Your Christmas present is here! Get up! Get up!" I thought, what kind of a Christmas present could be delivered on December 15? My father was virtually incoherent, wildly waving around a copy of the *New-York Tribune*.

"Take a look at this," he exclaimed as he opened the newspaper. I saw pictures of several ballplayers, including me. The headline was "Yanks in Big Trade." The subheading announced an eight-man deal—four former Yankees to the Boston Red Sox for four of that club: "Herb Thormahlen, Del Pratt, Muddy Ruel and Sam Vick go to the Sox for Harry Harper, Mike McNally, Wally Schang and Waite Hoyt."

I damn near collapsed. I had become a New York Yankee. My father revealed that he had been reporting on my progress to Ed Barrow—who had resigned from the Red Sox and joined the Yankees' front office as general manager—at Barrow's request. I now knew why my father kept asking about my condition. Barrow trusted my father's evaluation and never knew the extent of my arm trouble. My father was telling him I was in condition, so he took a chance and brought me over to New York.

Talk about sailing on cloud nine! I was ecstatic. I didn't know it yet, but I was about to enter one of the most glorious eras a ballplayer could ever experience. Better than all else, I would come to know the privilege of making a vital contribution to the pattern that would prove itself in 1921 and become the basis for all success by Yankees teams from then on. I had no tangible reason to believe that the Yankees would be the American League champions that year, but some small inner voice prompted an eager desire, telling me that this would be big.

I couldn't wait to go to spring training in Shreveport, Louisiana. Things began to happen, and my life began to take form. I didn't sign with the Yankees right away, however, because they didn't offer me a penny more than I had been getting with the Red Sox. I wanted to hold out for another $600. Can you imagine this? $600.

I stopped by the Yankees' office, and Ed Barrow told me to get my contract signed because I couldn't go south with the team unless I did so. He insisted he wouldn't give me another nickel. He said, "I really don't know whether you can pitch or not." Finally, he relented. "I'll tell you what I'll do," he said. "You don't necessarily have to win, but if you *appear* in twenty games, I will give you a thousand dollars extra." That satisfied me, and I prepared to leave with the Yankees.

The day before I was to go to spring training, I boarded an elevated train at Prospect Station, and who's sitting there but Dorothy Pyle and her mother. Dorothy was the girl whose father used to drive us to Coney Island and give us five dollars to have a good time. Then it broke off. Gee, she was a welcome sight. She looked gorgeous. Here she was, just sitting there, and she was absolutely stunning.

I sat with them, told them that the next day I was leaving for Shreveport, and asked Dorothy if I could write to her. She said she'd love that, so I sent letters to her from spring training. I kept writing to her, and Dorothy's letters back were just lovely. I couldn't wait to get back home to see her. When I returned with the Yankees for the start of the season, I called her, and we went out together. That began the romance.

During spring training in Shreveport, I got blood poisoning again, this time in my left thumb. A doctor had to lance it, and it came around, fortunately. The really good news was that I was back with the Babe. I pitched to him in one of those six-inning intrasquad games and pulled the string on him, which means changing the pace with a slow ball after a fastball. He swung and missed it by about a foot. Babe turned around; called over to Miller Huggins, the manager; and said, "Why the hell don't you make that kid throw what he throws in a game? He don't throw that in a game." Well, I certainly threw that in games, but Babe never noticed it. We had a big fuss, just because I threw him a slow ball.

Off the field, Babe seemed to like the fast lane. Harry Harper, a left-handed pitcher, was my roommate at the time. The night before Easter Sunday he said, "There's a party going on out at this private home." Harry had rented one of the first cars with an electric gear shift. We went to this place that was about fifteen miles out into the country. A band with a couple of singers performed, and it was a really nice party. I looked around, and there was Babe Ruth and a couple of fellows from the Dodgers, whom we were playing against at the time in some exhibition games.

After a while, we noticed a girl who was paying a lot of attention to Babe. He decided to leave, and she followed soon after. Harry had much more experience than me in such matters and said, "Gee, I don't like that. I don't like that at all. She looks like trouble." We waited a few minutes and then went out and got into Harry's car, the one he had rented. We sped up and went about five miles down the road. Sure enough, there was Babe's car and the two of them were standing outside it. She had a gun in his ribs and was saying, "I want my money; I want my money."

I don't know what she wanted the money for, but Harry got up behind her, hit her on the arm, knocked the gun out of her hand, grabbed her, and said to Babe, "Get in the car and take off," which he did. We took her in our car to a police station and told her to get out.

Ruth had a gun pulled on him a second time down there. I was sitting with Wally Schang in a dining car on the way to the next city where we were going to play, when Ruth came walking through in a hurry. It wasn't two minutes later that this woman came bouncing through, also at a fast clip. Wally, whom we used to call "Brick" because he was so strong, said, "Oh boy, something's doing." He hopped up from the table, turned to the left, and ran up a couple of cars. This woman had Babe pinned against a door, pointing a pearl-handled gun at him, demanding something or other. Wally wrestled her to the ground, and she was put off at the next station.

Babe was a wild man and always in some kind of a fuss like that. He left Shreveport under a cloud because his deportment wasn't the best in the world. He was kind of a loner. You hear all these stories about Babe Ruth and the people who roomed with him. I've read pieces saying I roomed with him. I never roomed with Babe Ruth at all. His roommate for a while was Ping Bodie, and then it was Freddy Hofmann. He had two or three roommates, but they always managed to be let go from the team after they roomed with him. I think it was Bodie who once said, "I never roomed with Ruth. I roomed with his suitcase." Babe was seldom in.

When I first met the Big Fella in 1919, he was one of the finest left-handed pitchers in baseball. He was kind of a good-natured goof who had no idea what glory and fame lay ahead of him. He forever reminded me of a powerful, shaggy dog. He had charm. Women went nuts over him, and he was nuts about them too.

Babe was never conscious of what went on around him. The affairs of the world, its trials and tribulations, never bothered him. A different set of men ran the world, and as long as they didn't interfere with baseball, they could do as they darned well pleased as far as Ruth was concerned. That also went for musicians, artists, doctors, lawyers—in fact, anyone in any other kind of business but baseball.

I often wondered where Babe thought the baseball fans came from, but if they were out at the park, he was satisfied. He had no business sense whatsoever. Salary meant nothing. Money was just metal and paper to be exchanged for whatever he wanted. He received some thirty thousand letters a week. He had no secretary and couldn't read—much less answer—all those letters by himself, so he just opened and read the pink, blue, and green ones, and those that smelled of perfume. Then he tore up the rest.

The Yankees ballplayers, including me, would sort out some of the others. We found that Babe would tear up letters containing checks for as much as $1,000, $2,000, and $3,000, sent to him as royalties for the use of his name. Goodness knows how much money Babe threw away by tearing up his mail.

I received but a fraction of fan mail compared to the Babe, of course, but answered every single one with diligence. Few envelopes contained a check for me, but at least one of them, which I received in 1949, well after my time with the Yankees, brought something money couldn't buy. It was a very neat, precise, and sincere message of appreciation for my broadcasts of Cincinnati Reds games during my second career as a sportscaster. 'Twas from a girl named Betty Derie—whom I did not know.

Receiving her letter was a deceptively small memory because it repeated itself over and over again. Our correspondence continued, and over time Betty became my assistant, helping me respond to fan mail along with other various and sundry tasks. When my second wife Ellen's health declined and our life together became nothing more than memories and nostalgia, Betty was there for both of us.

Betty was also one of the most knowledgeable baseball fans in the United States and completely informed in the classics of art and the theater. She and I connected in so many ways. As fate would have it, Betty became an assistant to Warren Giles, president of the National League in Cincinnati, which is how I finally first met her in person, over lunch. I found her to be truly gracious, thoughtful, generous, understanding, modest, and yet sophisticated.

So indebted was I to Betty as a helpmate that, in 1970, I arranged a special banquet in her honor, in celebration of her birthday, at the National Baseball Hall of Fame in Cooperstown. My hope was that she would be inducted as an honorary member for her service to the National League.

After Ellen passed away, Betty became my third wife. I was eighty-two at the time and reluctant to burden her with my declining condition, but my niece Ellen Frell Levy convinced me that it was the right thing to do, for Betty and me.

Betty will forever occupy a special compartment within my heart and soul.

Maybe Babe Ruth got something as valuable as I did out of his pink, blue, and green envelopes, but I can't imagine it. It hardly mattered because his relationship with fans manifested itself on an entirely different level than mine, given his uncanny way of delivering his greatest performances before big crowds. On a Sunday in New York, with the stands jammed, the Babe would really lay it on.

One time, in a game against the Philadelphia Athletics in 1921, my first year with the Yankees, that proclivity of his came at my expense. Everyone knows it's the desire of every pitcher to win 20 games. A pitcher always feels that if he wins 20, he's a made man. By the last Sunday in the season, I had won 19. We won the first game of a doubleheader against the Athletics, and Miller Huggins told me to "just take a few innings" in the second game. So, I started the game, simply as a workout, and was leading 6–0. I thought, *This is my 20th game*, and boy did I want that win. The innings went on, and in about the seventh inning, the crowd started yelling for Ruth. They wanted to see Babe pitch because he had been a pitcher. We had the pennant won, so it didn't make any difference.

Huggins says, "Waite, take a shower and let Babe finish the game." Babe finished the game all right. I heard this yelling and shouting in the clubhouse and couldn't figure out what it was all about. I asked the clubhouse attendant, who said, "The Athletics tied the score." Well, of course when the team ties the score, then the first pitcher of record is out. He's relieved of any responsibility for winning or losing.

There went my 20th game.

To top it all off, Babe Ruth hit a home run in the ninth inning or something and won the game for the team and also for himself as the pitcher. If you look in the record book, you'll see that Ruth is credited with 2 wins as a pitcher that season, one of which should have been my 20th victory.

You can size up Ruth two ways. You can, if you want, and some detractors will, talk about Babe's ego and his misdemeanors, his infractions of the moral and physical training codes. You can point to dozens of things in Ruth's background and make him out as an unstable character. But that's not how I, or other fellows who played with and against him, look at it.

The present-day ballplayer probably looks upon Babe Ruth as just a big, powerful guy who could hit the ball a long way, and often. But Babe's home runs were only part of his contribution to baseball, the major part to be sure. However, it was Ruth, beyond all others, who saved the national pastime after the Black Sox scandal—not by home runs alone, although the public certainly worshiped the King of Swat.

It was Ruth's infectious personality that caught baseball fans full blast. It was the publicizing of his character traits, which made the fans realize that after those Black Sox players had proved so dishonest that this big guy played ball just because he loved the game. He embraced it with all the zest and abandon of a kid playing Commando. Some ball players don't like to admit their love for baseball is strong. They think it is childish. Ruth wasn't like that. He would have played ball for a room and three meals a day. He loved the game that much.

Today, we're rather used to the home run. But in the early '20s, ball fans sat with their mouths wide open when Ruth came to bat. He managed to accept the hero worship and treat it with a sense of proportion. He took time to visit kids in hospitals and autograph baseballs. On a table in the Yankee clubhouse, there were always from six to eight dozen balls for him to autograph.

He did everything with an extravagant flourish and carried others along with him. Players on the same team who originally were low in confidence suddenly caught it from Ruth. The players on the other teams caught it. The league became imbued with it, then the other league, then the Minor Leagues—and soon all of baseball.

Ruth became a great teacher. He taught not only through words but also through action on the field. Yes, he was confident, but when at times he slumped, he worried. Yet even his worry was constructive because the big guy was so conscientious about his work. He never rested until he studied his way out of a slump. In that way, he set a fine example.

Every game was an adventure to Babe Ruth, a glorious adventure. Only when his ability began to give way to time did he begin to sulk. That was because of his refusal to believe it was all ending. His heart and his head refused to respond to the ravages of time. Finally, he had to admit it. Life had captured him. It was ready to tame him. It brought him out of the forest, stopped his blissful wandering and imprisoned him in the confines of retirement and boredom.

The game of baseball owes more to Babe Ruth than it can ever pay, although he still owes me for that game against the Athletics in 1921, when he flat-out robbed me of my 20th victory.

13

Turn of the Twenties

SO MUCH HAPPENED IN 1921 THAT I almost can't remember it all. I look back with some nostalgia because in the middle of the season I was still taking that long trip from Brooklyn up to the Polo Grounds where we played before Yankee Stadium was built. That was tiring, so finally Freddy Hofmann, Bob Shawkey, and I got together and rented a furnished apartment on Riverside Drive.

It was a bonanza. We had a lot of fun over there. It was a very fine arrangement and quite different from the Minor Leagues. Life had taken on a different aspect entirely for me, and it was just beyond belief. As a young guy in the limelight, I thought everything was going swimmingly for me.

Well, almost everything. In the summer of 1921, I did find the going rough for a stretch of some three weeks when I couldn't win and found myself in the doldrums. I was in a discouraging vacuum, which bid to become a pattern had I not found a cure. I finally managed to make a constructive adjustment in 1921 by remembering what John McGraw had told me during spring training in 1917 about varying my speed tempo by breaking up the rhythmic twirl of my arm.

I stopped my free, overhand, delivery and adopted a twisted, knotty, crouching style, used by the great Grover Cleveland Alexander. I hid the ball as much as possible until the second of release. Providentially, it worked. I used the style effectively throughout the balance of the season.

I wonder why fortune decrees that you have periods of success sometimes, where nothing seems to go wrong, and everything is on the upswing, both on and off the ballfield.

In 1921 a young lady sat down a few box seats from the players' bench every day. The seats ran all around the Polo Grounds, and in center field were huge bleachers arranged in a circular fashion. We had to walk under those bleachers to get to the clubhouses, which were in two separate buildings—the visiting team used one and the home team the other.

On this particular day, perhaps at the end of May, I came through under the bleachers, dressed to catch the train to go back to Brooklyn (I didn't have the apartment on Riverside Drive yet), and the young lady was standing there. She introduced herself and was very much a sophisticate if you know what I mean. She was a showgirl and also a terrific baseball fan. She said, "I see that next week you're going to be in Chicago," which we were. "Strangely," she said, "that's where I'll be too, staying at the Chicago Beach Hotel, right across the park from the Cooper Carlton, where you people stay."

A liaison formed between us that lasted the balance of the summer, and everything was hunky dory. As it turned out, she also became entangled with Babe Ruth, which was part of the reason he and I had that locker room fistfight and didn't speak for two years. Babe came to me one day and asked a few questions about her. I guess I said some things he didn't like. Apparently, he cared more about her than I did, and his feelings eventually boiled over into our brawl.

In the meanwhile, of course, I was also seeing Dorothy Pyle and becoming very attached to her. At the time, she and I had become fast friends with Joe E. Brown, a comedian whom I had met in Boston when he was playing in the Greenwich Village Follies.

Joe was one of the funniest comedians and eventually became successful on Broadway before migrating to California for a career in the movies. He used to come to the ball games and do somersaults off the players' bench into the field, drumming up publicity for the Follies. He was a small fellow with a wide smile, which, when he broke it out, wrinkled the corners of his eyes and puckered his face in a rather homely but warm personality. Joe was a great ball fan, and later on he became part owner of the Toledo club in the Minor League American Association. His son Joe L. Brown eventually became general manager of the Pittsburgh Pirates.

The funny thing about Joe was that he went to all limits to prove he was a baseball player but he couldn't stop a *basketball* if it were hit through his legs. He used to claim he started with the Yankees, which he never had. Oh gee, he was something. He was a very good guy, and his wife, Kathryn, was a jovial, wonderful woman. They used to come over and have dinner with Dorothy and me before we were married. Joe was a great party planner and actually set our wedding date—February 2, 1922.

Dorothy, as my fiancée, attended the 1921 World Series along with my future in-laws. My mother and my father, who had so much time, hope, activity, and desire invested in my success, were there too.

I don't like to talk about the '21 World Series, the Yankees versus the Giants, because it sounds like I'm boasting a bit. Since I had won 19 games during the 1921 season, I was sure Miller Huggins would start me in the Series, but Hug opened with Carl Mays, and we beat the Giants, 7–5. While I was warming up in the bullpen for the second game of the Series, I heard a voice behind me say, "So that's the young punk who thinks he's going to beat us." It was Ross Youngs, the Giants' right fielder, and he was just ribbing me, but of course I took it personally.

When I took to the mound, he and the Giants did everything they could to get at me. At the time I had endorsed Lifebuoy Soap, and the Giants apparently had seen me in the advertisements. At one point, on my way back to the bench, a cake of soap flew out of the Giants' bench and landed at my feet. I picked it up and fired it right back at them, just missing John McGraw's right ear. I actually think the Giants were more nervous than I was. I pitched all nine innings and held them to just two hits, and we won that game, 3–0.

In the fifth game, which I also pitched for nine innings, we won 3–1, which put the Yankees up by a game. In the eighth and deciding game, I once again went the distance, but we lost, 1–0. By the time the Series had ended, I had pitched twenty-seven complete innings and did not allow a single earned run, meaning that the only runs scored were a result of fielding errors, not my pitching. Only the legendary Christy Mathewson had achieved something comparable.

I have always believed that the pride of achievement was more stimulating, satisfying, and rewarding than all else. Impressionable people work and hope for recognition and money. Such recognition was mine at a very early age, just twenty-one years old. Even though the Yankees lost the '21 Series, I was happy with how I pitched, especially because I had opposed John McGraw, the manager who started my career with the Giants at fifteen but also nearly ended it when he consigned me to Rochester after three seasons in the Minors.

To celebrate my pitching performance, Dorothy's family asked me to dinner. My mother and father had hoped that I would be going to dinner with them. There I was, a youngster, foreign to such involvements, with no idea what to do. I was caught between two fires: loyalty to my father and mother or to the girl I was going to marry. What was a young fellow to do? I didn't know what to do.

It would have been a mistake no matter what I had chosen. If I had gone with my mother and father, it would have hurt the others. I decided to go with my future wife and in-laws, which made my mother and father very mad. Instead of just being disappointed, they were bitter about the whole thing. This opened a rift that developed into a separation that was never repaired and brought on recriminations with which I was unable to cope.

The problems originated in the insinuations of Uncle Joe, who seemed to be the catalyst in all these ugly complications. For some reason or other he didn't like Dorothy's father, Harry Pyle. So, he transmitted that feeling to my mother and father.

Sometimes I think it wouldn't have mattered which family it was, that my parents just didn't want me to get married. Aunt Anto came to me after the World Series and said, "You know, we're so disappointed." When I asked why, she said, "We think you should have bought your mother a mink coat." Or, "You should have bought them a house" or something of that nature.

In other words, they were trying to control the situation and did not want me to get married. They wanted to bask in my limelight, and so they told me I was too young to get married. Perhaps they were right.

Dorothy had some very good friends over in Elizabeth, New Jersey, who wanted us to live there. They asked us to come over and look at a house that was for sale. It wasn't huge or very pretentious. It was colonial style, and, gee whiz, it was a wonderful place. They said, "Why don't you buy this house and live near us? When you're married, we'll introduce you socially to our group, and it'll be a lovely life for you."

When I went home and said I was going to do this, my mother and father said, "*What?* What do you mean, you're going to buy a house?" It was entirely foreign to their economic way of thinking. They had different ideas. I don't know what they thought I was supposed to do, but nevertheless they were very mad at me.

Later on, about three weeks after our honeymoon and before I left for spring training, Dorothy and I were living with the Pyles. I got home one day, and my young bride said to me, "The most awful thing happened today. That aunt of yours called up my mother. She said she thought that you should come around and see your family more often. Then your aunt said that she thought it was a terrible marriage and that it wouldn't last a year."

Of all people, this aunt of mine was butting into our affairs! It got so bad that my wife and my own mother didn't speak. They did try to effect a reconciliation by meeting at the Ansonia Hotel, where we first lived following our marriage. They were supposed to patch up the differences but instead it turned into one of the most bitter arguments that could possibly have happened.

Neither of them wanted to see the other ever again. I don't know why my mother would accuse my wife of doing anything wrong because Dorothy was a lovely person. Although I loved my mother, she could be antagonistic and had a sharp tongue when she wanted to. As I look back on it, I have to say that I believe it was my mother, encouraged by my aunt, who started all the trouble.

I can't claim to be completely innocent in all things related to my relationship with Dorothy either. Just before she and I were married, I was on a road trip, and Ed Barrow, our general manager, brought Mrs. Barrow and his daughter, Audrey, with him. She was a little younger than me, and boy, I tell you, she was something. Audrey was a knockout. She and I kind of hit it off, so Barrow and his wife invited me up to dinner with them. Audrey had very high expectations; I mean, she was going to be an expensive girl. I was very much interested in her.

After the '21 Series, Colonel Jacob Ruppert, the Yankees' co-owner at the time, gave us a dinner down at the Commodore Hotel. I was sitting next to Ed Barrow, who turned to me and said, "You know, son, I believe that you should start to think about settling down." Then he said, "I'll tell you what I'll do. If you marry this winter, I will pay the expenses of your wife to join you at spring training camp." To this day, I think he said it because he thought I was going to marry Audrey, his daughter. My commitment, however, remained to Dorothy.

Following my wedding with Dorothy, we took a brief and not very glamorous honeymoon to Atlantic City for a few days because I planned to bring my new wife to spring training. I believe this came as rather a surprise to Ed Barrow, but he was faithful to his promise and paid Dorothy's way. We went to Hot Springs and then to New Orleans, because we trained there, and it was delightful.

It was a great time for me, but obviously not without its conflicts and certainly full of disappointments and expectations left waiting.

In spring training of 1922, at New Orleans, we were booked to play the St. Louis Cardinals. Sad Sam Jones was to pitch the first five innings against the Cards. I had the assignment to take the last four. It was to be my first experience with Rogers Hornsby, the National League batting king who had hit a "meager" .397 the year before.

I watched the great "Rajah" during batting practice. He stood far back from the plate, in the rear corner of the batter's box. Blinded by my great love of my fastball, I thought, *What's the problem here? Pull him up with an outside pitch, then crowd him with the fast one, high and inside.* This formula had worked wonders against the Giants in the World Series the October before.

Hornsby had three bullet line drives off Jones for three hits. Then came my turn. I went to work on Hornsby. He singled sharply to right field. *Bad pitch,* I thought.

In his second appearance against me, I shot that high, hard one inside. Rog drilled it over the left field wall for a home run. Five straight hits. I was beginning to respect him! In the ninth inning, I looked toward center field. Elmer Miller was playing in. I motioned him back. Elmer didn't move. Hornsby hit the bottom of the center-field wall, his sixth straight hit.

One of those things, I said to myself, thoroughly of the opinion Hornsby had simply had a big day. The lesson was, "Never underestimate the batter," much less one of the real geniuses of all time. I could have added, "Never try to throw a fastball by any batters." I wasn't that receptive to lessons or advice, even my own. I believed my style was adequate, my knowledge complete, and my development at an end. I figured I was the finished product. It seemed I was bound to learn the hard way.

The ensuing year was one of dissension and cordial dislike within the Yankees because the two club owners, Colonel Ruppert and Colonel

Houston, were fighting. Ruppert liked Miller Huggins as manager, but Houston did not. Meanwhile, there were some fist fights among the players, and on top of that the Giants, owners of the Polo Grounds, refused to extend a lease to the Yankees beyond 1922.

The Yankees changed its training camp from Shreveport, Louisiana, to New Orleans, and the town was a veritable night club. New Orleans was fascinating. Antoine's, the Old Absinthe House, and the playboy emporiums banded together in one section of the city. The Little Club, a nightery featuring crawfish and beer, was directly across from the side door of our hotel. It was a gathering place for the players at times. I must insist, beer was the staple drink. The guys were *not* rolling over under corn liquor, or "white lightning."

But Bill Farnsworth wrote for the *New American* or *Journal* (I forget which), and the headlines were a thing of beauty: "Yankees Training on Scotch." The details set forth that whenever Huggins needed a substitute—a pinch hitter or runner—he would telephone the Little Club and say, "send out so and so—I need a hitter."

I'm making it sound like everyone was out of control, but we weren't. All of us were conscious of Hug's system of fines for excessive off-field behavior. There was a $500 fine for staying out after midnight—a penalty that most of us risked at one time or another. Caught taking a drink also cost $500. Playing cards for money was $250. It cost $100 for failing to show up at the ballpark, unless your excuse was ironclad, such as having lost a leg en route.

Frantic antics on the field also came at a price. Hug never wanted a player to make a fool of him or ridicule his judgment in public, as I learned on several occasions. Like most determined pitchers, I hated to be relieved and always felt that the very next batter was the man I could get rid of, if given the chance. One day, when Huggins gave the sign to remove me from the mound, I banged my glove down and kicked dirt into the air. Huggins watched my performance without apparent emotion.

"That little act," he told me, "will cost you a hundred."

"Only a *hundred?*" I shot back. "On the *Yankees?*"

Hug did not even blink an eye. "All right," he said. "Make it two hundred."

Another time, after being hoisted from the mound, I stormed toward the dugout and let my glove fly. It hit the back wall of the dugout with a smack. Huggins looked at the glove, looked at me, and then addressed the open air: "The next man who throws his glove that way will pay two hundred bucks for the privilege."

So, the next time I wanted to express my disgust at not being allowed to fight my own way out of trouble, I flipped the baseball high into the air, without giving a damn where it came down. Huggins calmly watched the flight of the ball and, when it landed, said, "Any pitcher who throws a ball up like that will be fined $200."

Soon afterward it came Sad Sam's turn to be taken out of a ball game, and Sam, bearing all of Hug's warnings in mind, took hold of the ball as if it were hot, tenderly between thumb and forefinger, and set it painstakingly down on the rubber, like an egg. When he started for the dugout, Huggins announced to nobody in particular: "Anybody who does what Jones just did with the ball will be fined $200!"

That added yet another item to Hug's catalog of fines. I cannot remember them all. But one that might suit some ball players today, especially when flying from one time zone to another after a night game, was the $1,000 price tag for "taking an airplane ride."

Hug wasn't the only one imposing discipline at the time. Judge Landis, who was the baseball commissioner, issued a proclamation before the '22 season that no ballplayer was allowed to play exhibition games after the season was over without his permission. I don't know why he put that rule in force, but Babe Ruth, Freddy Hofmann, and another pitcher did go on an exhibition tour without asking Landis and were suspended for the first month of the 1922 season.

So, we started the season without those fellows. Ruth had become a prolific home run hitter, and consequently we missed his prowess. I can never understand the vicissitudes of life that occur in our daily pursuits. I mean, here we missed the big fellow very definitely, but after the month was over, we were in first place without him. Yet it was a time of turmoil.

About two-thirds of the way through the '22 season, a fellow named Herb Hunter, who had played with the New York Giants and had been in Japan for three or four years coaching Waseda University, secured Judge Landis's approval to approach a number of American players about forming an All-Star team to tour Japan and possibly parts of China over the winter.

He canvassed the big leagues and did a pretty good job lining up some players. He finally came to the Giants and the Yankees and asked Joe Bush, Freddy Hofmann, and me if we would go. He also asked Herb Pennock, then of the Boston Red Sox. It sounded like fun, but we had to get permission first.

We knew that Colonel Ruppert was very sensitive about losing and never to approach him on any subject when the team was on a bad streak, which we were at this particular juncture. Finally, the losing streak ended. We were still playing at the Polo Grounds and had beaten Detroit or another team in a double header. Joe Bush pitched the first game and beat them something like 12–2. I pitched the second game and won, 2–1.

After the game, we showered, got dressed and beat it upstairs to Colonel Ruppert's office, where he was sitting behind his desk. Bush was first to speak and asked the colonel for permission. Ruppert said, "Vell"—when he got excited, he would lapse into a little bit of German dialect. "Vell, Bush," he said. "Go ahet." He said, "Go over dere and haf a gut time and see da vonders uf Japan and China. . . . Don't forget old Colonel Ruppert—send him a postcard vonce in avile." And he said, "Hey, by de vay, Bush, nice pitching out dere today. Nice pitching. Twelve to two, dat's the vay to vin dose ball games!"

So, he gave Bush permission, and I said, "Well, if Joe is going, I guess it's all right if I go too, isn't it?" He said, "Stand aside, stand aside, get avay, Hoyts, get avay!" He called me "Hoyts." He always put an "s" on the end of my name. He used to call Babe, "Baby Ruths." I said, "What's the problem?" Colonel Ruppert says, "Dat lousy pitching you do, dat's de problem. Dat 2 to 1 pitching. Why de hell don't you vin 'em 12–2, like Bush?"

Close games clearly made him nervous, but Colonel Ruppert gave me permission to go on the trip anyvay.

Toward the end of the '22 season, the team was doing fairly well, but we were only a couple games ahead of the second-place team, the St. Louis Browns. We only had to win one game out of the last five to take the pennant that year. We played Cleveland at League Park and in the last game of the series, were shut out, 5–0.

Then we had four straight days off. Instead of the club taking us back home to New York and allowing us to be with our families where we would have found some surcease, contentment, and rest, we were sent to Boston. We spent four days off there, not even practicing, just sitting around in our hotel, worrying about whether we would win the one game out of the last four we needed to claim the pennant.

We were so nervous we could hardly hit. We got beaten by Jack Quinn, 2–1, and by Rip Collins, 1–0, so now we had to win one out of the last two. I was the pitcher that Saturday. I had the Red Sox beaten 3–2 in the ninth inning, and of all things I loaded the bases with one out. Hug replaced me with Joe Bush, and we won the game, 3–2. We only won one game out of the last five we played and entered the World Series against the Giants for the second straight year.

We went into the 1922 World Series in a miserable hitting slump. Strangely, the most runs scored was three in any one game. I took one on the chin, 3–0. We only tied one game, 3–3 in that series, and an umpire inexplicably called that game because of darkness, even though the sun had not yet set. Fans went into an uproar, and Judge Landis ordered the receipts turned over to a charity. We didn't win a game in the '22 Series and ended on a very bad note. It was a very discouraging operation.

1. Mother and child: Louise "Lucia" and Waite Hoyt

2. At age four: But baseball was my game!

3. "Everybody's a good fellow." Addison and Waite Hoyt, circa 1918.

4. March 9, 1917

5. Schoolboy
at Middlebury
College, 1918.
Retouching
by Alan Radom
and Jeff Seaver.

6. With the Nashville Volunteers, 1918.
Credit: National Baseball Hall of Fame.

7. (*left*) Dorothy Hoyt

8. The top of the hub

9. Delivering the palmball in 1925

10. The Bambino and the Schoolboy.
Credit: National Baseball Hall of Fame.

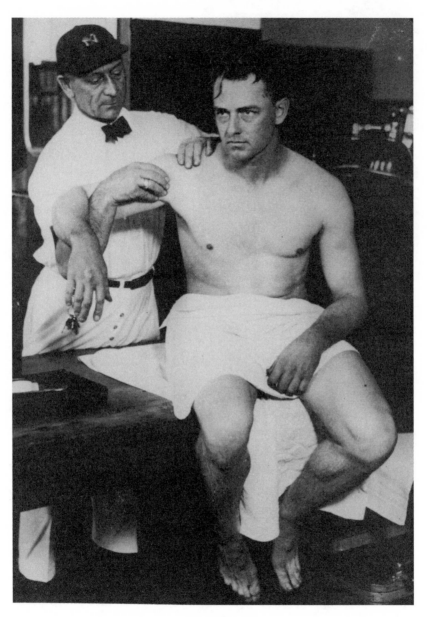

11. A little PT

12. (*left*) Ellen Hoyt. Credit: National Baseball Hall of Fame.

13. The luckiest men on the face of the earth: Babe Ruth, Waite Hoyt, and Joe Dugan listen as Lou Gehrig says farewell. Photo retouching by Julie Manners and Jeff Seaver.

14. Vaudeville days: J. Fred Coots and Waite Hoyt

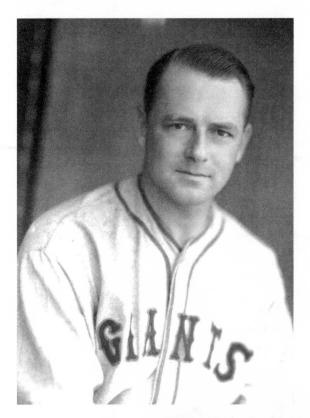

15. (*left*) Great Big Fella

16. The voice of the
Cincinnati Reds, 1942

17. Hall of Fame, class of '69 with baseball commissioner Bowie
Kuhn: (*left to right*) Stan Coveleski, Stan Musial, Waite Hoyt,
Roy Campanella. Credit: Hollis Studios, Cooperstown NY.

18. Induction celebration: (*left to right*) Christopher Waite Hoyt, Judy Hoyt, Ellen Hoyt, Christopher Waite "Chip" Hoyt Jr., and Waite Hoyt. Credit: Andy Paranya, Ostega Hotel, Cooperstown NY.

19. The artist as an older man

20. The 1927 Yankees

14

Art of Baseball

AROUND OCTOBER 22, AFTER OUR 1922 World Series debacle, our All-Star team left for Asia. It took us eleven days to cross on the Empress of Canada, a party of twenty-five players from various teams, including Dorothy and some of the other wives.

We went up through Mukden in Manchuria, down to Peking, on to Shanghai, Hong Kong, and Manila, then back to Kobe in Japan, over to Honolulu, and then back home. There was no drinking, per se, on that trip and no misbehavior over something like twenty-six games. I won a no-hit game but was also beaten when I threw a curveball that didn't break, and the batter hit it over the left-field fence. The opposing team scored five runs against us in one inning because we made three or four errors. We just played bad baseball that day.

In our free time we toured, and I was smitten by Japanese artwork, especially Satsuma pottery and cloisonné. It was interesting to go around to different factories and watch people use little wires to form a design, fill it with some sort of enamel, and then burnish it. They were also remarkable in their painting. They took brushes with little bamboo handles, honed to a tip. You'd be surprised how they could paint a flower or a design and then duplicate it without measuring anything, just by instinct and by hand. I couldn't get enough of that. That didn't include their work in silk. The designs on kimonos were absolutely beautiful. It was an education just being around the artists over there.

Ballplayers are not very intrepid cultural sightseers as a rule, but I was always interested in art museums. I'd go to the Metropolitan Museum of Art in New York City. My in-laws took residence almost across the street from it, and I would go there to study paintings by the different masters, as well as the sculptures.

I would love to go to Florence to see the art there. I did cross the ocean one time to Italy, and on the same boat was the Pietà, returning from Boston. It was housed in a steel compartment in the afterdeck on our boat, the *Cristoforo Columbo*. I never saw any of it because it was fastened inside to whatever it was resting on. The ship had a swimming pool adjacent to the chamber carrying the Pietà; the pool was lowered and raised to balance the boat so that the masterpiece wouldn't rock. When we finally arrived in Italy, it was an education to see the hoists flip this thing down onto a railroad flatcar to be taken to a museum. I did go see the Pietà later, when it was in place.

I've always been inclined toward that sort of thing. After Lindbergh had flown the Atlantic, I canvassed the entire ballclub to see if somebody would go with me to see the *Spirit of St. Louis* on display. Nobody was interested.

When my teammates were gambling, playing poker or bridge, I would always sit off in a corner and read. I was so interested in the French Revolution, the British War of the Roses, the times of Caesar, Genghis Khan, and the Renaissance. I just read everything I could, always bringing at least one—and sometimes four or five—books with me in my bag wherever I was on the road.

I remember reading a great novel, called *Sorrell and Son*, one rainy Sunday afternoon in Detroit. It was the story of a schoolteacher in Britain, a professor who sacrificed everything to raise and provide for his son. It was so beautifully told, and it affected me so seriously, deep down in my heart.

My love of reading is how I met Ford Frick, a newspaper columnist and radio sports commentator, principally in New York City, who later became president of the National League and, subsequently, the baseball commissioner. The Yankees were headed West, and this fellow was sitting in a sleeping car, off to one side all by himself, reading a book. He looked rather lonely, so I went over and introduced myself. He was so gentlemanly and cultured. Later on, he lived in the same resort hotel in Florida where I did. He also lived not far from me when I had a house in Larchmont.

Ford stimulated my desire for books and became a close friend of mine. There was within me a great deal of appreciation for anybody, like Ford Frick, who loved art and the graciousness of life. I love pretty things. Now, I just used a word that is very seldom heard in baseball. They don't *ever* say anything is *pretty*. They might say it's handsome, but *pretty* is a feminine word. It is also an aesthetic word; you say a picture or a scene is pretty. I think it is a lovely word.

Much later in life, I developed an interest in creating pretty things by becoming an artist myself, as a painter. When I first came to Cincinnati in the 1940s to start my career as a radio sportscaster, I didn't know anybody and wasn't invited anywhere. So, my second wife, Ellen, and I went out in the country a couple times, and I tried to paint. I was so bad at it that I gave up.

Then came a rainy spell, which, when I was broadcasting for the Cincinnati Reds, meant the Reds didn't play for a protracted time. Ellen came home one rainy day with one of those numbered sets, and she said, "I don't know if I should give you this because you'll think I think you're a softie or something."

I got kind of a kick out of the numbered sets. Then one day I was working on one of them and thought, *What the heck, I can do as well as this freehand.* I threw the numbered sets away and started painting with oil on my own and did pretty well for a while. Right around that juncture, say, 1954, an artist in Cincinnati named Ed Fern painted a portrait of Ellen. I went up to watch Ed work and took such an intense interest in it that after the portrait was finished, I asked him if he would give me lessons.

Well, that was the funniest thing in the world, him giving me lessons, because he had a slight tendency toward the spirits that would paralyze—in other words, he drank a little too much. We were doing a still life at one time and it had a glass of wine in it. Every day when I'd come in, the wine looked a little lighter in color than it did the day before. Ed had been nipping at it and kept adding water to make up the difference.

It was a little difficult to get Ed pinned down to the lessons, and he used to borrow the money in advance. He'd say, "Could you loan me enough money for five lessons?" Oh, he was a character, but he was smart as a whip. One day he called me up and said, "Don't you think we should sojourn to the country today for a little outing? Perhaps we can get a little something out of the landscape." We stopped along the way at a local delicatessen to get some sandwiches and he'd always insist on a few cans of beer. I wasn't drinking beer at the time.

We were out on a hillside, on this dirt road that he claimed he owned, and on one side was a rather scenic little farmhouse. He said, "Gee whiz, that'll make a nice little subject." He never used an easel. He'd just stand the canvas up against a tree and sit down and paint. A little after noon he said, "Do you think it is time for a dash of the critter and a little respite? Perhaps we could feed the inner man." He talked like that. So, we sat down and opened the sandwiches and drinks. Well, Ed left his picture leaning against a tree and along came a dog who lifted his leg and let fly all over the painting. I said, "Ed, looks like you got an addition to your painting over there!"

Then I didn't paint for a long, long while, until one day we were out at a place called the Fox and Crow in Cincinnati. A man named Bob Fabe, who was one of Cincinnati's better artists, had an exhibition there. The colors and pigments of bright hue and the compositions of his work really attracted me. I didn't know whether he was a ball fan, but I called him up and said, "Mr. Fabe, would it be possible to come over and talk to you about painting and baseball?"

I went over, and that summer he and I became the closest of friends. We painted next to each other, and it turned out beautifully because I learned from him just by watching him work. He'd say, don't do this or that. He was more or less my instructor. By the end of the summer, I gave a one-man exhibition and sold thirty-nine out of forty paintings. Of course, as much as I love to paint, I don't believe there will ever be much of a market for an "original Hoyt."

I know my limitations, in baseball as much as in art.

Somewhere in the past, some wildly enthusiastic sportswriter, seeking superlatives to describe the work of a baseball pitcher and writing more lyrically than factually, said, "Pitching is an art." The chronicler explained the classic way in which the pitcher applied his skills: the graduation of speeds, the application of control to varied spots, the nuance and timing, and the form and pattern of his masterpiece.

Other gentlemen of the sports pages have suggested the "science of pitching."

I prefer to think of pitching as a craft, with the big league pitcher, of the Warren Spahn or Whitey Ford type, as the master craftsman. A phrase most often used about such men is, "Oh, he's a smart pitcher." That's an overworked observation if there ever was one. Pitching does require an element of intelligence, but beyond all else, the success of a Major League hurler depends on his ability to be exact over a long working period. Call it control or what you will, but more descriptive in my mind is the word *exact.*

To the average baseball fan, and often in the minds of young pitchers, *control* means merely the ability to get the ball over the plate. The top-flight moundsmen also throw the ball to minute and imaginary locations: high, low, in or out, and often with design, near but not within the strike zone.

This, then, requires an applied skill, using the tools at a pitcher's disposal: his ball, his arm, his legs, his wind, his body, his power, his stuff—fastball, slider, curve, knuckleball, sinker, fade away, screwball, palmball, and change-of-pace.

I would say, then, that a pitcher is more the artisan, for in the individual sense he manipulates his tools and his talent with a deftness peculiar to his native ability and pursues perfection first through apprenticeship and then through the avenues of experience, learning his trade through a rugged process of trial and error.

In addition to his basic skills, there must be the desire, patience, willingness to learn, tolerance of setbacks, temperament, and a distinct understanding of to what extent his capabilities will take him, as well as what sacrifices he will make to reach his goal.

The one characteristic, beyond the manual manipulation of stuff that elevates the start beyond the norm, is his superior pitching savvy. *Stuff* is that instinct found in most successful people that tells them when to act—or when not to—and to what limits their activities should extend.

A pitcher learns his trade principally in competition—accepted and rejected advice alone is worthless. Lessons learned from victory and defeat, and much more by defeat than success, as John McGraw tried to tell me early on in my career, have no substitute. Mistakes are always punishing, and baseball pitchers remember punishment all their lives.

While mistakes are punitive—and too many times actually ruinous— they argue well for the pitcher's sense of humor, in that he can look back and laugh in wonder about some of the results of his lapses.

Mistakes are not difficult to catalog. We make mistakes in judgment, which are very prevalent in the young and inexperienced. There are mistakes in mechanics: control and lack of proper delivery, such as inadequate body action, wrist snap, step, or another defect. On occasion, a pitcher might get by with a few flaws in a game, but not often. Such miscalculations usually wind up in a disaster.

Losses come to pitchers through bad breaks or just plain old lack of ability, either temporary or chronic. In rookie years, all this is tolerated with the balm of advice, but there comes the day when the manager feels a pitcher should be making more progress, showing more understanding, and shouldering more responsibility. I took all of this in large doses.

The bad spells I had during midsummer of each season seemed to defy explanation. Heat didn't bother me, but the batters did. In four of my first five seasons with the Yanks, I had the midseason doldrums. I chalked up no wins for three or four weeks; just a couple of successes in those periods would have elevated me above the 20-victory mark. It was harrying. Winning was too pleasurable and necessary to take this sitting down.

The Yankee pitching staff had always been one of high character, with men who unselfishly helped each other. That was one of the rewarding features of playing with a gang in which the feeling of camaraderie was so pronounced—another heritage passed down to clubs of later decades.

Coming out of Saint Louis one night, I sat in my berth talking to Herb Pennock, who occupied quarters directly opposite mine. Pennock, in my opinion, had developed into one of the master craftsmen of his time. He was a slender, graceful, smooth-working machine of left-handed perfection. He knew my plight as well as I did.

I thought that he might give me some new angle or that I could benefit from some consensus of opinion as offered by pitching mates in the bullpen or the men's smoking room on the train, or when I was not around. Ball players have a way of freely criticizing each other, not through meanness or the desire to belittle, but more from the point of analytical understanding.

Pennock said, as he squinted an eye, "Well, *boysan* (a term we had used as teammates on the Japanese tour), first of all you're using your fastball too much (echoes of Huggins). You throw them that fast one on the first pitch, and you give away a sense of speed and timing. Even if you get it over, you have established them at the plate. From then on, you haven't many variations to fool 'em."

I observed, "I know you throw that sidearm curve on the first pitch and get it over for a strike. Then later, the big overhand curve, or the screwball. Or you cross them with the fastball." Pennock's fastball wasn't a ripper.

"Yup," he said, "and that first sidearm curve is my worst pitch. Luckily, most of the batters take it. So, I still have other stuff in reserve. What is your worst pitch?"

"My curve," I admitted.

He said, "Why not start throwing that on every first pitch except to rank first-ball hitters or guys who murder you. Nine-tenths of the rest of them will take the first one. Then you can work around 'em and set them up for that fast one, or a change-of-pace pitch."

Herb's advice worked well. I came out of my slump, and over the next three years won approximately 65 while losing 23. Perhaps I earned it as I leveled off in temperament, using a more cautious approach that was less impulsive and more calculating in pitching pattern and execution.

A pitcher, like a good artisan, should take a personal inventory, recognize his or her constraints, be guided by those, and not try to exceed them. An artisan has a similar kit of tools. He may not have a complete set—not all tools for all situations—so he must learn to use to his advantage the implements he has in his box. A carpenter realizes he cannot fashion a joist for lack of a particular implement and becomes more proficient in applying those he has at hand. He knows his limitations.

Yet, to those who have not reviewed their limitations and begun the experience of failure, I can readily understand the frustration and explosion of high hopes and dreams. By comparison, those who know their limitations become content with life and find pleasure in their accomplishments.

This does not mean that once you become conscious of your limitations you should stop experimenting. For instance, at thirty-two years of age, I learned to throw the slider. It took me two seasons to dare use it in a game. Strangely, I, who had never been a strikeout pitcher, fanned more than one hundred batters in 1934, thanks to my slider.

I believe in one infallible rule, which might seem to deny my theory of "know your limitations." It is wise to ask questions and keep asking them. If your basic, inherent talents do not permit an ascendancy to exalted heights, at least you can improve your quality of production. The slider, without suddenly launching me to league leadership, did keep me around a few more years.

I chose baseball as my craft because it's something a lot of other people can't do, which is why baseball players are paid so much. It's true that an artist sometimes is poorly paid, even though he can do something that somebody else can't do. This is what breeds confusion. You know that something is true, but then a similar thing doesn't hold the same content of truth.

Sometimes I feel like a man with his feet firmly planted in midair.

• • •

After completing our tour of Japan, we crossed over to Korea, and the University of Korea asked us to play a game. We had to shovel the snow off the field in the morning, and I pitched in two-degrees-below-zero temperatures. We then proceeded by train up to China, into Manchuria and Peking—only twenty-one years after the Boxer Rebellion—and onto Shanghai and Manila, back to Kobe and then Honolulu.

On the way back to San Francisco, sailing from Honolulu in early February, a little pamphlet, which amounted to a newspaper, was left under our cabin door each morning. It was mostly headlines, coming from the radio room upstairs, but it would report on the stock market and the news, along with a little section reserved for sports.

Dorothy got up one morning, and there was the paper under the door. I sat down to have breakfast, opened this paper, and it said, "Waite Hoyt traded to the Boston Red Sox for Herb Pennock." I thought, *Oh my God*. My heart just dropped from where it's usually located to the pit of my stomach. This meant going from a pennant winner to the last-place club in the league. Oh boy, was I sick . . . sick at heart. I had never suffered a disappointment like that. It was worse than being let go in Memphis, a setback beyond all setbacks.

Don't forget, this was between the 1922 and 1923 seasons, and I had

had good years for the Yankees. I just couldn't believe such a thing was possible. Dorothy was almost nauseated by the news, and we could hardly bear to come out of the cabin. When we did, some said they were sorry, but since Herb Pennock was also on the boat most didn't want to take sides, so they just didn't say anything.

We reached San Francisco about four days later, and my Yankees teammate Lefty O'Doul wanted to play golf. I was sitting on a bench waiting to tee off on the fourth hole, and another teammate, Joe Bush, said to me, "Waite, I want to tell you something," he said, "and I hope you'll take it as it was meant, constructively, with good grace."

I said, "Okay, what is it, Joe?"

He said, "You weren't traded to the Red Sox. It was a frame up, a practical joke. You know, at times you have a little way of becoming a bit precocious and overconfident in yourself. We decided that you needed a little taking down and thought that this would be a good way to do it."

By George, I wanted to learn lessons in life but didn't know what to say.

When I look back and consider the different incidents in my life, I have never been humble. I have tried to be, but without much success. More recently I have been—since 1945, when the big incident in my life occurred—but back in those days I was riding the crest of a wave of success and wasn't thinking much about anybody else, mainly just concerned with my own welfare.

Being newly married, the world was very roseate, and I was at the height of my self-assurance. I guess at different times I had a way of aggravating people. I'm not ashamed of having been that way. I'm not reluctant to talk about it because I believe we should admit to our failings in life, and this was one of mine. It did me a lot of good and taught me a big lesson.

Perhaps part of the problem was that I had set myself apart sometimes—improperly or tactlessly—to pursue activities that were on the aesthetic side: the art, the reading, and the general refinements of life. I believe this was genetic, that it came from my father and my mother, this appreciation of the stage and of artistry. That remained with me, and it was a very powerful force, more powerful than I was ever able to exert my energies toward, because I was overpowered by the profession I was in. I never gave full play, while I was playing ball, to the gratification of my actual desires.

I never really allowed myself to portray my aesthetic side because it brought derision from the fellows I was playing with. If they ever read this, they would pooh-pooh it and say, "Why, that so-and-so SOB. When he was playing, he was one of the playboys of the business." Well, I wasn't exactly a playboy, but I didn't let anything deter me, either.

I love the excitement and feeding of the mind and the soul, artistically, athletically, and otherwise. That nervous energy directs me toward constant activity. I didn't just sit around the hotel lobbies like some of the other ballplayers. The fellows who sit around like that usually are drones. We have drones in baseball and in all walks of life. I was never a drone.

Good, bad, or indifferent, at least I was excitable.

15

Young and a Yankee

WHEN WE ARRIVED BACK HOME FROM Asia, in February, it wasn't long until spring training for the 1923 season, which proved to be a banner year because we would win the world championship. We also discovered that Dorothy was pregnant.

Dorothy and I decided to leave our apartment on Edgecombe Avenue, which sat on a high bluff overlooking the Polo Grounds. We moved to Larchmont, New York, to a very charming Tudor-style home there. We entered a period of domesticity when our son was born in July. We named him Harry, after Dorothy's father, and were very proud of him.

Lovely days up there, in Larchmont, lovely. Radio was just coming into prominence then. They were these huge contraptions of batteries that took up two-thirds of the side of a living room, with big horns and that sort of thing. It was one of the marvels of the age. Little did I realize that later in life I would make my living announcing baseball games over that type of machine.

I can't tell you how happy we were in our home in Larchmont. We had the greatest vegetable garden. Now, I was city born and bred, so what did I know about planting tomatoes, beans, and even corn? But we planted them, and I even got down to the point of knowing what a cut-off worm was. We had to put screening around the tomato plants to keep away these bugs that would cut them down. The tomatoes we grew were as big as grapefruit. I lived a life of gardening and took a keen delight in it.

I was still a youngster, just twenty-three years old. Although all those years in the Minor Leagues had taught me things that were on the decadent side, life in the Major Leagues was charming. Aspects of the future were very bright, cheery, and optimistic. I was just a young guy making good, and it was so wonderful. I acquired my first real automobile, a Cadillac. Now, don't get high notions—it was secondhand.

Everything was so strictly Americanized, as you picture the home and the family. Dorothy was very much in love with me and also with Harry. Then, just a couple of years later, our little girl, Susie, was born. There was this devotion to the cradle, to the diapers, and to be gentle and tender with the child. Life was given over to rearing and caring for our babies.

Dorothy was an excellent mother, but I didn't grasp being a father. Mothers understand very well because they have a natural instinct for it. They know what to do and how to handle the baby. A young father like me, twenty-three years old, was not the wisest guy in the world, and I handled our babies like they were Haviland china. I would have liked to have known what to do but felt it was outside my domain.

It's like they used to say in the old days. One fellow asks another, "What do you know about electricity?"

And he says, "I know enough to leave it alone."

I married a girl who was my sweetheart, and we were very much in love. All of a sudden the babies appear, and the mother unintentionally sets the father aside. She still loves him as much as she ever did, but the babies become the featured object. I believe that when a young couple marries, they should spend a few years together and enjoy each other before accepting the responsibilities a baby compels.

In my second marriage, that occurred. Ellen and I traveled a lot, went to different countries and enjoyed each other and life. The world opened up before us, and we weren't pinned down to a home in a little town, letting the rest of the world slide by. I don't know what young couples talk about before they're married, and I'd be silly even to try to guess, but I don't think they sit down and say, "Oh, when we're married we can't wait to have a baby." They get married because they believe they're the only two people on earth who are going to share life's problems, its benefits, and enjoyments. They want to be able to enjoy each other as they did when they were younger.

So many problems arise in the first few years, especially if youngsters arrive, and it breeds a misunderstanding between the husband and wife. It leads to problems because it requires extra money, clothing, care, doctors, and other responsibilities. I do think couples should wait a while, so they can learn to fit their personalities and characters together, learn to understand each other so that when the realities set in, they are prepared to meet them. You don't learn how to do that pitching.

Right in the middle of all this was constant bickering between Dorothy's family and mine. Her father was a real fine man, a gentleman, a good fellow. I liked him, and he liked me. Her mother, on the other hand, did odd things. I was making good money, and there was no necessity for her intrusion. However, Mrs. Pyle would arrive unsolicited from Brooklyn with a load of items—especially after our second child, Susie, was born—baby dresses, socks, and other clothes. That was fine and duly appreciated. But then she would tell people that she was buying all of these clothes because I wasn't buying anything for them.

My own mother was just as guilty. When I went over to see her, she always said something mean or caustic about Dorothy. So, I stopped going. Then Dorothy wouldn't let my mother see the children. I felt trapped between two families. Who was I supposed to placate: my wife's family or my own mother? There was an attempt at reconciliation between my wife and mother but instead of an affable conclusion it wound up in a bitterness that was never ameliorated. There was that constant strain.

It does strike me that we have personal interactions; we are human beings. Even professional ballplayers have emotions and reactions that play like little subtonic discords in one's soul. They accumulate and affect behavior patterns. You become rather loose and irresponsible. A twenty-three-year-old kid doesn't know what to do. His mind cannot make the adjustment. I believe this has been the cause of many divorces or breakups of what otherwise would have been happy marriages.

Of course, I wasn't exactly the All-American boy and became careless in my associations.

It was a remarkable baseball year, however, in 1923, under Miller Huggins, who assumed real control over the Yankees, including the authority to dictate over Babe Ruth. Winning the championship that year justified Colonel Ruppert's confidence in Huggins, so he made him the manager after he bought out Colonel Houston's share of the team.

Then came the announcement that the Giants, from whom the Yankees rented the Polo Grounds, were not going to renew the lease, and we would have to look for our own field. The Giants ran into a stone wall because they didn't realize Ruppert had enough money to build his own stadium. They braced the wrong fellow. They thought possibly that Ruppert would come around and advance the rent, which he didn't do. Ruppert hurriedly bought the land from the old Astor estate across the Harlem River and built Yankee Stadium, which opened in 1923 and stood a three-quarters of an hour drive from our home in Larchmont.

The thing opened in a blaze of glory. Bob Shawkey pitched the first game in Yankee Stadium and Babe Ruth, true to his style and achievements, hit a home run. The infield and outfield had grass like a golf green. It was so perfect. This was the pièce de résistance of all baseball fields anywhere for ever and ever, it seemed. The stadium had a health club in it, which was never used, and it had all the latest gadgets, including something like a sauna bath. It had more in it than the public ever realized. We were just in seventh heaven, the Yankees, playing there.

We went on a road trip a month or so after the stadium opened. When the weather started to turn warm, the Yankees rented it out to a rodeo. To prevent the horses from digging into the lovely turf, they put mats down, covering the infield and part of the outfield. When they took the mats up, there wasn't a blade of grass left. The mats had smothered the grass and beaten it to death. They did not reseed the infield and outfield, but instead brought in sod. The whole aspect of the grass was changed.

The whole nature of the Yankees was about to change too.

In June 1923 I was out at the new stadium, watching batting practice. It was so early in the afternoon that regular batting practice hadn't started, but two or three of the stars who felt they needed a little extra work were alternating with the pitchers. There was Ruth, Wally Pipp, Everett Scott, and Aaron Ward. The gang was standing behind the batting cage, some with one foot resting on a bolster rod.

From the direction of the Yankee bench appeared two men, Miller Huggins and a young, smooth-faced Atlas trailing him rather shyly, his shoulders sloping. I was impressed, not so much by the young man's physical appearance but that he rated the personal escort of the manager.

We, who were to become his teammates, had just taken our first look at Lou Gehrig.

Hug stopped by the batting cage and asked the guys leaning against it to lend the kid a bat. Ruth handed over his club, which weighed some forty-eight ounces. Gehrig stepped into the batting cage, twisted his back foot once or twice and set himself. He missed a couple. He dribbled a pair to the infield. He seemed anxious, nervous, his timing too quick. From the aisle behind the box seats, behind the Yankee bench, came a raucous yell: "Show the big fella that he isn't the only one who can hit 'em out of the park!" Gehrig had brought along his own cheering section.

Lou seemed to take heart. Swinging Babe's bat was no light chore, but Lou gripped the handle tighter, cut at the next pitch—and *wham*—the ball took off, higher and higher, long and far away, into the section they then called Ruthville, high over the railings of the right-field bleachers. Babe's eyes popped. "Jesus," he grunted. The rest of us watched in amazed silence, stealing a glance at each other after Gehrig banged yet another into the same area—and then another. Members of his personal cheering squad couldn't restrain themselves, yowling in high glee, "Atta boy, Lou! See that, Babe? You got company!"

Indeed, he did. Larrupin' Lou Gehrig had arrived at Yankee Stadium.

Lou and I didn't take to each other right away. He reminded me of the first boy to raise his hand in school and say, "I know, teacher"—a teacher's pet. I have the greatest respect and fondness for him now, however. I didn't fully realize it until years later, after I had left the Yankees and we were no longer teammates, but in many ways Lou Gehrig, because of his personal qualities, was somebody whom I would have liked to have been.

Ed Barrow signed Lou to a contract, which was dated for the day after he was to play his last game for Columbia University. The Yankees were already well on the way to a third straight pennant, so the arrival of the power boy barely created a ripple in the press. Gehrig played just a few games in '23, relieving Pipp at times. Huggins thought he needed more experience and sent him down to the Minors in Hartford.

Gehrig did not play in the World Series with us that year. That was the Series with the game in which Casey Stengel hit the inside-the-park home run and lost his shoe between third base and home. I didn't pitch much in that Series, only $2\frac{1}{3}$ innings, and allowed four hits and a base on balls. Talent and luck deserted me.

131

The 1924 season was no better for me and much worse for the team as a whole. There was nothing funny about the 1924 season. I can't even remember any comedic incidents. It played out more like a tragedy. In the middle of the season, we had beaten Washington five straight games; we were the same club we had been in 1923 that won the pennant by sixteen games.

So, in 1924 we were sailing along and thought we could beat Washington anytime we wanted to. But Washington started to catch on, and all of a sudden there was a wave of enthusiasm for the Washington ballclub and Walter Johnson, its great pitcher, who had never been in a World Series. Everybody, it seemed, wanted to win for Walter Johnson. All the other ballclubs in the American League were pulling for Washington against us because we had won the pennant in 1921, '22, and '23. No matter what town we were in, it seemed like everybody wanted to see us lose.

Babe Ruth, meanwhile, was living the life of Babe and having a great time. In his early years, he was not generally a favorite with his teammates and certainly not Miller Huggins. But his home runs were pulling people into the park, his popularity was immense, and his communication with the fans was faultless. Privately, "Gigge," as we generally called him (a contraction of his first name, George), was having domestic problems.

It all came to a head in 1925 when he was fined $5,000 and suspended by Judge Landis, the baseball commissioner. He was also rebuked by many because of his infatuation with a beautiful showgirl and his annulment from his first wife, Helen. Babe was called to account and made a promise to reform, which he did to the surprise and pleasure of those around him.

Washington beat us over Labor Day weekend, 1924, in New York, and took first place. We went from New York to Boston, where Miller Huggins called a meeting and said, "Now, we're going on this road trip, and to win the pennant we'll have to win at least 21 out of 24 games to stay in the race." Well, we won 21 out of 24, but Washington still took the pennant. That was one of my first objective lessons in not having done my best all season long or living up to my potential.

When a season ended in those days, the fellows split up. Some went to Texas, others to the West Coast, and some to Maine. They went to all points across the United States. The Yankees ballclub was breaking up. Those of us who were going back to New York, of which there were a few, waited at the Pennsylvania station at North Philadelphia, a raised platform, like 125th Street in New York. It had been a misty, foggy day, and by then it was raining.

I stood there off by myself, looking out at the city, because it was October and darkness arrived early. It was about seven o'clock and the city lights were diffused into an eerie glow. I had rarely felt so gloomy.

I thought to myself, *How could we ever blow this pennant? How could this team ever lose?* When you lose like that, you think you're never going to win again. I thought, *For goodness sake, there goes the last chance probably that we'll ever play in the World Series. We had a chance this year, and we certainly blew it.* You could cut the dejection with a knife. I'll never forget the penetration of that thought into my mind and my heart.

Sometimes the public doesn't realize that professional athletes have emotional upsets and very serious dejections—and very high elations. The ones who don't have no imagination. If you have imagination at all, you have peaks. If you have nervous energy, you have peaks. This was the depth of depression, the nadir. In the middle of the season, instead of assuming we were going to win easily, we should have put on a drive and turned it on a little bit because we were the better club.

Losing in 1924 was so hard to take. It certainly didn't feel good at the time, but I now realize it was good because I survived it and was able to rise above my shortcomings and defects of character. I suppose you have to suffer defeat to learn how to accept it and survive.

The season passed, and Huggins told Ruppert that the club had to be rebuilt. During spring training in 1925, he informed Aaron Ward, our fine second baseman, that he would not play regularly anymore. Everett Scott, who had played 1,230 consecutive games at shortstop, was at his end. Earle Combs came up in '25, and after two years in the Minors so did Lou Gehrig, who replaced Pipp after Wally was beaned by Charlie Caldwell during practice. Little by little, the Yanks took the shape of the club it was later to become, but not before finishing in seventh place in 1925.

In came Tony Lazzeri, Mark Koenig, and other fellows. Transitions were taking place, and the Yankees finished the 1926 season with a record of 91-63, winning our fourth pennant and advancing to our fourth World Series, the last game of which made history.

The New York Yankees and St. Louis Cardinals were tied at three games each, as we headed into the seventh and decisive contest.

The day looked like a setting for an Alfred Hitchcock mystery—raw, cold, drizzly. Yankee Stadium was shrouded in a shallow ground fog, like an English moor. The playing surface was just as boggy—soft—and uncertain for footing. The weather was so bad that the crowd was slim for a seventh game of a World Series.

I had won the fourth game, 10–5. In the seventh game, I faced the Cards' clever knuckleballer Jesse Haines, who had shut us out in the third game 4–0. I cannot recall ever being as nervous as I was the night before that final game.

To keep my mind off the responsibility, I went to Madison Square Garden to watch an exhibition tennis match featuring the magnificent champion Suzanne Lenglen. There was plenty to divert me. Between sets, while Lenglen and her opponent were off the floor, Al Schacht and Nick Altrock, the hilarious baseball clowns, staged a match of their own, without racquets, in pantomime. The crowd was in stitches, watching Al, who was garbed so exactly like Lenglen and whose features so closely resembled hers—only without the finesse. It looked like Lenglen giving a burlesque imitation of herself.

After Al and Nick retired, there was a long wait because Lenglen would not come out. She claimed she had been insulted by Al's characterization. However, as it was "play or no pay," she finally appeared.

The next day, I had my own problems. I was still nervous, but that was nothing new to me before a ball game. I always suffered somewhat; in fact, it was a healthy indication. Times when I had not worried, I didn't last long. I sat on the training table watching the hands of the clock approaching warm-up time. My hands perspired. Finally, I went out. The drizzle was slight, still a day not suited to good baseball. It was a day for tragedy or glory—depending on one's hopes and dreams.

For three innings, all was well with the Yanks. Babe Ruth poled one of his long home runs, sending us into a 1–0 lead.

Then in the fourth inning the Cards added another player: fate. Rogers Hornsby, leading off for the Cards, slapped a grounder back at me—one out. Sunny Jim Bottomley sliced a single to left field. Lester Bell rapped a grounder to Mark Koenig, the start of what seemed to be an inning-ending double play, but the inning was far from over. The

World Series was to be decided right there. Koenig booted the ball, with Bottomley safe at second and Bell safe at first. Chick Hafey, one of the National League's toughest batters, hit a short, high-fly ball to left field, just behind the shortstop. Koenig went out, Meusel came in. Each thought the other would catch the ball. Neither did. The bases were loaded.

Destiny was having a field day. Bob O'Farrell came up. I was bearing down—all power and skill on every pitch. There had been two bad breaks, but I had seen nothing yet. O'Farrell hit a fly ball into short left center. Meusel and Combs were after this one. As Meusel had the better throwing arm, Combs moved aside to allow Bob to get into throwing position. It seemed an easy catch until Meusel took his eyes off the ball to estimate time and position. The ball hit his shoulder and dropped to the ground. One run scored, tying the game, 1–1. The bases remained loaded. Up came Tommy Thevenow, who ultimately was named the most outstanding player in the Series.

I squared away to pitch to Thevenow. The count reached two strikes and no balls. I have heard time and again since then that I made a serious mistake in allowing Thevenow to hit an 0-2 pitch. The critics said I should have made him hit a bad ball. Well, that is exactly what Tommy did. He hit a curve six inches outside the plate. The bat broke in half, with the big end flying out and sticking straight up in the mud. The infielders, because of the three-on-base situation, were playing in. The ball flew out over Lazzeri's head, barely reaching the outfield and embedding itself in the mud. Two runs scored; the Cards led, 3–1. One of the weirdest innings in World Series history had left the Yankees trailing.

In our half of the sixth inning, a pinch hitter went in for me. We scored one run and seemed to be coming back—3–2, Cardinals.

Came the seventh inning, and Jess Haines was pitching with some difficulty, as he had raised a blister on a pitching finger. Combs led off with a single. Koening sacrificed. Ruth was walked intentionally—and I might point out that Ruth represented the run that would put the Yanks ahead, so you can judge the respect in which Ruth was held. Meusel grounded into a forced out at second base. Gehrig was next. Lou had won one Series game with a single and hit a double to help win another. Haines blew two strikes past Lou but then tore that blistered finger. Jess walked Lou, but not purposely. The bases were loaded.

Then came the scene from which evolved one of the greatest dramatic efforts of all time. Hornsby patted Haines on the back, excused him, and pointed to the bullpen, which was a long, long way down beyond the left-field wing of the Yankees' grandstand.

The crowd turned expectant eyes in that direction. It was hard to see. The misty, foggy, October afternoon had grown darker. The gloom was real for Yankees fans.

A figure more like that of the fanciful concept of the specter, gaunt and bony-shouldered, shuffled slowly forward at a knock-kneed gait. His cap was perched atop his head like a scarecrow's.

He was the approaching figure of doom. His identity through the drizzly mist was apparent only by his odd manner of walking. He emerged into focus. It was the great Grover Cleveland Alexander, one of baseball's immortal pitchers, who had pitched a complete 10–2 victory only the day before. He had also won the second game, 6–2.

He was being brought into pitch to the robust, long hitter, "Push 'Em Up" Tony Lazzeri.

Lazzeri, then in his rookie year, was faced with his first crucial test. Old Pete on the mound looked at Lazzeri with cool indifference, his leathery jaws munching on tobacco as he prepared to pitch.

He delivered, slicing the outside edge of the plate with his side-arm curve for strike one. He cut a pitch outside—1-1. Always a quick workman, Alex came in with a fastball. Lazzeri met and drove it. The ball started twenty feet fair as it began its course toward the left-field grandstand. The fans jumped up screaming. A grand slam? No. The ball slowly curved, veering to the left and landing in the seats, five feet foul.

Alex had been in that spot before. He carefully drew a bead on O'Farrell's glove. Pete broke off that curve, a sharp, viscous, snapping pitch. Lazzeri took a roundhouse swing . . . and struck out. Old Pete registered no emotion at all. He shuffled to the bench, hardly disturbed, and lingered outside the dugout to smile at a cheering spectator. Pete retired three batters in order in the eighth, and our World Series hopes were formally extinguished in the bottom of the ninth when Babe Ruth was called out at second—some say while trying to steal the base, while others contend it was a failed attempt at a hit-and-run. (If the latter, John McGraw would not have approved.)

Old Pete won 373 games in the regular seasons of his brilliant career, yet that one incident in the seventh inning of the seventh game of the 1926 Series, the perfect execution of Lazzeri's strikeout, gained him more renown than the sum total of all other victories. Forty-six thousand fans had seen a dramatic episode that would come to be the central theme of a story, screenplay, and movie, *The Winning Team*, with Ronald Reagan starring as Grover Cleveland Alexander.

I sat there downcast, of course. Along with my 1–0 loss because of a fielding error by the third baseman in the fourth and decisive game of the 1921 Series, it was one of the two soul-ripping, heart-tearing, saddening experiences in my career as a pitcher.

Nevertheless, I was entirely mesmerized by the art, science, and skill of Pete Alexander. It was like watching a master artist with a brush. Alexander did not just work the corners of the plate; he painted every outer inch of the strike zone. Each pitch came in at a different spot—up, down, high, low. I have never seen a pitcher use more control, more intelligence, more natural pitching exactness than Alexander that day. He was a brilliant executioner, with a composite blend of art, touch, and timing.

It was the finest pitching I had ever seen, yet that defeat stayed with me not for a little while but, as you must discern, to the present moment. That is a vignette of a baseball pitcher whose emotional structure was destroyed by forces he could not control. We do meet such episodes in life, do we not? I was learning, by addition and subtraction, the vagaries of life and the transitions from good to bad and back to good again.

As it was, I had been out for five weeks of the 1926 season because of a lame arm, which comes with a small story attached. After pitching one afternoon in Philadelphia, Herb Pennock asked Babe Ruth, Joe Dugan, and me if we would attend a street carnival. One of the booths featured a game in which contestants threw a baseball at a pyramid of five papier-mâché bottles. If they knocked them off the counter in three throws, they won a doll and a box of candy. It was so easy, and Esther Pennock soon had her arms full of dolls and candy. Finally, the proprietor came from behind the counter and said, "You guys are breaking me." So, we agreed to back up five feet, started throwing wildly, and gave back all the prizes.

The next morning, my right elbow was swollen to three times its normal size. I went to a doctor who told me I was out for the season. I told Huggins I had hurt the arm playing against Philadelphia, and he sent me to a doctor in Rochester. I was there for a month, soaking the elbow in a cauldron of almost boiling water with hot salve and bandages at night. Then, every day I had a massage, until one day, without notice, he suddenly, while rotating my arm, flipped it. There was a click, and the offending cartilage or whatever it was snapped back into place. I am sure I would have won 20 games in 1926, but being under a handicap for more than five weeks, that ambition was buried.

Speaking of which . . .

16

The Merry Mortician

DOROTHY'S FATHER WAS A FUNERAL DIRECTOR, and a very good one. He was very much a gentleman and highly astute. He proposed that I learn the business under him, for $35 a week, when I wasn't pitching. I didn't do embalming or anything like that; I helped run funerals and became involved in sales.

I could have made a lot more money doing other things, but I worked there because Dorothy was an only child and she felt the business in the end would come to us. People started calling me the Merry Mortician, and that name stuck for a while. I didn't like that at all.

In the off-season of 1926 I became a little discouraged with what was taking place in the mortuary business and was asked to join the Brooklyn Visitation Basketball Team in the American Basketball League. I was not good enough as a basketball player to compete in the league but sufficient to play the exhibition games. I played many such games and earned $1,000 a month, which was a helluva lot better than $35 a week as a funeral director.

I went to talk to my father-in-law and said, "What is the future here for me?"

He said, "What do you mean?"

I said, "Well, is the business going to be left to Dorothy, and am I to presume that there will be some substantial income from this?"

He said, "No, I'm going to leave it to Dorothy's mother."

So, I said, "Then where do I fit in?" He said I could buy the business from her, which I was not prepared to do.

As much as I pined for the normality of a conventional career of some sort and knew I needed to plan for the future, I really was not cut out for the business world. This was not news. Back at the end of the '23 season, the people who lived next door to us in Larchmont, the Drummonds, wanted to know if I'd like to go into the real estate business, or just work for them over the winter. I wasn't doing anything else, so I said, "Yeah, that would be really nice." Their oldest daughter ran the office, and old man Drummond was a pleasant fellow with a typical Scotch burr in his voice. We were very cordial with each other.

One day, a young fellow and his wife came to Larchmont and stopped into the real estate office, looking for a home. I showed them some houses but knew the place they liked best was very poorly built. The front door frame was out of plumb, and there were cracks and splits everywhere. It was really just a heap of boards, plaster, and shingles. The fellow told me he had $3,000 to put down. He looked like a kid who worked very hard for his money, and I hated to see him waste it on a poor investment.

When he came back the next week, I talked him out of buying the house. He then thanked Mr. Drummond profusely for my honesty, which of course finished me off as a real estate salesman. It also ended my cordial relations with the neighbors. Drummond couldn't get over that I had told the truth about the house, but I felt that if someone needed my advice, I had to give it.

I had a long history of failure as a salesman. When I was about eighteen, I took a position for the Christmas holidays with Frederick Loeser & Company, a department store in Brooklyn, and was put in the sports department, at a counter selling flashlights. These small devices ranged anywhere from thirty-five to fifty cents to a dollar. I was rated according to the sales I made each day. Well, you could sell a hundred of these cheap little flashlights, and it wouldn't amount to anything.

So, I took myself out of there without being asked and went over to the ice skates because it was a devilishly cold winter and a lot of ice skates were being sold. I enjoyed myself, especially with the ladies trying on their ice skates. That lasted for a while, and then I went over to the bicycles because they cost fifteen or twenty dollars apiece. I did pretty well there, and they wanted me to stay on after the Christmas holidays, but I had to go to spring training.

I'll never forget that experience in the sporting-goods department. A woman came in one day and wanted a baseball uniform for her little nephew. The only baseball uniforms we had were scratchy and not made of good material. "Madam," I said, "don't buy this uniform for the youngster because he'll be awfully disappointed. It won't last any time at all, and you're just wasting your money." She went to the head of the department and told him he had a wonderfully honest salesman back there who told the truth and she appreciated not being sold something not fit to be bought. The manager came around to me and said, "What are you trying to do, ruin the store?"

That same winter, my cousin got me a job selling crocheted buttons for a firm that, strangely, was in the same building as the New York Giants. The sample case weighed about thirty-five pounds. Oh, it was heavy. My route was on Third Avenue in New York City, and I was given the addresses of possible customers, about one every block. It was so bitterly cold. I had to stop in doorways to get warm before I could go to the next stop, all the way up to Ninety-Sixth Street, toting this case.

Finally, over in Brooklyn was a huge place that sold all sorts of novelties, embroideries, linens, and things, where I sold an order, eighty-six dollars. I made the sale on a Saturday and showed up for work on Monday with this order in hand. The gentleman who owned the firm, a lovely guy, a very compassionate sort of fellow, came to me about two days later and told me he couldn't fill the order because the customer's credit was no good.

"Waite," he said, "If I were you, I'd look for some other method of earning a living. You're not a salesman."

My only real successful business enterprise was as an entertainer during the off-seasons throughout the 1920s. Carried by my celebrity with the Yankees, I went into vaudeville, and that's how I met Jimmy Durante, the Marx Brothers, and many other stars. I met Mae West on a night train going out of Cleveland. She asked me to tell her all the dirty stories I knew, and then she'd clean them up and use them. I had a good time with her.

I appeared onstage with a kid named Tommy Gordon in Brooklyn. He was considered the greatest ad-lib comedian of the time but was not a good fellow to work with. He was pretty much an alcoholic, and I had a hard time keeping him straight. I played three shows a day and appeared alone at Reisenweber's Café, which was a big night club on Columbus Circle. I did a supper and a night show there, taking the subway back and forth. I was only at Reisenweber's for two weeks but was making $2,500 a week. In those days that was real money, more than I was making with the Yankees.

I continued on the stage with Tommy for about ten weeks, and we played places like Bridgeport and New Haven. It was a talking act, with no singing, and the chatter was rather inconsequential, kind of silly. It really was my name that was carrying us through these places, not any theatrical ability. I liked it, although I wished I had been a better performer. I didn't feel free on the stage. I didn't feel loose. But the money was irresistible.

After the '28 baseball season, I was offered a fabulous sum to perform sixteen weeks around New York. In fact, I would net around $1,200 in sixteen weeks, more than double the money I was paid in twenty-four with the Yankees. I accepted and teamed up with a premier song composer and producer named J. Fred Coots, who wrote songs like "A Precious Little Thing Called Love" and "Love Letters in the Sand." His most famous tune was "Santa Claus Is Comin' to Town." For a time, I was erroneously credited as the song's cowriter, and my image was featured on the sheet music. I paid Coots a liberal salary and also had to pay my agent a commission. In 1929 we played the Palace Theatre in New York, Chicago, and Cleveland. We did really well.

At the Palace, I appeared onstage first in a Yankees' uniform, although I took the spikes off the bottom of my shoes. I didn't have on the cap, but I had "New York" or "Yankees" across the chest. When I went off-stage, Coots played a medley of all the songs he had written, giving me time to change, and then I reappeared, this time in a dinner coat and tuxedo with a carnation in my lapel.

Dorothy and my son Harry, who would have been about six years old at the time, came to a performance at the Palace in New York, the mecca of vaudeville. At one point, Mae Questel, who later was the voice of Betty Boop, sang a song that had sort of a flirtatious theme. The idea was that she came over and picked a petal or two off the flower in my lapel, sidled up to me in a provocative way, and tweaked me on the ear. My little guy, who was sitting in about the tenth row, yelled out, "Mommy! Mommy! She's hurting Daddy!" That was the best part of the act.

In the audience one night, in about the fifth or sixth row, was a man named Ben Piazza. He was with MGM, or an outfit like that, and a most delightful man. After the show, he came backstage and said he would like me to take a movie test. When I got back to New York later that winter, I went down to a studio, I think on Fifty-Seventh Street.

I had no idea what I would be asked to do. They had me stand in front of a camera, just ad lib, share a few facts about myself, and then turn my head verrrry slowly to the left and then back to the center camera to look straight into it. Then I had to look right very slowly and turn my head in certain ways. This was all new to me, and I didn't do a very good job. I was a flop.

I guess I have a strain, perhaps inherited from my father, of enjoying being out in front of people. A certain artistry was supposed to be connected with the stage. Although I can't say that what I was doing was art, the feeling was there, and I envied those people who did have the talent to perform before a live audience.

The dead—now, that was another story.

Remember, I was still in the funeral business at the time. One of the other funeral directors who worked for my father-in-law was an awfully nice kid from Pennsylvania named Dick Meehan. I told him in 1927 that I would back him if he would open a mortuary in Larchmont. The firm became known as Hoyt & Meehan. My father-in-law was very bitter that I took one of his best funeral directors and financed him in this venture.

That summer, there was a death in Larchmont, and Hoyt & Meehan was called on to prepare the remains for transportation, provide a casket, and so forth. Where do you think the burial was to take place? In Brooklyn! And my father-in-law was to handle the internment.

The remains and the casket had to be transported in a vehicle with a canvas cover that buttoned down over the trunk. Dick Meehan said to me, "You know, I've got to get this body over to Brooklyn, but I don't like to leave the place alone." Well, the Yankees were playing at home, so I told him I could take care of it for him.

I'm not making a joke out of this because there is some respect to be shown to the gentleman, but the funny thing is I was pitching that day. So, I drove the vehicle down to Yankee Stadium and parked it in the lot. I pitched the game and then drove the body over to Brooklyn.

I imagine that was the first and last time anything like that ever happened at Yankee Stadium.

Eventually, we had to close the business because Dick Meehan had pneumonia, and the serum doctors gave him made him go blind. Last I heard of him, he went to Worcester, Massachusetts, and was operating a drugstore.

17

The Roaring Yankees

THE GRANDEST, MOST SUCCESSFUL AND COLORFUL of all the years I played baseball was 1927. We went into first place after the first game, and we were never out of it the whole season, winning 110 games. In 1969, at the celebration of baseball's one hundredth season, the Baseball Writers Association of America voted the 1927 Yankees the greatest club of all time. That may be true, but maybe not. Many other teams have bona fide claims to greatness, but I'll be satisfied with the accolade until some other club establishes an uncontestable record and set of figures.

Despite all the clamor about other Yankees greats and teams throughout the decades, I am sure the teams of the twenties initiated the style, set the pattern, and, through wisdom and management, built the almost invincible organization that came to be known as the Yankees dynasty.

This was the season Ruth set his record of 60 home runs. It has often been said it was easy to pitch for the '27 Yanks because of the murderous hitting. This is outright baloney for one reason: if a pitcher didn't start the game well, he didn't last long, and someone else was pitching in no time. I hold a fondness for the '27 season, as I led the league with 22 wins and 7 losses, in earned run average at 2.63, and in winning percentage at .759. I was among the first five in fewest bases on balls per nine innings, 1.90, and third in complete games, 23.

It was also the year I broke into radio. NBC had its offices down near Wall Street, and as I recall I was contacted with a request to do a fifteen-minute program each Monday night in September. Because the Yankees were home all of September and we had the pennant won by Labor Day, I thought it would prove a fine experience, not realizing I was experimenting with what would become my livelihood. The reward for my first radio effort was a pen-and-pencil set.

We took the winner's share of the 1927 World Series by practically scaring the opposition to death. The Pirates won in the National League with a batting average of .305 and had seven men hitting above .300, but the mere sight of our assassins taking turns driving the baseball out of the Pittsburgh ballpark took most of the fight out of them.

The Series opened in Pittsburgh, and I was asked to pitch batting practice. Huggins made no special request of me to lay the ball in there to help our sluggers show off. I just pitched in the regular batting-practice style, and one after another, the team teed off on me, as I was glad to have them all do. Earle Combs, Mark Koenig, Babe Ruth, Lou Gehrig, Bob Meusel, Tony Lazzeri—just their names are enough to give pitchers nightmares still. Every one of them powered the baseball out of the playing field again and again. More than that, the lower end of the order—Dugan, Johnny Grabowski, and Pat Collins—also stroked my pitches up against the far fences or into the seats.

I could see the Pirate players watching in numb silence. They had their own hard-hitters—the Waner brothers, who could belt the baseball too. But they were relatively small men who looked like schoolboys in the company of the towering Yankees sluggers. They shook their heads as they watched and left the field in silence. After that, they never had a chance, and the Yankees won four games in a row. The first game was mine, which I won with the eighth inning help of our new sinker-ball relief man, Wilcy Moore.

The winter of 1927 I devoted pretty much to staying home. Then came 1928. We lived high that year, with salaries better than ever, World Series money burning in our checking accounts, and more in the offing. I had vaudeville money besides. My pitching, I discovered, was a matter of concentration, and I stuck to my plan of demolishing each batter as if he were the last out of the game. My contract that year called for a $2,500 bonus if I equaled my record of 22 wins. (Huggins had told me that I could win 25 every year if I would concentrate.)

Our 1928 season was very much a repeat of 1927, as the Yanks won the pennant again, but not without a struggle. We had a series of injuries—and in August we blew a thirteen-game lead. The Philadelphia Athletics caught and passed us. Labor Day morning they were in first place.

Before an estimated crowd of eighty thousand, we played the A's in a double header that day. The crush of the crowd was so overwhelming that it was impossible to get a car within ten blocks of the park. I had to show my credentials to get a policeman to ride my running board before I was allowed to come through the lines.

George Pipgras pitched 5–0 to win the first game, and I beat them 7–3 in the second. We held on to win the pennant by 2½ games. The Athletics were a mighty team, but we were mightier. Nothing seemed to stop us. If one man got hurt, we came up with a Durocher or a Tom Zachary to fill in and keep us winning.

We knew in our hearts that when we beat Philadelphia we had clinched the pennant but did not make it a certainty until we beat Detroit on September 28. Then we uncorked a wild celebration at the Fort Shelby Hotel. Babe Ruth got management to add two extra rooms onto his suite, and he had couriers bringing up drinkables all evening. Lord knows how many invited and uninvited guests were there. Babe at one point climbed on the piano and warned that the party was going to get rough. But no one went home, and the racket continued until dawn.

I had to pitch later that day, and my teammates were barely in condition to walk to their positions. I was aghast when I noticed that my catcher, Pat Collins, had his pants on backward. Even though we had clinched the title, this game carried extra importance for me because, according to a newspaper report, I was one game short of the 22 wins I would need to match my '27 record and collect a $2,500 bonus. After about five innings I was ready to give up but decided to get my licks in if nothing else. I got a base hit; when I trotted down to first, I found my old friend Harry Heilmann playing there. He had put the Tigers ahead by doubling off the scoreboard, and I wanted no more such stuff from him. "For God's sake," I ribbed him, "this game means $2,500 to me!"

"Oh, why didn't you tell me?" Harry replied sarcastically. When he came up to bat, he drove a ball right back at me, very nearly taking my ear off, for a hot single. But then, God bless him, he tried to steal second and was thrown out. Then came our next turn, with Babe Ruth up to bat and three men on base. Babe had barely closed his eyes the previous night, but he waved his hand to indicate it was in the bag, and then drove the ball over the fence for four runs, more than enough to win it for us.

As it turned out, the win was my 23rd, and more than enough to earn that bonus. The newspaper report that I had only won 21 games was wrong!

I didn't have any inkling at the time that the 1928 World Series was my last as a Yankee and was probably my most prosperous year in baseball. The Series, which the Yankees took from the Cardinals in four straight games, was as spectacular as the season had been—even more so when you consider that almost every Yankee was sporting a bandage or a bruise of some sort and Earle Combs could not play at all.

We were the first team ever to win the World Series four games straight two years in a row. Moreover, we used just three pitchers. I won the first and fourth game, Pipgras the second, and Zachary the third. Between the three of us, we pitched *four complete games.* In 1914 Dick Rudolph, Bill James, and Lefty Tyler in a sense performed the same feat, but James, after winning his start, relieved Tyler the next game two days later, so all three did not pitch complete games. Of course, the Babe was the greatest. In the final game, in St. Louis, he hit three home runs in three successive times at bat and even had the bloodthirsty Cardinals fans cheering him.

It may have been the extra money and soft living that brought me overweight and out of condition to Saint Petersburg the following spring. Now, don't forget we were in the middle of the halcyon days of the twenties when the market started to rise. Everything was very prolific and lovely. Women broke out with little clay pipes of pastel colors, pink and blue, and then the ladies started in on colorful cigarettes, like English Ovals. These cigarettes were long, and the women employed a graceful sweep of the hand while smoking. It was common to see two ladies sitting together in a cocktail lounge in a hotel. Office workers went out at five o'clock for cocktails. People didn't do that previously; it was unheard of. That started the three-martini luncheon idea, back in the 1920s.

This was the age of Prohibition, and with it came the drinking, cocktail parties, and nightclubs. There were speakeasies, and morals began to loosen. People began to see others in these public places drinking in the afternoon and evening. The whole world in the twenties changed. I'm talking about the sophisticates—those who went to the theaters in New York and frequented nightclubs. All of a sudden, the forerunner of the jet-set appeared at places like the Stork Club, where Sherman Billingsley would give perfume to the ladies, offer cigarettes to the men, and serve champagne.

It was another version of the same idea in the suburbs. When I'd come home from Yankee Stadium, my wife would greet me and say, perhaps, "We're going over to the Parson's tonight. Freddy Parson called up and said he has a new form of cocktail, the Rum and Honey." Everybody had pet cocktails and was always inviting friends to come over and sample them.

Our neighbors were lovely. They weren't doing any harm, but I can't tell you how many roasts were left in the oven because somebody would say, "Come on over, we have a party going on" or "Somebody has discovered a new cocktail." They'd turn off the oven and go to the cocktail party.

Of course, I was hitting all the smart spots in nightclubbing and luncheons. I remember spending an afternoon in the restaurant 21 Club with a friend, and I must admit we got a little bit tight. It came to the point when it was time to go to dinner, so we went to the Paradise, I think it was. I was feeling pretty good, meaning I was a little bit schlockered, as they say. The club, up a flight of stairs, was a huge place. When we walked in, the master of ceremonies greeted me, and I specifically asked him not to introduce me from the floor. The MC had that habit of announcing prominent people: "Mr. Johnny Jones is here!"

We sat down and ordered dinner. I was still kind of woozy and, sure enough, the master of ceremonies came out and introduced four or five people who were sitting ringside. He finally got around to me and introduced me as "the great Yankee pitcher." I was supposed to stand up and take a bow, and right at that moment, the waiter put down the first course of dinner, a plate of soup. I was kind of mad about the whole thing because I had asked not to be introduced. I stood up, took what was supposed to be a bow, went to sit down, slipped, hit the edge of the chair with my fanny, and fell forward face-first right into the plate of soup. When I looked up, the soup was dripping from my chin. I was a fine sight to behold!

It was the height of the theatrical world, performing down on Broadway: Al Jolson, Eddie Cantor, Ed Wynn, all the girl singers and dancers, and—gosh—the Ziegfeld Follies. I became very friendly with Eddie

Jackson, Lou Clayton, and, oh so many other performers. I joined the Friars Club through Joe Laurie Jr. and learned a different attitude toward facing the world. Theatrical people projected themselves more than ballplayers did. A lot of ballplayers were reticent about public speaking and presenting themselves. They were not gregarious like my vaudeville friends. All the theatrical people I met were wonderful. Later on, in 1931, when I was with the Philadelphia Athletics, George M. Cohan sent for me. It was the most flattering thing in the world. I sat in his hotel suite with him for three or four hours and talked baseball. It was one of the best evenings I ever had.

Theatrical entertainers are a breed unto themselves. I guess all entertainers are—circus and show people. They seemed to live in worlds by themselves, as did ballplayers, although in baseball, you rise to the peaks and sink to the depths and must be able to handle both. You can engage in a profession like acting, in which you feel the thrills and sensations of extreme pleasure and heights of accomplishment, as well as the cellar and dregs and disappointments of defeats and loss. Yet actors don't get the same kind of nostalgic remorse because they can go on from one character to another and endure much longer than a baseball player can.

The twenties were just a hilarious, wonderful, exotic, unbelievable ten years. Everybody felt rather free and easy. The nightclubs were flourishing, and it became the thing to do to go to the theater and then a nightclub. During Prohibition in the twenties in New York, there must have been, at different times, 150 nightclubs. They weren't all going at once because the Prohibition agents would descend and close some of them, and then new ones would spring up. Some of them endured— the Silver Slipper, Melody Club, Surf Club, and the Paradise. Oh, there were so many. Jimmy Durante and Lou Clayton used to perform at the Silver Slipper. I don't think El Morocco was going at that time, but I have a hard time remembering them all.

I also got to know the gangsters because they owned most of the nightclubs. They were real nice guys in a way. You might be thinking, *How the devil can you say they were nice guys when they were so vicious?* Well, they were not vicious with the general public, only against each other. The public was their patron who supplied them with money by going to their clubs. If you went into a nightclub, they'd seat you at a table, and two tables away would be Larry Fay or Legs Diamond or the owners of the place, and they'd send you a drink. I met mobsters like Dutch Schultz, Lucky Luciano, Owney Madden, and George "Big Frenchy" DeMange at various nightclubs.

Meeting Al Capone in Chicago in the twenties was rather an incident.

During Prohibition, if you wanted a glass of beer when you were on the road, you'd ask somebody on the hosting team for the best places to go. So many clubs closed so rapidly that places you had been just a month or two before would be gone, so you had to ask someone for advice. One time, when we were playing the White Sox at Comiskey Field, Bob Meusel, Herb Pennock, Joe Dugan, and I were directed to Capone's club.

Dugan was a wisecracker who was always talking out of the side of his mouth. So, he said to the bartender, "Say," he said, "how do you get to meet the big boy?" Now, Dugan was only kidding.

The bartender said, "Are you serious?"

Dugan said, "Why, certainly."

The fellow said, "Wait a minute," went into the back, and pretty soon came back out and said, "There'll be a car here in twenty minutes."

We couldn't get out of it at this point. We couldn't say we were afraid or didn't want to. In exactly twenty minutes, this big, black limousine pulled up in front of this place. It looked rather ominous because we'd heard about the bulletproof limousines these fellows rode around in. They put us in the limousine, and off we went. They took us to a hotel—I can't remember the name—the Wentworth or whatever it was in South Chicago.

We unloaded and went inside the hotel, where a fellow met us and said, "You're the ballplayers."

We said, "Yeah."

And he said, "Well, I just want to tell you this. It's a cage elevator, and we want you to keep your hands out of your pockets. On each floor you'll see a couple of fellows sitting on chairs outside the elevator doors. Don't think anything of it. When you reach the floor where you unload, turn to your left, and you'll be taken to Mr. Capone's door."

So, we went up the elevator and then down a corridor. Our escorts knocked on the door and then announced us. We entered the room, and there's Al Capone sitting behind this big desk with a grin on his face. Up above Capone was a picture of George Washington, Abraham Lincoln, and, on the far right, Al Capone. So, Dugan, the wisecracker, stepped up to Capone, shook his hand, and said, pointing at the pictures, "Three great men: George, Abe, and Al."

Capone thought that was the greatest thing, so he said to some handy guy, "Bring in the grape," meaning wine. So, in came the guy with a hand truck, and on it was a couple of cases of champagne. We stuck around there for about an hour drinking with the guy. He was very cordial, and I couldn't believe everything that was ascribed to him, but nevertheless it had to be so.

At another place on the continuum, as fate would have it, I also spent time with J. Edgar Hoover. He and my second wife, Ellen, became good friends. They once were driving somewhere together and ran out of gas on the causeway between Miami and Miami Beach, so they went wading until an armored car arrived to pick them up. Another time, we were out together for dinner at some joint, a nightclub. A female impersonator was dancing around, singing this lyric: "Could I care for that big boy there? I certainly could." The idea behind the gag was that this dancer had a hotel key, and he'd throw it on some table. Well, Hoover's sitting there with his hand open, and the goddamn key fell right in his hand.

Anyway, we ended our afternoon with Al Capone in one piece. The fate of my decade with the Roaring Yankees—and my life with Dorothy—was another matter, however.

The breakup of a marriage has seeds that grow and develop. For Dorothy and me, those seeds were planted during the twenties. It was very disconcerting. I look back upon the day and think so much could have been averted, and some common sense might have been introduced. That wasn't to be because my mind was wrongly set.

There was an accumulation of disagreements and differences of opinion. Dorothy was not inclined to play hostess to theatrical people, to whom she was not accustomed. Getting home late was not well received either. I recall so many incidents of discord because of late arrivals.

I was too excitable, too adventurous, too investigative. I wanted to see what made life tick. It was not that Dorothy did not like to travel. After all, she went with me to spring training in Hot Springs and New Orleans. She went to Japan and China with me and loved it. Later on, we were pinned down with children, and I must confess I wasn't the most attentive father in the world, a great fault of mine.

When you live with somebody, it isn't a question of sharing money, clothes, or this or that. It's a question of sharing beliefs, amusements, and desires, of sharing problems and finding help from your mate, having her interested in what you're doing and you being interested in what she is doing. You must sacrifice part of yourself and so should she. I didn't make good on my responsibilities, but Dorothy did. She was very attentive to the children. I placed myself in roles, in the theater and other outside activities—I don't mean baseball—which had destructive overtones.

What I mean to say is that I was not true to Dorothy. Certain women exerted appeal upon me, and I succumbed to them. I cheated. I don't believe that Dorothy knew that at all; there weren't any repercussions along those lines. It was more that my personal behavior became foreign to her way of considering life and what should be, or who her husband should be. As the decade ended, both my marriage and career were set on a downward spiral.

Then came the loss of my mentor, Miller Huggins.

18

Little Big Hug

MILLER HUGGINS WAS THE GREATEST MANAGER who ever lived. He was a remarkable fellow.

I could tell you stories about Huggins all night long and what a wonderful man he was. He didn't use profanity, and what he had to say was very wise and to the point. He'd just call me into his quarters, which was equipped with a desk, a couple of chairs, and a couch. It seemed like a psychiatrist's office.

He'd sit me down on that couch and tell me about all the things I *wasn't*. I managed to pass *that* test all right, because I had so many shortcomings that you would need a computer to list them. Sometimes it seemed to me that I was in Hug's office more than I was out on the ballfield.

Huggins was never one for belaboring his players. The little guy always preferred an appeal to intelligence rather than the heavy hand of authority. We very seldom heard praise for an outstanding performance and no criticism for a bad one. We were thought of as collecting the high dollar for work well done—and that was expected. Failure was recognized as part of the picture, but it couldn't dominate, or we would be gone.

Hug could sympathize with bad breaks and reasons beyond those of human control or even those commensurate with the defects of human nature. Rank stupidity he couldn't abide. He wouldn't tolerate the neglect of lessons that should have been learned but weren't, especially in the labors of more experienced players.

His counsel had a lot of force but, for me, would flow in one ear and out the other because the inflation of my self-esteem made me a little bit indifferent to his advice. I had this complete confidence in myself. After all, in my first four years with the Yanks, I won 74 games and lost 47. I had won 19 games in a season twice and 18 once, just missing the coveted 20-game circle three times by narrow margins.

Yet, Hug nagged me about my tendency to use my fastball so constantly—without variation of level, speed, or design and "entirely too much satisfaction with yourself." Huggins's admonitions were borne out only too often, but I was too cluttered by ego to recognize the situations when I saw them.

Just a few weeks after the '22 season opened, I was pitching a game to the Red Sox, which was tied from the ninth inning through the fifteenth. What happened next was funny, and it wasn't. This fellow came to bat, with someone on second base. First base was open. I heard this whistling from the bench, and Miller Huggins was pointing toward first base, meaning, walk him and put him on base. I didn't want to do that. I wanted to pitch to him because I was confident of getting him out. What's more, fans would start booing at me because they couldn't see Hug's orders from the bench. So, I yelled to him from the pitcher's box with my usual lack of tact: "If you want to tell me something, come out here and tell me, don't sit in there!"

Gee, that made Hug mad, of course, and I wound up walking the fellow anyway. The next batter was Joe Dugan, who would be traded to us from the Red Sox a couple of weeks later and eventually became my roommate. He doubled down the left field line and won the game for the Red Sox in the fifteenth inning. When I got back to the bench, Huggins said, "What's the matter with you? You act as if you don't want to pitch!"

And I said to him, "Look, Hug, if I didn't want to pitch I could have lost the game in nine innings. I don't have to go fifteen innings to lose a ball game!"

It happened that a fellow named Fred Lieb, a newspaper writer, witnessed our argument. In those days, the press box used to be at field level, and reporters could see from there right into the bench. I don't remember this, but I've been told I raised my hand as if I were about to strike Huggins. Lieb said I had thrown a punch, which I didn't at all. I didn't even start to. The story the next day in the paper said, "When last seen of Hoyt, he was dragging Huggins's body through center field to throw it in the Harlem River." Then Lieb wrote that I had been suspended for two weeks.

When I asked Huggins if this was so, he said, "Goodness, no!"

I later argued about this with Lieb and he said, "How dare you question me! I am a newspaperman!"

I said, "Question you—why, you said I was suspended and I wasn't, so why don't you ask Huggins about it?" He did, and Huggins told him that I wasn't suspended but that he just wasn't going to pitch me for ten days.

"He's only a youngster and needs to listen," Huggins said, "and by these things he will learn."

Sometimes I felt incapable of learning. George Burns, who played first base for the Athletics and Cleveland for most of his career, could hit me as if I had tossed the ball underhand. He clobbered me. He was one of a half a dozen to whom I was a delight. Johnny Bassler of Detroit was another. Johnny Hodapp and Lew Fonseca, both of Cleveland, were as well. But George Burns hit me as if he owned me. Against me, his average was mountainous.

I threw him everything but my glove. The results were always the same: catastrophe. I asked Huggins, "What can I do about that guy?"

He said, "Not much. I'd say throw your fastball with every ounce of power you own, everything you've got."

Burns came to New York with Cleveland. I thought, *I'll waste a curve on the first pitch his first time up. After that, only fastballs.* I threw the curve all right—six inches outside. Burns, with his usual confidence against me, reached out and slammed it into right center—a double. When I reached the bench, Huggins asked knowingly, "And what did you throw Burns?"

I replied, "I thought I'd waste the curve, then—"

Huggins cracked, "I know. You were thinking again! Give your brain more rest and your arm more work."

Another time, I was beating the Philadelphia Athletics at Yankee Stadium in a low-score, one-run-margin game. The A's started a rally, with one run in, two on, and Bill Lamar, a fine left-handed hitter batting about .350, at the plate. I pitched him high and outside and Bill smacked the ball to left center for a triple. The ball game rolled along with it, now out of reach.

This time, Huggins's anger was real.

He called me into his office. There he was, seated in that oak, swiveling desk chair of his, puffing at his pipe like a donkey engine. Out came the pipe. His lips trembled. "What kind of dunce are you?" he demanded. He just looked at me. Words at that moment couldn't equal the disgust of that look.

I felt I should say something, but what? "Look, Hug—I pitched Lamar where I always have—high and outside. He just hit the ball. Lotsa times I get him out."

Huggins shook his head in pity. "Look," he said, as his voice took a tolerant turn. "I am not criticizing you for where you pitched the ball but rather when you pitched it. You've been around here a long while. You've watched others. You should know by now what is what and when is when. Can't you get it into that thick head of yours that, in a batting rally, each succeeding hitter gains confidence from the guy ahead of him? If one fellow hits safely, then four or five guys will hit safely in succession. They start to believe fate is riding with them. You have to jockey 'em around a little. Make 'em wait. Set 'em up. You can't just walk right up on their front porch and let 'em hit the first good ball, and a fastball at that. Well, you've learned another lesson, and earned another loss. Don't make those mistakes so often."

Then he just turned away.

In many ways, success in pitching, like success in any occupation, depends not only on an individual's ability to win out over tough competition but also on victory over oneself. This, to a point, had been my most lamentable failure. I possessed every requisite I could ask for, physical or mental, yet I was still far short of my goal or at least the peak Miller Huggins repeatedly said I should attain: league leader, winner of 25 games.

I did manage to lead the league but never did reach the 25-win mark. Many lessons were to be learned, and perhaps many fruits of conquest withheld from me until such time as I could prove to myself—and to those above and beyond baseball managers and mere mortals—that the rewards were justified.

Huggins did his best. He used every known tactic with me, including understanding and patient explanation. He tore me down, and he built me up. "With your stuff, you should lead the league every year. Your attitude is wrong. You're enjoying life too much. It's all too inviting, too heady. Why not give yourself a chance? You're not giving 100 percent to yourself, your pitching, or the Yanks. You have friends in the grandstand in every city. They're down at the bench visiting with you, probably flattering you. Other things seem to take precedence over your work."

"What's wrong with saying hello to people you know?" I asked.

"Nothing, when it's held within bounds," Hug replied. "But whenever you borrow from your on-field concentration, you whip yourself. It's all too easy. Take it more seriously. This is a business, not a game. Work at it, and it will bring you great returns."

Then he'd stand up, and with the side of his hand he'd make a slicing motion across my shoulders. "Pitch there, not there." To accentuate the second *there*, he'd use another slicing motion across my shirt, front-letter high. It was Hug's contention that I should pitch six inches above my usual levels when I used the fastball. (Those were the days when the strike zone was larger.)

He'd tell me, "You're one of those fellows who starts slow. You have bad first innings. Waite, from the first ball you throw in a game until the last out, you must pitch as if there were three on base. Never let up."

There's great importance to this because it fits so closely in relation to my character, attitude, and my entire life: impetuous, impatient, and impulsive—all the ims, I guess.

Hug's admonitions fell on an empty soul. His fatherly advice was ignored. This went on for a few years. I think he adopted me as his protégé in a sense. He kept needling me, and yet I continued pitching the way I pitched. It's remarkable that he wasn't discouraged with me because of my self-satisfied attitude.

· · ·

Even though we won the World Series in 1928, the season actually marked the breaking up of the team because nearly every man on the squad was on the sick list at one time. After enjoying a prosperous off-season on the stage, earning $1,200 a week in New York, Chicago, Cleveland, and Buffalo, I checked in for spring training in 1929 far overweight. I really had to strain to get into shape.

I had become more an actor than a ballplayer, and my interest in pitching was not as intense as it should have been. I did win 9 out of my first 10 starts that season. Then I came down with cellulitis and never pitched any really good ball thereafter. Poor Miller Huggins had a dismal year himself. In August he called a clubhouse meeting and tried to talk some fight into us—or get any reaction at all.

Soon afterward, Ruppert visited Huggins in the dugout. "What's the matter with the team?" he demanded. "Why aren't they winning?"

"They're through," Huggins said. "They're tired. It's time to start thinking about next year. We can't take the pennant with this club."

In mid-September 1929 I started a game against the Cleveland Indians, with Joe Hauser playing first base for them. I used to get Joe out pretty easily because I could pitch high and fast to him. But I was having a bad day, and Hauser hit a home run off me. I was pitching out where I usually threw to him, but he got around on the ball and knocked it into the right-field seats.

Huggins was not on the bench that day because he had developed what looked like a boil, or a carbuncle, on his right cheek. He was in the clubhouse, putting a heat lamp on it. I'm not acquainted with the facts on these things, but as I understand it, he was doing the worst thing you could because the heat generated the germs and spread them. What jackass told him that a sunlamp was the right treatment for the dreadful infection on his face, I'll never know.

I came into the clubhouse, knocked out by that home run, and Hug said to me, "What happened to you?"

And I said, "Well, Hauser hit one into the seats off me, and they took me out of the box, so here I am."

He said, "Sit down, I want to talk to you." I sat down alongside him, and he said, "Waite, how old are you?" And I said, "Hug, I was thirty a week ago, September the ninth."

"I'd like to say something to you," he said. "I knew that you were not going to have a good season." One of Hug's attributes was that he was able to diagnose and predict the entire fortunes of every player on his club before the season started. Oh, he was a shrewd manager. He said, "I told Colonel Ruppert in spring training this year that you were going to have a bad season. You came down fat in the chest, and I just knew what was going to happen."

Hug looked me straight in the eye. "I have always discovered in my relationship with athletes that they cannot do after thirty what they have done before," he continued. "You cannot recuperate. Say you had a bad evening or night before or you've been ill; your recuperative powers are not as great as they were. I wish you would listen to me about that." We had quite a talk along those lines, and it was not only interesting but also informative. It was very sound advice, but Hug wasn't finished yet.

"Tomorrow," he said, "go down and get your paycheck. You're through for the season. Get in good shape this winter, come down next spring, and have the year I know you can have."

That was my last visit with Miller Huggins. Sadly, what was thought to be a carbuncle or a boil developed into severe blood poisoning. Hug was taken to the hospital, given blood transfusions, but died within a week. I sensed that everything was going to be different from then on in baseball, and it was . . . it was. It was never the same again. I had some fairly good years and some not so successful. Some of the years I don't even like to think about.

Miller Huggins's death took a lot of the life and determination out of me. I went to his funeral, sat in the back of a little church down in lower New York City, and cried like a baby. If there was a single Yankee who did not cry that day, I don't know who he was.

He's buried in Spring Grove Cemetery in Cincinnati, about an eighth of a mile from where I'm to meet my eternal rest. Matter of fact, every once in a while I go out there, and as I pass by his grave, I hear this whirring sound because he's spinning in his grave. As Joe Dugan, my roommate said, "We killed poor, little Miller." Perhaps we did.

After Miller died, Ed Barrow, the general manager of the Yankees, learned I was going to do vaudeville again. He asked me not to. He said, "To tell you the truth, Waite, it disturbs me. It changes the rhythm of your life." He thought it would encroach on my dedication to baseball and pitching. Well, I had led the league in pitching for a couple of years, so I didn't pay much attention to him and went onstage anyway.

What Ed Barrow predicted was exactly what happened. It was a different mode and method of living. I was on stage generally next to closing at around 10:30 in the evening, and because Larchmont is about twenty miles from New York City, I got home sometime after midnight. A lot of these theatrical people, after the shows, would go to their favorite haunts for a snack or sandwich and sit around and talk. I felt I had rapport with them, so I'd join in. I became distinctly out of shape.

First choice to succeed Miller Huggins was Donie Bush, but Donie, by the time Barrow reached him to offer the job, had already signed to manage the White Sox. So, the mantle descended to the man Miller himself had wanted to succeed him—Bob Shawkey, my fellow pitcher and former roommate. Bob was a good fellow, in his own world. I happen to believe that the big world, as we know it, is made up of a great many smaller worlds, in which certain cults, sects, or conglomerations of people live one for the other. Once in a while, my world might overlap somebody else's world.

Shawkey lived in a world that ran counter to my beliefs and philosophies. We just didn't mix. It was difficult for me to take him seriously as manager because he simply lacked the necessary temperament and knowledge.

One of Bob's first public statements shortly after his appointment prompted headlines in New York sports sheets: "Shawkey Says Hoyt Has Lost His Fastball." As this was in December, it seemed a bit premature, and of course it didn't endear Shawkey to me. Indeed, it set up the strain of enmity, which didn't help our personal relations and carried over into the season and onto the ballfield. On one or two occasions in spring training, I thought, erroneously or otherwise, Bob was pulling rank unnecessarily. Our relations became short of cordial.

After several minor skirmishes, Bob and I one day went head-to-head. I was pitching against the Philadelphia Athletics in Shibe Park. It was the slugging team of Al Simmons, Jimmie Foxx, Mickey Cochrane, Mule Haas, and Jimmy Dykes. (Haas and Dykes will probably wire me, thanking me for including them as sluggers.)

Simmons was at bat when I threw him my fastball. He hit it into the lower deck of the left-field seats, a home run. When I reached the bench, Shawkey said, "What did Simmons hit?"

"A fastball," I replied tersely.

"You should have thrown him a curve," Shawkey said. "After this, I want you to throw him a curve."

I cracked, "If I threw him the curve, he wouldn't hit it into the lower deck, he'd hit it clear over the pavilion."

On the train that night, the situation almost had a sequel. A newspaperman slid into the seat next to me to ask, "What did Simmons hit?"

"A fastball," I dutifully replied.

He said, "Say, Waite, what happened to your fastball anyway?"

I snapped, "It's back in the lower deck at Shibe Park where Simmons hit it."

I once said it was great to be young and a Yankee, but I wasn't so young anymore. As for being a Yankee, well . . . my departure was humiliatingly sudden.

On May 30, 1930, a neighbor of mine, Freddie Parson, came over to my home while I was having dinner. In a wavering voice he expressed lament about my being traded. This was a fact I did not know. I hadn't been told, even though I had left the stadium only an hour before. Freddie had heard it on the radio, and I heard it from him.

Nobody else ever informed me that Mark Koenig and I had been traded to Detroit for Harry Rice, infielder Yats Wuestling, and Ownie Carroll. Although I held my trade to the Tigers as a personal affront by Shawkey, I know now, with the kindness of receding years, he was probably right. It pleases me to say that I look back on the happier times I had with him and even today feel a warm kinship whenever we meet.

That said, being traded from the Yankees was a severe blow from which I never recovered. None of the other clubs in the league operated with the same philosophical intent, imbued with the same confident spirit nor the same rigid discipline as the New York Yankees.

Had Miller Huggins not died in 1929, I believe I would have been a Yankee for life. He was not out to win any popularity poll among his players. He was stern and rigid. He was also fair and sympathetic. I could have gone on playing for him until I could no longer lift my arm, but that was not to be.

Hug and I had become quite close by the end of the 1928 season, and I know he could have kept my desire burning and helped me to concentrate, in my off hours, on the job of staying on top. I had just begun to learn the lesson that all champions must learn, that staying on top is often a fiercer struggle than getting there, that it requires concentration above the average and ambition that lasts beyond the victory through defeat, injury, and distraction.

Hug was gifted at motivating his champions, including me. He knew not only how to win the current ball game but also how to keep his self-satisfied athletes from taking victory for granted. He could awaken their desire for higher and higher attainments. He could maintain discipline too, without staging temper tantrums or calling names. He had the respect of his players, and they wanted his approval.

I regret exceedingly that I did not heed his advice, almost the inverse of my supremely conscientious teammate, Lou Gehrig, who laid his whole baseball life on an altar of self-sacrifice. In his early Yankee days, Lou was beyond the understanding of many of his more calloused teammates. He seemed complicated merely because he was of direct and simple honesty. None of us could conceive of a man being that true to himself, his work, his neighbors, his life. While many of the Yanks, including me, were having a good time and taking bows, Lou was studying the art of playing first base, trying to improve himself. It wasn't until I was gone from the Yankees, divorced from Dorothy, and down on my luck that I came to realize what Lou Gehrig was really made of, that he did have the stuff of a true-life hero inside him, that he could and did think deeply, that his mind was broad and interests wide-ranging.

Part 3

19

Skating with Lou

IT'S DIFFICULT FOR ME TO WRITE about Lou Gehrig because I feel ashamed about the way my teammates and I sized him up at the beginning and how we ridiculed him. He was like a kid, sort of juvenile in a way. Many of us thought he was a mama's boy. He had quite a lot of the college boy, or boy scout, about him. This grated on some of our hard-bitten players, many of whom had never attended college, much less an Ivy League school like Columbia University.

We also had to eat more eels—eels!—in the clubhouse because Lou would go down to Sheep's Head Bay and catch them. His mother would fry up these eels, and he'd bring them down to the clubhouse. Sometimes he brought pickled eels, in jars. A few of the ballplayers would express profane disgust. Miller Huggins would have none of that. "For goodness sakes," he said. "Don't hurt the kid's feelings." So, we ate the eels.

We didn't want the darn things. They actually tasted pretty good, though, a little like bluefish. Eventually, we all came to know Christina Gehrig and to relish her cooking.

Lou's recompense for the unselfish sacrifices his parents had made in giving him his chances were not only admirable but also so intense and his attitudes so dedicated, they almost seemed like a form of penance. Lou excused himself from most all pleasurable activities (except fishing for eels) and was not at all inclined toward dates or feminine society until the period immediately prior to his engagement to the very lovely Eleanor Twitchell of Chicago, whom he married in 1933.

After I was traded to Detroit, Lou and I didn't cross paths again off the field until after I had parted ways with Dorothy and endured a sort of penance of my own with both the Detroit Tigers and Philadelphia Athletics—which sometimes reminded me of my days in the Minor Leagues. I had always known the Yankees were first-class and harbored a mild contempt for the bush-league atmosphere of other clubs. Once in Atlantic City, when the Yankees were traveling home with the Dodgers, we had left our boardwalk hotel while they sought out some third-class inn on a side street. Not until I arrived in Detroit did I realize how startling the difference truly was, however.

The Detroit bench saw continual draping around the water cooler and talk of everything but baseball. Some players even turned their backs on a play. The locker room was not always picked up unless we remembered to do it ourselves. Lockers were dingy and equipment often tacky with use. The atmosphere of intense concentration and disciplined effort was almost wholly gone. Such changes had an effect on me. On the mound I still centered my whole mind on winning, but off-diamond it was easy to shuck off all concern about my role on the team, just as if it were a job in a factory that did not bear thinking about at home.

I could never quite resign myself to being a Detroit Tiger. More than that, the self-image that I had almost subconsciously erected over the past decade began to tarnish and fade. The fellow I pretended to be and the one I knew myself to be could no longer live comfortably in the same skin.

So, I did what many another fellow does when he wants to keep an illusion about himself alive—when he wants to hang onto that feeling that he can lick the world if he wants to, or when he prefers not to look his real self in the eye and admit he is not master of his own fate: I began to drink more than I ever had before. I started cultivating a wise-guy, "I'll do as I damn please" attitude. No one was going to tell me what to do with my evenings, when to hoist a glass or put one down.

Bucky Harris was the Tigers manager, and I've always felt bad because he had acquired me from the New York Yankees with wild, expectant hopes that I would prove to be a big help to his pitching staff. He had been a friend of mine and had so much confidence in me, but I wasn't in good condition at all.

Bucky didn't make a big deal of it. The most he ever did was grab hold of the spare tire I was developing around the middle, shake it a bit to remind me of its size, and say, "Get rid of that, and your troubles will be over." But my troubles went far deeper than a ring of fat under my ribs. I was fed up and mad at the world.

I did win a few ball games for Detroit. As usual, once a game began, I developed a fierce desire to win. On the mound I always tried my damnedest and snarled to myself if I had to be taken out. It was in my time off that my drive and desire failed me. What was the use of sacrificing good times and good company for a game that would treat me this way?

Baseball, I told myself, had given me about all it was going to give. It was no longer possible to concentrate on the game once my uniform was hanging in the locker. In my first season in Detroit, I appeared in 26 games and won but 9 while losing 8 (I had won 2 and lost 2 of the 8 games I had worked that year for the Yankees). The next season, I was far worse. Working in 16 games, I won 3 and lost 8.

At the time, I was in the middle of my separation and then divorce from Dorothy, which came to a head at the dinner table one night in the fall of 1930. We were more or less bantering with each other. There wasn't any bitterness, no arguments or anything like that. I reached over, sort of chucked her under the bicep of her arm, and made it quiver. She made an angry retort of some kind, and then I got upset and said, "Well, if you don't like it there's no point in me staying here."

She said, "No, there isn't."

I don't remember the exact dialogue, but it made me mad, so I went upstairs, packed, and moved into the Alamac Hotel in Manhattan. Eventually, Dorothy moved in with her parents in Garden City, Long Island, along with the children.

The problems I accrued after 1928 through 1930 were my own doing. When I was having domestic problems, I knew what was occurring. I was not strong enough in my mind or determination to handle them. I made many mistakes for which I am sorry. I had been indulgent and impulsive and a great many other things. I had disappointed Dorothy as a man, her husband. The inevitability of our divorce was my fault. It contributed to my downgrade, both personally and professionally. I now weighed almost 200 pounds, which was about 20 pounds heavier than I should have been. I was drinking too much.

It was an odd hop-skip-and-a-jump year when things were good, bad, and indifferent, but mostly bad. Then a sort of desire, or perhaps it was hope, was reawakened in a peculiar way. One night in Detroit, in 1931, it was hot as sin. Gee whiz, it was hot—must have been one hundred degrees. The phone rang the next morning at about eight o'clock and the voice on the other end said, "Is this Waite?"

I said, "Yeah."

And he said, "This is Eddie Collins."

I thought it was somebody playing a practical joke. Collins was a star of the Philadelphia Athletics. Why would he be calling me? So, I said, "Cut the malarky" or some such and hung up the phone.

A few minutes later the phone rang again, and he said, "No, Waite, this *is* Eddie Collins. Really, it is."

I said, "Well if it's Eddie Collins, then what do they call you?"

And he said, "Cocky."

Only ballplayers called Eddie Collins "Cocky," so I knew it was him. I said, "What in the world can I do for you?"

He said, "Connie Mack would like to see you in his suite at the Detroit Leland Hotel. Please be there at ten o'clock." I was shaky, and oh, boy, my tongue was fat and thick. I felt terrible. I had little idea what Connie Mack, manager of the Athletics, might want with me.

I managed to rouse myself, get some orange juice, coffee, and breakfast and then walk over to the Detroit Leland. It was so hot. I had a blue shirt on that was black with sweat by the time I arrived. When I entered the hotel and rang, I was told to come up to a suite of rooms to see Mr. Mack. Now, you must understand that Mr. Mack called all ballplayers "mister," and we returned the courtesy.

"Mr. Hoyt," he said, "I asked you to come over today because I would like to ask you a question or two."

I said, "Yes, sir?"

He said, "Do you think you could pitch for me on the Fourth of July afternoon?" Now, this was about the first of July.

I said, "Mr. Mack, please help me understand. One ballclub is not supposed to tamper with the players of another club. Is this legitimate? Have you cleared the way?"

He said, "Everything is taken care of; don't worry. I'm just asking you if you can get in shape well enough to pitch for me on the Fourth of July."

I wasn't in good condition, but I said, "Yes, sure," because the Athletics were in first place by about ten games, and it was obvious they were going to win the pennant.

That afternoon, still with Detroit, I was coaching third base, and the coach's box was near the Philadelphia bench. The Athletics players were yelling, "Go in and change the uniform, get the blue sox on!" They knew I was coming to Philadelphia.

So, I pitched on the Fourth of July for the Athletics and beat the Boston Red Sox.

I subsequently won 6 games and lost just 1 with the Athletics before Labor Day of 1931, when I pitched against my old mates, the Yankees. For seven innings or so, I was doing better than all right. I had them shut out, my acute desire to beat them slowly becoming a reality. The sequence of subsequent disastrous events is hazy in memory now. I can only recall the Big Babe coming to the plate with a man or two on base. I hadn't pitched against him, as I recall, since leaving the Yanks the year before. Now he was up there with all his menacing power— power previously exerted on my behalf was now to be used against me.

I only knew one way to pitch to Ruth: throw the ball shoulder-high and outside, and try to curb his clout with speed outside. That was mere conjecture. I had seen him hit all speeds to all fields. The percentage told me to pitch away and high.

He fouled the first two fast ones. Then I wasted a pitch, too far outside, but I had him leaning in. I figured sometimes gambles paid off. Perhaps if I drove a fastball inside, over his hands while he was still in the act of leaning in toward the plate, he'd pop it up or dribble into the infield.

I threw the ball exactly as planned. With the reflexes that only great batters enjoy, Ruth brought that forty-eight-ounce mace around with terrific force. There came the recognizable thud. I had heard the sound too often to be mistaken. Instinctively, I looked into the wide, blue yonder. Yes, there it was—the ball soaring on its majestic flight high above the right-field wall. Instead of descending, it seemed to gain in altitude.

Like an admiring fan, I watched the ball take off over the street behind the right-field wall—over the first row of marble-stooped houses, beyond the rooftops of the second row of houses. My admiration turned to amazement as I watched the ball drop behind that second row of dwellings.

What a sock, I thought. *Who could ever hit a ball like that, that far?* What delight I took in being privileged to see such a drive. Suddenly I remembered. The man off whom Babe Ruth had hit that tremendous homer was . . . me. Coming out of my mesmerized state, I remembered to be mad. I had many home runs hit off me, but never one like that, before or after.

I wound up that season winning 10 games and losing 3 for Connie Mack and the Athletics in half a season, which is the equivalent of about 20-6 if the pace kept on. That was good pitching, even though I was out of shape.

The Athletics, as anticipated, made it to the World Series in 1931. Just prior to the first game, during the three days or so between the end of the season and the Series, I was staying in a suite at the Warwick Hotel in Philadelphia. Who appears on the scene but Dorothy, who had come over from New York! She rang the door and sat down. I am still not sure what she wanted.

We spent the afternoon together, and she had lunch with me. There wasn't any bitterness or an argument. She took off and went back to New York. Maybe she hoped—I'm flattering myself now—that I wanted to make some effort at a reconciliation. I knew that could never happen. She and I were divorced soon after. In New York at the time, a state law said that the only way you could get a divorce was because of adultery, and she couldn't prove that. So, she went to Reno to finalize the matter there.

I was beaten by the Saint Louis Cardinals in my sole appearance in the 1931 World Series. They scored 3 runs off of me, as I recall, and won the game, 5–1. The Cards also won the Series. I stayed in Philadelphia for a while after the World Series and then went back around Christmas to an apartment I had in Larchmont. I still wasn't taking care of myself very well.

The time for baseball contracts came along in December, and Connie Mack cut me by something like $2,500! This aggravated me because I had won 10 games for the man. I couldn't understand it. I wrote him back and objected, and he replied by sending me a yellow slip, releasing me. I still don't know why he cut me loose.

I was out of a job and didn't know what to do with myself. I knew I had to get back in shape, so I decided to try working out on the indoor ice-skating rink at Playland, an amusement park in Rye, New York. It was just wonderful. My sessions started at eleven o'clock each morning. It was healthy, refreshing, and invigorating. I skated until eleven at night with a couple of hours out for lunch and dinner. I set aside certain periods for speed skating because the added energy helped my conditioning.

Lou Gehrig also liked to skate and happened to be there to condition his legs. I got to know him in a whole new light, as we talked and shared our philosophies. Lou held his own on subjects like cause and effect, and programs for living that opened my eyes and ears. It was hard to believe that this was the same person whose outlook I considered to be at the level of just a kid when we were teammates on the Yankees.

I have to dig in to remember my impression of Lou shortly after his installation as a Yankee regular. I do recall him being so fired up with zeal and the cold, college spirit when I was in the box pitching and in trouble. He'd come trudging over to me, ball in hand, punching the air with his fist, yelling in a disconcerting voice, "C'mon! Stay in there! We'll get 'em!"

Lou's intentions were sincerely praiseworthy, but his exhortations sometimes upset me more than the batter did. I had to tell him, "For God's sake, Lou, stay back there. You play first base, and I'll do the pitching!"

Lou's life was not a succession of humorous episodes or glamorous outings like mine. His upbringing was completely different from mine too. To make Lou a ballplayer, his parents, who were simple-hearted people with no money to spare, had to do without many comforts, but they sent Lou to Columbia University. They also enabled him to play baseball when it might have been natural for them to insist that he get to work to help support the household, or at least learn a trade. Lou's trade was baseball, however, and he very early decided to make a living at it, not for himself but for his family.

Lou was in professional baseball for ten years before he married. His family was always his mother and his father—his mother, particularly. Lou's thoughts and devotions were entirely mother-directed. She was as fine and noble as any character study could make her, and his efforts on her behalf were hard to miss. It was his mother who persuaded his father to let Lou buy a baseball glove long before Henry Gehrig could tell first base from a sack of flour. Once Henry had seen his boy in action, however, he became a fan who delighted as much as anyone in the mighty blows that Lou could strike with his bat. So dedicated was Gehrig to his determination to repay those who had helped him and so duty-bound to prove to them their investment of time and energy was worthwhile, he was somewhat slow to advance into even a modest degree of sophistication.

For years, Lou seemed like a lamb running with the lions. I'll never forget, late in the 1926 season during our strenuous struggle for the pennant, when we were playing in Chicago. We had but five or six games left to play. The Chicago pitcher was giving us a fit. He had us handcuffed. Ruth wasn't doing so well. None of the Yankee batters were exactly knocking spectators out of the stands.

In the late innings we came to life and put a couple of runners on base. Gehrig came up to bat. A base hit might have given us the win, but Lou popped out. He shuffled back to the bench, and the inning continued. The Yanks were rallying, but through the excitement we heard a peculiar sound at the end of the bench.

Lou was crying—actual sobs.

This incident in Chicago is not meant to portray Lou as a mewling adolescent or expose him as a case of arrested development. This is no indictment of Lou Gehrig. Perhaps it is instead my own deep envy, for he cried the clear, clean, pure rain of the soul.

Whereas Gehrig sobbed because of his imagined failure in a pinch, the more calloused world salved the ego by condemning any influence but those that came from our own storehouse of weaknesses. Gobs of cynical, muddied profanity spilled from the mouths of the hardened sophisticates of the diamond—a cover-up we used to rationalize our own defects. Such was our façade, and it accentuated the fullness of Lou's later days, when he developed a character that was broad, sincere, and dependable.

Sophistication is not necessary to an admirable state of being. It might have been better had I retained Lou's youthful embrace of life, his faith in people, and a belief that the greater segment of mankind is pure, without guile and tempered by humility. From the first day Gehrig appeared in a Yankees uniform, through Babe Ruth's last day in the same uniform, Lou had to play second fiddle. He was not relegated to that status by decree of any kind, for even as Gehrig would tell you, "I know Babe has everything. He's the greatest. I know what he can do when he has to do it. I'm lucky to be playing with him, much less trying to outdo him."

That was so true. I've been quoted as saying, "Every New York Yankee and his wife should teach their children to pray, 'God bless Mommy, God bless Daddy, and God bless Babe Ruth.'" I've also been credited with "The secret of success in pitching lies in getting a job with the Yankees."

I was one of Lou's former teammates who came back to honor him on Gehrig Day, July 4, 1939. Standing in line along the third base path, I listened to his inspired message as he told the ushers; the ball players; his manager, Joe McCarthy; and last but not least the people who had cheered him for many years how sorry he was to leave: "I consider myself the luckiest man on the face of the earth." It was a simple statement from the heart, an unashamed brushing away of tears, then the slow, sad, turn, and painful shuffle into history.

I saw Lou in Joe McCarthy's office a year or two after the terrible disease had taken its toll. His face blossomed into a big, boyish smile. He said, "Excuse me for not getting up. I got hit with a line drive." I always think of him as a person who was forever conscious of his blessings—a state of mind many of us never wholly attain. His story was not like Ruth's: broken into segments of brilliance, the fantastic, the earthy, the rise and the fall, the adventurous. Through Gehrig's life flowed one stream of consciousness—gratitude.

Later on, in comparing myself with Lou to try to learn from him, I began to consider who really had the greater wisdom—the boy who learned to conceal his sensitivity and idealism beneath a crust of wise-guy sophistication, or the boy who occasionally made himself look ridiculous in his teammates' eyes because he acted the part he had been raised to believe a good person should play. Of course, Lou was not quite so simple a person as that formulation may make him sound, and neither was I. Essentially, I think Lou became what he was because of a devotion to boyhood ideals of manliness, courage, self-sacrifice, and strength.

That he made his way through, eventually, to earn not only the affection but also the worship of many a hard-boiled baseball player is an indication that even the most sophisticated of us knew that Lou had something basically fine about him, that right from the start he had the makings of a hero. Lou Gehrig represented something of value to me, not an empty product of trial-and-error but the result of sacrifice and self-determination. He was a prime example of what most fathers would like their sons to be. It was pleasant knowing, too, that it was someone else out of baseball whom I could talk to and learn from.

Those days spent with Lou at the ice-skating rink were fruitful and pleasant. I also went on a crash diet, where I ate just one meal a day, quit drinking, and went from 200 to 169 pounds in about a month. My weight loss was both dramatic and public, to the point where I started receiving letters, mostly from women, asking for diet advice. The problem was that my best pitching weight was about 180, and the weight loss weakened me.

I looked great, though, and then went down to Florida, to the Philadelphia Athletics training camp, to present myself and see whether Mr. Mack would reconsider. I booked myself on a train, but at the last minute, for some reason, decided to purchase passage on a boat, the *Shawnee*, instead.

I don't know why I did this.

It turned out to be another of those moments where predestination simply walked through the door.

20

Dear Ellen

SHE WAS BLONDE AND STATUESQUE, WITH Betty Grable legs and lips like Marlene Dietrich, standing up straight and tall, like an elegant armoire with the top drawer pulled out. She wore this amazing green outfit that I'll never forget. I was seated in the saloon, just before the ship sailed, and she came through the doorway from the inner to the outer deck to wave goodbye to somebody standing on the pier.

I thought, *Good grief, now there is something!*

It was Valentine's Day, 1932. The *Shawnee* took off; that night, a soiree of sorts took place. I met up with a police officer I knew, Inspector Formosa, and was sitting with him watching people dance. The girl in the green dress was with a fellow who seemed pretty well lit. She was trying to get away from him, and he was making an ass of himself. So, I went over, patted the guy on the shoulder, and suggested he back off. He stumbled away, and I escorted this beauty to a chair. We sat down and later walked around the deck together. She was bright-eyed, with a manner as lively and inquisitive as a puppy's.

"Why are you going to Florida?" she asked.

"Could be for work, and could be for fun," I replied, playing it cool.

"Oh. What kind of work do you do?"

"I play professional baseball," I said, waiting for her to be impressed.

"Baseball? You mean that's a living?"

I was not feeling too encouraged at this point.

"Well, I know baseball," she said brightly. "I've seen a lot of games at the Montclair Athletic Club!"

My God! I don't think she knew a baseball from a football—much less anything about me. But so what? We danced on the boat on each of our three evenings together, and that's how my affiliation with Ellen Burbank began.

We both got off at Jacksonville because I had to take a bus across the state to Saint Petersburg, the hub of where the ballclubs trained. She was going to visit the Mellons of Pittsburgh on some island they owned down there. Her father was Abraham Lincoln Burbank, who was quite successful running steamship lines at the time. Ellen, I soon learned, traveled in high-society circles.

The Brooklyn Dodgers were training in Clearwater, which is only some twenty miles from Saint Petersburg. The Yankees were training there also, so I worked out with them for a while. Joe McCarthy had replaced Bob Shawkey as manager, and my arm felt so good. McCarthy said to me, "I like having you here with us, Waite, but I think it's bad policy, so I'd rather you didn't train here anymore."

I left and went to see Max Carey, manager of the Brooklyn Dodgers. I explained my situation and asked him how he felt about it. The Dodgers made me a very generous offer of a bonus—so much down, so much if I lasted until June, or something like that. I told them I had to clear things with Connie Mack first. When Mr. Mack saw that I had taken off all that weight and looked so well physically, he said, "I'll pay you what you wanted if you come back." The offer from the Dodgers was better, though, and that's how I returned from the American League to the National League.

I didn't do well for the Dodgers at all, however. I was like a fish out of water, living by myself in the New Yorker Hotel. In June of that year, a batboy named Babe Hamberger unceremoniously delivered my walking papers to me as I sat in the Dodgers' dugout. So, I applied to Bill Terry of the Giants. I had an oral agreement with them that they wouldn't give me a bonus for signing with them, but I would receive a very liberal salary. They signed me in the role of a relief pitcher, but Terry told me that if I started any games there would be a $2,500 bonus. To make a long story short, I started about 9 or 10 games. Although I lost more than I won, the Giants were seventh in the league at the time, and I wasn't getting much support in terms of hitting and fielding. The team wasn't great, but I was pitching well, and my earned run average was respectable.

When I joined the Giants, Terry told me to play an exhibition game in Jersey City to get into condition. It was a very sparse crowd, but there was this girl in the box next to the Jersey City bench, looking at the ball game through opera glasses. Opera glasses! It was kind of noticeable. I thought to myself, *My God, that's the girl in the green dress who was on the boat!*

After this exhibition game in New Jersey, I dressed in a hurry and went to find the beautiful girl who watched me pitch through opera glasses. How Ellen ever found that ballpark in Jersey City I'll never know, because later on I learned she was hard put to find her way around the block. She had the worst sense of direction. Yet somehow she found that ballpark.

We ran around together the rest of the summer. She had this big Packard automobile that seemed to be a block long. It was a convertible and heavy as hell; it was like driving a truck. Her brother lived in Scarsdale, which wasn't far from Larchmont, so she used to go up to visit him. I would go see her over there, and we became very chummy. We had very nice times together.

The day before the season ended, with the Giants playing in Pittsburgh, Bill Terry and I were sitting on the porch of the Schenley Hotel. Bill said, "We're having a meeting this week, and you will be retained. We like your work." He told me to go see Horace Stoneham, the owner of the Giants, and ask him for the contract. I went to see Horace Stoneham . . . and he let me go.

Unfortunately, I got to drinking again. I know it sounds as if I was a chronic drinker or an alcoholic, but I was not, absolutely not. I drank about as much as anybody did during the halcyon days of the twenties. Because of Prohibition, liquor wasn't easily available, so when it was around we sometimes drank too much because we never knew when we were going to get another drink. On the road, if we wanted whiskey or any sort of hard liquor, we'd ask the bellboy. If he could get us some, it was $15 a quart.

We'd invite the newspapermen up in those days. Ballplayers and reporters had great rapport. We'd sit, have a few drinks, and talk. There was nothing untoward about this, nothing chronic. I did do too much drinking just prior to, or during, the divorce from Dorothy. I admit to that but cooled off soon after. Then, in '32, after the summer, I began drinking again, which was why the Giants let me go. I began to think about doing something else for a living.

Out of indolence, inability to choose a course, or a desire to put off the fateful decision, I went back to my skating program, trying to get back into shape by skating in wide circles. I was going in circles in my mind too. One thing I knew for sure: I wanted to marry Ellen and devoted a good part of my time and energy to courting her. In a way, she was responsible for the decision I finally made about whether to continue playing baseball. During a visit with her and her brother, Sonny, at his house in Scarsdale, we were talking about my pitching and whether I was going to play the following summer and for whom. Ellen was a great kidder, and she said, "You're not going to do any pitching because nobody's going to want you."

So, I said to her, "I could get a job in an hour."

I had no idea whether this was true, and Ellen and Sonny both continued to tease me that I couldn't get back into baseball if I tried. I took the bait, reached for the phone, and called the Pittsburgh Pirates. I don't remember what prompted me to try Pittsburgh first—maybe because Ellen's family was well-known there. I really was just showing off and was not prepared to talk contract terms with anyone. Somehow, I got through to Mr. Benswanger, president of the Pirates. I told him I was in very good condition. I had stopped drinking at the time. In addition to a salary, I proposed a bonus for signing, and he countered with a bonus if I stayed through the season. He said he'd call me back in fifteen minutes, which he did, and said, "We will send you a contract."

Ellen could not understand this bonus business, and I am not sure she ever did see any logic to it. "You mean you get paid just for taking a job?" she would say, wearing a puzzled frown through all my explanations. Pay for working she could understand. But pay just for showing up? It made no sense to her at all. I kind of agreed.

I felt a resurgence of all my old ambition and desire when I set out for Paso Robles, California, for spring training with the Pirates. I was at ease with myself again, confident in what I could do and determined to do it. My grudge against the world, against baseball, against myself—all had washed away. Best of all, Ellen and I were engaged to be married.

That old Pirate crew was a jolly one, one of the best teams I ever belonged to. There was never any better company in the world than the Waner brothers, who could invent more ways to enjoy life in a day than any ten men could think of in a week. Then there was Remy Kramer, the veteran pitcher who roomed with Big Poison (Paul Waner); Larry French, a twenty-three-year-old pitcher who was headed into one of his best seasons with the club; Heine Meine, another pitcher who had won 19 games; Pie Traynor, the permanent third baseman, starting his thirteenth season with the club; and a dozen others great and small.

Sadly, my father died while I was with the Pirates. He had contracted angina pectoris, a form of heart trouble. While on the road for Swift & Company in 1936, he died in a hotel in Detroit, alone, at age sixty-five.

My father had the talent to be successful, but the fates were against him. He had a blithe spirit and a joie de vivre. He was so good to people, so optimistic and indulgent with everybody. We had an expression in baseball: everybody's a good fellow. You'd say, "Today's a great day. Everybody's a good fellow." That was his philosophy almost every day. He never believed that anybody was ever deliberately dishonest. I hope I inherited some of that. I didn't fully appreciate him because young people don't always recognize good values. It's only when you get older that you understand the virtues of the people who passed before you.

When my father died, some property in Troy, New York, was left to my sister and me, and I wanted to see it. My mother joined me in Albany, and we had connecting rooms. I was in bed when she came through the connecting door and sat down next to me. The tears started in her eyes. She said, "I haven't got you for long, Waite, but at least I have you for this day or two, just you and me." She said, "How I long for you and some time to talk to you about our past and the nice times we had, the Christmas Eves and the trips to Coney Island."

She went through this whole reminiscence of my boyhood, and regardless of the fact that I was a crusty professional ballplayer at that point, I started to cry. It was a pathetic, sentimental exposé of our hearts and minds. I remember it as a lovely episode. My mother later became very sick for quite a while with a series of infections under her arms and later on developed breast cancer. In those days doctors weren't as thorough in their treatment, and she had both breasts removed. She lived about nine years after that.

On a happier note, Ellen and I were married during my Pirates years, on May 12, 1933. I really buckled down on my pitching too—never more so than on Labor Day that year, in the second game of a double header against Saint Louis. Dizzy Dean was my opponent, and my desire to beat him was as fervent as my urge to live and breathe. Lord almighty, it was a hot day! Ellen came to watch. She always felt right at home in Pittsburgh; her upstairs box seat put her in full view of most of the spectators and, of course, the ballclub.

I did not get off to a particularly good start. Terry Moore lined the very first ball I pitched deep into center field, where it hit the statue of Barney Dreyfus, the team's owner, and rolled all the way back to the infield. Before any of us could lay a hand on the ball, Terry had crossed the plate. I put my whole soul and mind into my job from that time on. The only way, I told myself, was to be numb and dumb. I saw nothing, I heard nothing, I thought of nothing. Between turns on the mound, I would sit on the bench in almost a mesmerized state and stride like a zombie back to the mound.

We put enough runs across to set us ahead, but in the ninth inning the heat began to oppress me. The sweat ran in a river down my back. I could feel it trickling on my legs like rain running down the pillars of a porch. My hair was as wet as if I had stood under the shower. Dust from the mound rose up in almost invisible clouds and half choked me. The feet of my stockings actually squished when I moved.

My heart was thumping so hard a man on third could have heard it . . . and a man *was* on third. As I put my head down to study the ball in my glove, I could spot those candy-cane-striped Saint Louis stockings at every base. I moved off the baking mound onto the grass so I might absorb at least a breath of coolness. I took off my cap and wiped my forehead on my shirt. As I fixed my cap back on, I looked up to where Ellen sat.

By all the saints, she was lolling there as if she were on a park bench a mile away, her feet on the rail, a newspaper open in her hands, completely absorbed in reading it! Every damn fool in Pittsburgh could see and recognize her and have himself a laugh. The fury roared in my head until I was nearly blind. *God*, I thought, *I'll get this over with and see her at home!* I threw a pitch that went wide, but the umpire called it a strike. I needed one more and dared not glance again at Ellen. I fired a pitch to the next man, and he popped out. We won the game, 3–2.

As I dressed and showered, I rehearsed what I would say to Ellen. I got home, swung the door open as her cheery greeting sounded: "Hello

Mathewson!" This knocked me off stride, but I swallowed hard and started to roar out my catalog of her delinquencies: Everybody knew her! The whole team could see her! Me, in one of the worst jams of the year and she—reading a newspaper! I could never forgive!

I stopped for a breath and she said, "Okay, if you're finished, I'll tell you how *I* won the game." I couldn't imagine what she had in mind.

"In the first place," she said, "I knew everybody could see me. The newspaper was upside down. I was pretending not to be nervous. I was counting my fingers over and over. I was praying under my breath. But I knew you would look up and see me, and by seeing how relaxed and confident I was, you would just relax too and get yourself out of the jam!"

I was speechless.

Ellen could be sort of a comedian, halfway between Fanny Brice and Carol Burnett. She had this delightful way of getting her phrases all mixed up. "A stitch in nine saves time," she would declare and then brush off my correction with "Oh, you know what I meant!" By far, my favorite story about Ellen was when I received word that I had been voted into the National Baseball Hall of Fame.

We were in Florida at the time, and I was out on the golf course when I was told there was a long-distance call for me. It was a newspaper reporter on the line who broke the big news. I immediately tried to reach Ellen, but she was not in our cottage; she was at the beach, so I left word for someone to tell her that I was in the Hall of Fame. Now, remember, Ellen was not overly familiar with the game of baseball. When she got the message, she exclaimed to her girlfriends, "Oh, can you believe it? Waite is in the *House* of Fame!"

Ellen was pretty, sweet, and lively as a firecracker. She radiated fun.

Dear Ellen,

Why do I love you the way I do?
   For your caring, your sharing,
   Companionship too
   Your smiles and your laughter
   Your warm, thoughtful way
   For the joy that you bring
   Every hour, every day

I'll love you for being
My sweetheart, my wife
With all of my heart, for all of my life

Your man,
Waite

I loved Ellen with every fiber of my body and soul from the day I met her until the day she died, November 23, 1982. I loved her intensely for forty-eight years and never more than as I did as her health slowly declined. I will always remember our happy days together and think of them and her always, constantly. She was beautiful every day of her life and my dearest, true Valentine girl, my lovely wife.

21

The Unartful Dodger

MY RELATIONS WITH THE PITTSBURGH MANAGEMENT were always exceedingly friendly, so when Bill Benswanger, the president and chief executive, called me to his box one day in 1937, I didn't think much of it. We were in Brooklyn that day, in the park where I had made my first attempt to break into professional baseball. When I stood at the box rail, Mr. Benswanger broke the news that I had been traded back to the Brooklyn Dodgers.

It was not a complete surprise to me, for I had not been turning out much mileage for the Pirates. I worked 27 games for Brooklyn in '37, won 7 and lost 7 and did not feel I had done too badly. Still, I knew I had better begin to consider once more that there was not much baseball left in me. As I coasted closer to my forties, it became more and more difficult to whip my muscles into shape. Each season the hill got steeper and my wind grew shorter, to use a simple metaphor.

A man could do other things for a living, but I had not tried too many of them and was not sure where I might get a foothold. Vaudeville had very nearly breathed its last. Hard times in the early thirties had closed many theaters. Motion pictures were now talkies, and it was obvious that silent movies would go the way of the horse and carriage.

Radio had been considered just a fad to old-timers, but it was big and brawny now. Something told me it was the field for me. Sometime earlier I had worked for WEAF in New York, providing an analysis of the day's ball game. I had caught on as a sports expert with a program known as *Grandstand and Bandstand*. This was a sort of "spectacular" designed to make the airwaves hideous for hours in a row!

There was a thirty-five-piece orchestra, a gaggle of experts on every subject under the sun—cooking, mending, cleaning, bridge, football, baseball, high society, and low gossip—all mingled endlessly with singing and instrumental music as well as comedy bits and small-time drama. I would often deliver my part, rush downstairs to write another while the music was on, then hustle back to the studio to deliver that, hop down to write a third, and then scurry on back to the microphone to inflict it on my audience. This routine developed my ingenuity and drained my energies as much as any job I had ever held in my life.

The following spring, in 1938, I remained with the Dodgers. I simply could not get started, however. During training at Clearwater, I put my foot in a hole while I was running and suffered a charley horse. My leg would not stop hurting, and I could not get any power into my pitch. I worked in 6 games, lost 3, and won none at all. Still, because I had always been strong and come back from worse afflictions than this, I had hopes of straightening out.

Then came May 16, a warm spring morning, when I found that fateful telegram from John McDonald awaiting me at my locker. My release was sent to me this way so that I would get it before noon and the club would not have to pay me for another full day. The Dodgers had tried to phone me at home, the wire said, but had been unable to reach me. Baloney. I was at home. Perhaps someone had forgotten to put in the nickel.

With great deliberation, I cleaned out my locker. This, I told myself, was really it—the end. There would be no more baseball for me. I said a fairly jaunty goodbye to my mates and walked out. I felt no anger, just a dreadful, hollow feeling and a conviction that I had exhausted the last ounce that baseball was going to give. I had been in the game for twenty-three seasons, far longer than most players, and had seen it grow from a sprawling and slightly ragged enterprise to a highly stratified and centrally regulated complex of systems, from Class D to the Majors, with regiments of scouts, instructors, coaches, statisticians, publicists, and accountants, as well as a coterie of millionaire sponsors.

I had pitched in the dead-ball days, when the outfielders played shallow, through the home run era, when batter after batter could drive an outfielder to the fence. I had been intimate with the men who had revolutionized the game, who had fought to boost salaries so that a baseball hero could rank with a movie star and spread the gospel of the game around the globe.

There was hardly a major star in the game whose path I had not crossed. Most of the famous ones I had played with or against. I had even pitched once to the great Nap Lajoie when he was winding up his career in Toronto. I had tried to walk him, and he reached far across the plate, bat in one hand, and slapped a single into the outfield. Ty Cobb had been a day-to-day opponent and had even felt my muscle, as he did every rookie, trying to measure the new man's strength against the day when he might have a run-in with him. I sat on a bench with the National League's answer to Cobb, the incomparable Honus Wagner, and listened to him tell stories about his hunting dogs.

I had seen the mighty Hank Greenberg as a raw rookie, patiently practicing his fielding, and faced the mighty Walter Johnson a dozen times. There was never a faster pitcher in the game. I had known Lefty Grove well and learned what a patient, friendly, and loyal fellow he was. The Dean brothers had been my opponents in their best days. My career had even led me into the company of several of the old Baltimore Orioles, pioneers of the fighting spirit in baseball. I used to pass Wilbert Robinson on Flatbush Avenue and stopped to talk baseball with him. Hughie Jennings was still in the game when I joined the Giants.

One of the great hitters of the century, Harry Heilmann, had been my close friend. I faced George Sisler and remembered when, with the game all but won, George turned an easy third out into a base hit . . . while the ball was stuck in the webbing of my brand-new glove.

There was hardly a great name I could think of that did not somehow trigger a memory of my career. Alexander Joy Cartwright Jr., a founding father of the modern game? I visited his grave in Honolulu.

Now, here I was once again, back where it all began, at Ebbets Field, where I had climbed the hinges of the gate and been chased across the park by Charlie Ebbets Jr. I thought back to the day Wheezer Dell's wife arranged to have me invited to pitch batting practice right here, more than twenty years before. What if she hadn't done that? How would that have turned out? It seemed I had been destined to play baseball ever since my father took me out into the yard and showed me how to throw, patiently helping me work my small arm and showing me how to release the ball to make it go straight.

It felt like the death of some dear friend, whose end we knew was near. The event, when it came, was still sudden and shocking. I went home in a mood of deep melancholy, with no notion of where I might turn next. Ellen was there to greet me. When I told her the news, she said, "It's a beautiful day to be released."

It would be convenient, for the sake of the story, if my exit from Ebbets Field on that May morning in 1938 marked the end of my association with baseball. But it did not. It did not even mark the end of my playing career, because almost immediately I accepted an offer to pitch for the Brooklyn Bushwicks, one of the strongest semipro teams in the country, which played near the Brooklyn border at Dexter Park in Woodhaven, Queens. The park's facilities were better than average for semipro, about equal to what a good Minor League team would offer at the time. The field was a little hard, and the deep outfield went uphill. The ball was livelier than the regulation Major League ball, and this meant more distance and a fiercer bounce. I was to pitch five innings on Wednesday nights and a full game on Sundays, with no practice sessions, for $1,000 a month.

This seemed like easy duty to me, but before the season was over I found my tail dragging deep in the gutter and began to suspect I had gotten the short end of the bargain. The Bushwicks played ball into late October. By that time, I had pitched 300 innings! Fortunately, my arm was still strong even if my legs had developed a slight creak. The pitching was hard work, too, for the Bushwicks met teams that were often loaded with Major League talent. During the regular season, we played a number of Black teams: the Baltimore Black Sox, the Pittsburgh Crawfords, the Newark Eagles—all of which would have given any pitcher problems. The mighty Josh Gibson, who drew comparisons to Babe Ruth, came to Dexter Park two or three times, and I saw him rocket some record-breaking home runs into the beyond.

Home was now in Montclair, New Jersey. That meant two hours traveling, parallel to the journey I had made by trolley and subway on that long ago day from my home in Flatbush to the Polo Grounds. Don't think I did not dwell on this sometimes during the long, hot ride, glooming over my baseball career and asking myself what I would have done differently had I known all that lay ahead.

Still, I was far from downhearted. The chance to pitch twice a week against worthy opposition had the juices flowing in me again, and I went out there on Wednesdays and Sundays full of determination and confidence. I did not feel completely out of circulation. The games I pitched do not stick in my mind because there were so many of them and they were so much alike. My first was a two-hitter, which I remember because I went into it wondering how much I had left in the tank and ended up pleased that my arm was still able to pour in the fast ball when needed. Yet, I knew the Bushwicks were the last stop on the baseball line. Besides, Ellen had just given birth to our son Christopher, and this gave me a new feeling of urgency and a conviction that I needed a permanent base. I could have gone to work for my father-in-law, in the A. L. Burbank Steamship Corporation, but I simply could not bear to get too far away from baseball.

Radio had long seemed the logical choice, but had I realized how little I knew about it and how dearly my lessons were going to cost me, I'm not sure I would have had the stomach to enter the business. The *Grandstand and Bandstand* sessions, despite their haste and helter-skelter quality, had been fun and paid well. But they taught me only a small part of what I needed to learn. In addition, and without realizing it yet, I faced the job of finally growing up, maturing emotionally and mentally, as well as physically. Baseball matures a boy too quickly in some ways. In other ways, particularly if he makes a success of it, it keeps him a child.

Certainly, there was a childish quality in my constant urge to climb on the merry-go-round whenever the music began to play and go on from day-to-day under a self-imposed obligation to have fun.

22

Radio Days

MAYBE RADIO APPEALED TO ME AT the beginning because it seemed to offer some degree of the freedom that baseball had. I would still be in the entertainment business and able to move in the circles I had grown used to. If I could work my way to the top, I would have an income comparable to what baseball had brought me.

What I had not yet admitted to myself, or at least had not articulated, was that baseball had never been just a game to me—it had been my whole life. I felt no relief in leaving it, just a lost and bewildered sensation. It was like the ending of a thirty-year marriage or, more than that, the expulsion from an environment that had been my whole world since I first put on long pants.

I don't suppose I had meant for baseball to become my whole reason for living and all of life itself. At various times during my career in baseball, I toyed with the notion of leaving the game. But I had grown up in it, devoted my whole soul to it whenever I put on the uniform, and kept coming back to it even when it cast me off. Instinctively, then, I undertook to become a baseball broadcaster. Looking at the job from a distance, it seemed a natural and easy transition. A little more experience with the ins and outs of broadcasting. and I'd be ready for the big time, I thought.

Jim Peterson, who had pitched with me in Philadelphia in 1931 and was a teammate on the Bushwicks, was the man who sealed my commitment to radio. He was with N. W. Ayer & Son, an advertising agency, and knew that sponsored programs were paying fat salaries. "Get your own program," Jim urged me. "Never mind what the starting pay is. You have to get on the air before you can get sponsored."

I initially caught on with WNEW, telling sports stories and anecdotes every weeknight, right after Martin Block's *Make-Believe Ballroom.* My program was to run fourteen minutes and fifteen seconds. This was my first experience with tight timing. On *Grandstand and Bandstand,* a minute or two either way never mattered. Now, to my dismay, when the clock ticked off the apportioned seconds, my words were strangled in midsyllable. Again and again, I would take off on a story about Ty Cobb, Honus Wagner, or Babe Ruth and suddenly discover I was talking to myself before I had even reached the point of the story.

Nobody ever told me about timing. I was expected to know about it or learn it as I plugged along. Like all broadcasters, I suppose I was overtaken occasionally with the feeling that nobody was out there listening. Apparently, the sponsors felt that way too, as none showed up to pay the tab for my broadcast or start paying me a salary I could support a family on. I was earning about 20 percent of what it cost me to live. I was paying a cost in discomfort too—the long, off-hour train rides to and from Montclair, the occasional nerve-wracking delays, and many cold suppers at 9:15 p.m.

If the program manager at WNEW had doubts about the size of my audience, they were set to rest one night when I invited a fellow from *Sporting News* on the air. He wanted me to help him get rid of some remainder copies of the publication by offering a free issue to anyone who would mail in a postcard before midnight. He came on the air with me to tell a few stories, and the next day we counted about seven thousand requests!

Unfortunately, *Sporting News* only had 450 copies available and had to go back to press to make good on its promise. This episode gave me heart because now I knew I was being listened to and became determined to stick with it until I could find a paying sponsor. The station was on a different timetable, however. While the baseball bugs were just beginning to stir in the stadium woodwork, WNEW let me go.

I grimly continued to hawk my skills all over the radio front—and learned the bitter lesson that when you get into another man's game you have a whole new set of rules to learn. Agency executives and radio nabobs were not throwing their doors open to baseball players. A ballplayer to a radio man in those days was a vulgarian who could not pronounce a three-syllable word and would probably call the Army

Corps the army corpse. What mattered in the thirties was the pear-shaped vowel, the resonant tone, the elocution school refinement, and lovingly lingered-on final note—the *hmmmmm!* or *nnnnnng!*—that betrayed how reluctant the speaker was to deprive the audience of the sound of his voice.

As an old-line vaudevillian and locker-room baritone, I was hardly equipped to send the ladies into a swoon over my consonants. But I stayed with it, convinced that a knowledge of baseball and a willingness to work my ears off would compensate in somebody's eyes for a shortage of loveliness. My first break came through N. W. Ayer and my friend Jim Peterson, in the form of a chance to do a pregame broadcast for Yankees games. It was timed, rehearsed, professionally produced—and sponsored by Silvercup Bread! A young fellow named Nick Keesley worked with me to help make the show a success. Then I learned another lesson in radio: success is not always enough. N. W. Ayer lost the Silvercup account to another advertising agency, and the whole show went up the flue.

Fortunately, my outlook had improved because even the radio executives recognized that I might actually be partly human. I built a file of contacts in the field, filled speaking engagements all over the New York area, and took on special one-shot assignments of one type or another. I learned the business in every way, especially how not to offend any listeners inadvertently. It was like learning the habits of batters. It finally became instinctive, like shying away from the high, hard pitch without advance thought.

I found that broadcasting was like baseball in other ways. A rookie was not welcomed by certain old-timers, and if they could make his way a little harder, they were happy to. Just as certain hardened citizens of baseball would try to teach a new boy a lesson, so too a pack of radio's throat-cutters counted every new name on the roster as a threat to their own daily bread. I had been through that mill before and knew that I could, to some degree, become the master of my fate.

I grabbed every opportunity to improve my knowledge of sports and sports broadcasting. Lou Little, coach of Columbia University, offered a football school for the press. I attended every class. Red Grange came east on a lecture tour, spreading the pro-football gospel. I went to his every lecture. I worked night and day on new formats, trying to hit on some approach that no one had yet tried. A chance came along to do a Saturday program in Schenectady, and I made the long trek up there every weekend.

Then in April 1940, the break of all breaks seemed to arrive: the Brown and Williamson Tobacco Corporation signed me to do a fifteen-minute sports review over WABC, every weekday evening at 6:15. It was a regular, well-produced, and fully sponsored program that would provide a salary equal to the best I had made in baseball. Unfortunately, in true theatrical tradition, the radio station preempted our time for other purposes, blew the program off the board, and left me adding up money I would never receive. This was one of the most dismal moments in all my life. Not since that train pulled out of Memphis and left my teenage self crying on the platform had I felt quite so desolate.

Brown and Williamson subsequently offered me a fill-in program on WOR following the Red Barber–Al Helfer broadcasts of Dodger games. This job really tested my ingenuity because there was never any telling how much time I would have. It might be ten minutes. It might be fifteen seconds. Whatever it was, I had to fill it. The good news was, it could also be thirty-five minutes! I just had to be ready to go whenever the sign was given. This meant extemporizing at length. I would just pretend I was sitting on a bench somewhere yarning with a friend, and in this way, I found I could spin out very nearly limitless numbers of baseball anecdotes. The strain this put on my brain was good for me and became my stock in trade, or at least one of the chief items in my cart.

I discovered that I had finally caught the tide in my affairs, the tide that Shakespeare said needs to be "taken at the flood." So, I took it. I had two sponsors, including one for a football program. I was ready to take any offer and got myself an agent, the William Morris Company. Ellen and I took a large apartment in Manhattan, big enough for parties and raising our young son. All I needed now was a steady play-by-play job with some baseball club, and my cup would begin to run over.

That job came rather quickly, but it was not quite what I had hoped for. The William Morris office asked if I would go out of town for play-by-play broadcasting. I did not hesitate. On the day after Thanksgiving, 1941, I traveled to Cincinnati to audition for the radio station there and the executives of the Burger Brewing Company. I returned home with a new job and a new home, in Cincinnati, Ohio.

Believe me, I did not leave for Cincinnati with a heart full of joy. I knew well enough that the move this time had to be for good, and I was not at all certain that I was going to take root and flourish so far away from Broadway and Yankee Stadium, so far from the places I longed to eat, drink, and play. It had never been a project of mine to lead a quieter life nor to limit the range of spots where I might satisfy my appetites or fondness for lively company. Buried in my mind was a suspicion that a city less impersonal and less pleasure-oriented than New York might reject me, deeming me an outlander and wastrel.

Would the locals put up with me? Would I ever really feel at home? It was not unlike the feeling that had filled my heart when I took the train for Lebanon to find a home among strangers and make a place for myself in a profession where I was still a novice.

Before I had time to brood on such matters, the Japanese planes had bombed Pearl Harbor. Matters of personal adjustment became petty indeed after that Sunday morning, for it was obvious that the lives of us all were going to be turned upside down. Baseball? Perhaps there would be no such thing in 1942. A cry went up that baseball be suspended because it was looked upon as a profession that was not contributing anything to the war. It was not viewed as useful.

Similar to popular opinion during World War I, some of the public saw ballplayers as virile, macho guys who should be at war, not at play. A certain sentiment ensued to suspend baseball and send all athletes to the army, navy, or other service. The question was brought up to President Roosevelt himself, who subsequently gave baseball the green light. FDR was a smart man who understood that people needed a diversion to relieve the tensions of the era. Baseball didn't make a lot of money but nevertheless helped relieve the nervous tension of the general public.

It actually was just as well for me that the nation had far weightier matters to consider than whether its baseball games were properly described on radio. It gave me a chance to learn my new job by hit and miss, to make all my mistakes when hardly anyone was concerned enough to notice them. Ellen and I were thankful that baseball continued and that I had work to do. We could not fret about a future that might never arrive. Like the rest of the country, we lived from day to day, doing without the things we could not have and grateful for what was left.

Wartime baseball was a challenge. Cincinnati had a center fielder who was totally deaf. Saint Louis had a one-armed right fielder. Every team had a catcher who could barely boost the ball to second base or a first baseman who had trouble bending his back. Ball games were often played in the morning to catch the night shift from the war plants. Only fourteen night games a season were played, with any one of them likely to be blacked out on a minute's warning because of an air-raid drill—or a real air-raid, for all we knew.

Play-by-play of baseball games was frequently disrupted by the ominous bonging of bells and repetitive fifteen-minute bulletins from the front: "We interrupt this program to bring you, direct from London, . . ." These summaries offered no news, and enraged baseball fans would flood the switchboard: "The winning run is on thoid! Put the game back on the air!" Brooklyn fans, many of whom would later fight and die in World War II, had no interest right then in any war except the one the Dodgers were waging.

Everybody had troubles at the time, and mine were trivial by comparison. Ellen and I were strangers in the stores and low on the list when it came to portioning out the goods that were in short supply. Traveling was difficult, and schedules were often completely hashed up. Nobody was shooting at us, however, and we had a steady income. A thousand other trials, both great and small, stood to toughen me up and shake me down into my new job. Luckily for me, other stations dropped baseball completely, while my sponsor, the Burger Brewing Company, took over sole sponsorship.

My partner in those days was Dick Nesbitt, the like of whom I had seldom seen for sheer eccentricity and devil-may-care. Dick had been a great halfback at Drake University and made a fine living as a football pro with the Chicago Bears. For years his punting records stood in the National Football League books. He had played recklessly and lived and worked the same way. He often appeared in the studio with hair uncombed and eyes still sticky with sleep, his trousers pulled hastily on over pajama pants, feet still in slippers and a pajama top for a shirt. In his "sports review" he offered material supplied by a syndicate, without previous reading, just pulling sheets out of a cardboard box at his feet. He never knew what he was going to say until he started to say it.

I could never be so offhand about the job, chiefly because I felt so inadequate for such a long time and knew I was going to have to give it my utmost every minute. In those days, we did "reconstructions" in which we would take play-by-play information off the Western Union wire and recite it over the air as if we were watching the game unfold in front of us. Usually, the play was sent in Morse code, in full detail, with sidelights, then quickly translated and typed up for our use. Sometimes it came over the teletype, reaching us within moments of the time the play took place. I broadcast games in the past tense because I was always behind on the action. It took a little time to get used to this arm's-length procedure, but after a while my confidence developed, sometimes too much for my own good.

One night the Reds were playing the Cardinals in Saint Louis. The Reds had loaded the bases, and Lonny Frey came to bat. The pitches came over the teletype one at a time: ball one, ball two, ball three, strike one. I earnestly reported them as they were given. Then the next line: "Lonny Frey walked—" No one had to spell it out for me, and I eagerly interpreted the dispatch into the microphone. "Ball four! Frey walked and the runner on third came in to score. The Reds have tied the ball game!" I had barely finished the sentence when my heart turned to ice as the teletype chattered on "Lonny Frey walked out of the batter's box to pick up—" I had already put Frey on first and brought a runner home!

My brain scrambled frantically to find a pathway out: "Wait a minute, folks!" I ad-libbed. "The umpire called Lonny back to the plate! It was strike two!" As I was talking, I realized that the run still counted if it had crossed without a play being made! I kept digging. "The ump called time and the runner had to go back. Manager McKechnie stormed out of the dugout! He evidently did not see the umpire call time. This is a real rhubarb!"

Lucky for me, the imaginary strike two was quickly wiped off the scoreboard when Lonny really did walk and the Reds actually tied the score. I thought some listeners might pick up on the discrepancy, but I heard not a word.

In those days, I was sometimes required to make deliberate mistakes because of a suspicion that our broadcasts were being pirated. So, for a long time I carefully misreported three unimportant plays in each game, but no fan ever complained, and no pirates were caught.

The deep and everlasting satisfaction I derived from my work did not mean that my job was not difficult or free of frustrations and near disasters. I don't believe anything I ever did with my life demanded more of me or gave me back half so much. The hours were often so long and the obstacles so steep that I look back on them and wonder how I kept my footing.

Once I almost didn't—on the final day of the 1946 season when the Cards and Dodgers were battling to the wire. The Cards played the Cubs that day, and the Dodgers played the Boston Braves at Brooklyn. The Cincinnati Reds were playing a doubleheader at Crosley Field. We secured the permission of all the clubs involved to reconstruct the Cards-Cubs and the Dodgers-Braves games while we were broadcasting the two Cincinnati games. That meant all the work had to be done from the studio. We needed three Western Union operators and a half-dozen helpers to keep the play-by-play flowing into my hands.

The Dodgers-Braves game started first, an hour before game time in Cincinnati. The Cards-Cubs game started when the other two were already going. For most of the afternoon, three games were on simultaneously. We kept three score cards and actually reconstructed every game pitch-by-pitch. (In addition, we reported pro football scores as they came in.) The only breathers were provided by twenty-second newsbreaks and station identifications. These gave me barely time to take a few sips of coffee.

Altogether, I was on-air for more than seven straight hours, talking just as rapidly as I could without turning the broadcast into gibberish. At one point I began to wobble. For a half-second, a black curtain seemed to descend over my eyes. But a quick sniff of smelling salts and a gulp of coffee refreshed me enough so I could keep going. I stuck it out just as I used to take satisfaction in toughing out a full nine innings, in spite of heat or enemy action. It was in my nature to finish any job once I started on it. When I finished, I had reported four complete baseball games. (The Cards, incidentally, won the pennant.)

With a feeling I had earned both rest and relaxation, Ellen and I took off for New York after this marathon session. We had half a dozen shows we wanted to see and more than that many restaurants with which to reacquaint ourselves. Unfortunately, when we reached New York, I took immediately to bed, wracked with chest pains and nearly delirious. There were hours of that nine-day stay that I do not even remember.

Of course, every baseball broadcaster has been hung up on a job that ran hours overtime. I routinely started broadcasting some twenty minutes before the game and continued on for twenty minutes past the last out. One Sunday in 1962, at Houston, Gene Kelly and I started to broadcast at twenty minutes to one. The second game began at 10:40 p.m., and we signed off at eleven o'clock, ten hours and thirty minutes without relief. There were not many sessions of that sort, but they wore me down to a point where I longed to get away from the job—just to loaf somewhere with no baseball game to talk about or even watch, and with no clock to regulate my life.

One winter, the opportunity came to me—no daily programs, just an occasional personal appearance. Ah, luxury—to lie about as I pleased, read books, paint, or dawdle. No two-base hits, no curve balls, no strike-outs, no baseball players! Strangely enough, after only a few days of this the days began to grow dull. Where my evenings had been filled with a sense of accomplishment and I sank into bed with a feeling of sweet satisfaction to lull me, now I fretted and stewed and found fault with life. I would tell myself, lying awake, that I had outgrown the game of baseball, that I had reached my goal in broadcasting, and that there was nothing left.

As I looked back on one or two of the games I had most enjoyed and felt my pulse quicken, I realized suddenly that baseball and broadcasting were the things I missed most. Without them, life had begun to slow down and shrivel. It was not that I had too much baseball; I had not had enough. Beside the hard work and frustrations were the glorious moments, the thrill of watching exhibitions of skill and courage and of seeing victory snatched from defeat at the final second. Baseball still had me hooked. When I admitted that to myself and began to look forward to getting back to my job, life had meaning again.

In addition to broadcasting baseball games, there were also wildly comic moments during my early days on TV, when the studio was a hodgepodge of exhibitions and demonstrations, with high-jumpers tripping on the heels of home run hitters. Archery champions appeared almost arm-in-arm with female wrestlers. We had an entire Canadian football team, in full uniform, demonstrate its version of the game.

There were bowlers, billiard experts, pistol shots, and boxers. In one exhibition, Gus Bell hauled off on a kapok baseball and twice drove screaming liners right square into the *Penny's Pantry* set. Then a shot-putter heaved the shot—not kapok this time—straight into the set too and knocked two shelves loaded with pans and dishes almost into the next studio.

Big Ted Kluszewski one time struck a ball so hard it severed a light wire. I stood hypnotized watching the wire twist slowly apart and the enormous light bulb and shade drop like a leaden parachute to the studio stage, where it exploded like a bomb.

The finest training I received as a radio broadcaster was in filling in the delays caused by rain. Other stations would shift back to the studio and play music—not our station. We had to keep the ball in the air so long as the tarps were on the field. Sometimes there was a twenty-minute gap to fill, but it could be as much as two hours. I would fish into my bottomless well of experiences, all the way from the Minor Leagues to the top of the Majors; repeat stories; offer opinions on playing and pitching methods; philosophize about the game, its traditions, its environment, or its future; or provide brief profiles of famous players I had known, not least of all Babe Ruth.

One of my saddest and also most successful evenings on radio came in 1948, the night of Babe Ruth's death, when I decided to follow the game with a eulogy. There was no preparation, no script, no research. I just raked through my memories and improvised for more than an hour and a half, sharing all I could recollect, sparing him nothing and still trying to give the man his full due. My sorrow and admiration were sincere, and no one took offense because I did not gloss over the rough spots. Indeed, this proved one of the most popular programs I ever offered and drew a warmer response than any other I had ever received since arriving in Cincinnati.

I knew the Babe himself prompted this reaction—even in death he dominated the baseball scene and made a better broadcaster out of me just as he had helped hundreds of other ballplayers, even those who have forgotten his greatness or come to belittle it. His name continues to comes up often when anyone talks about greatness in baseball. He remains the mightiest name the game ever produced, whether his home run record has been equaled or not. To this day, men use Babe's legacy to their benefit. Young ball players, without realizing it, owe some of their security and fat salaries to the man who turned baseball into a national institution. When measuring true greatness in this game, everyone has to start with the Babe, who did everything so well for so long.

Latter-day heroes are more often than not heroes to me too. Without question Stan Musial finished his career as the best-loved player in the game. Yet not even Stan the Man attained the eminence that was Ruth's—because the Babe was so much more than a ballplayer. He was the Game Incarnate, not just in this country but also throughout the world. I didn't really get to know Stan Musial until 1951, when I had an apartment at Redington Beach, Florida. It was one of those honeyed, semitropical evenings when voices sound so clear that people subconsciously hush them until they blend with the quiet lapping of the water. I looked up from my seat on the apartment patio to find Stan there beside me!

We sat and looked out across the Gulf of Mexico and watched the day fade over the distant Texas shore. It was a night for reverie, for waking dreams, and like all ballplayers we dreamed of baseball. Stan had led the National League in batting the year before, the fourth time he had won that crown. Four batting crowns was a career for most ball players. I asked him what he hoped for next.

"I'd like to do it five times," said Stan, in his gentle voice, made still more gentle by the mood of the night. "Just five." He seemed to be apologizing for wanting so much. Yet he went on to win the crown three more times and set new records from that season forth. When he retired in 1963, his name was spread throughout the record book.

Of all the heroes since Ruth, I count Stan as the greatest. It's not that Joe DiMaggio was not great or that Ted Williams did not earn the worship the Boston fans gave him. It's that somehow Stan seemed to epitomize the modern, dedicated ballplayer who won his prominence by work, study, and continuously striving to stay on top. Stan was warm with everyone and returned in good measure the affection the fans offered him. In the field or at bat, Stan gave the game his best efforts and was sincerely grateful for what it returned to him.

On the air or on the mound, baseball, to me, is more than a trade or a soft way of making a living. I know it is partly an illusion, but so are many other joys of life. I find myself trying to protect the game's illusions, which may be, after all, the only part of the game that is important. When broadcasting a no-hit game, for instance, I did not see myself as duty-bound to call attention to it. The ancient superstition that mention of a no-hitter would jinx the pitcher is one of the game's illusions. By respecting it, I helped the listener enjoy the feeling of sharing a unified struggle against the common enemy. Of course, the fans could figure out what was happening. Yes, it is a little bit childish, but it is part of the game and the fun of it.

Yet, just beneath baseball's innocent exterior, the other relentless dimension of my life continued to darken my existence: I was consuming far too many spirituous beverages. I had no sorrows to drown nor any wretched memories to anesthetize. I was just one of those thoughtless souls who had, at some time, decided that if two drinks made you feel good, four would make you feel twice as good. I always had taken a drink for enjoyment, and now perhaps I used it in part to subdue my chronic restlessness and partly to compensate for the heady, yet phony, excitement New York had provided.

Long before I recognized alcoholism or knew what it was, I was not a consistent drinker. I would stop drinking for long periods, but when I did drink, I couldn't handle it at all. Then the bouts with alcohol became closer, closer, and closer.

23

The Last Drink

I WAS SITTING OUTDOORS, ENJOYING THE perfume of roses, having breakfast on the porch beneath our trellis with Ellen on a beautiful morning in July 1945. Absentmindedly, I asked her what we were having for dinner that night. She told me it was my favorite dish. I don't remember what that was at the time. More to the point, I don't recall having dinner with Ellen that night because I never did.

I do remember lunch, which I shared with the president of Gruen Watch Company, Benjamin Katz. He had a martini or two and went back to his office. I stayed and continued to have double martinis, starting me on a three-day absence from my job as the voice of the Cincinnati Reds.

As a man I was an absolute failure. One side of me wanted this liquor. I have to admit, I had some damn good times drinking. I had some *roaring* good times. The best times I ever had I can't even remember because of the alcohol. I thought of myself as a high-class drinker, if you don't mind, who found the good joints.

This time I had disappeared from home for three days, living in a lavish suite in the Netherland Plaza Hotel in downtown Cincinnati. People were looking for me all over the city. I don't know why nobody could find me; I was right there! They found my parked car but couldn't find me.

I will never forget what happened at the end of the final day of the three: July 21. I wound up at the corner of Redding Road and Broadway. There stood the lousiest dump of a saloon that I had ever seen. I went into this place and asked for a drink. I wasn't particular about whether it was good whiskey. My hands were shaking, but I got the glass up and the whiskey down. I stood there drinking this thing, feeling a little better, and the bartender said, "What's the matter with you?"

And I said, "Nothing."

Nothing! That was the last drink I ever had.

I went back outside, to the curb of Redding Road and Broadway, and thought to myself—and I'm going to ask your indulgence about this—*Jesus, are you really going to let yourself go this way?* It was possibly the only sane, sober thought that I had about myself. I thought, *Waite, for God's sake, don't do it.* I started to cry. I stood there and cried for a long while. Then I called up Good Samaritan Hospital and was put through to Sister Andrew.

She said, "Take a cab. We're waiting for you."

It was pride that made me heed Sister Andrew and get in a cab. It was pride that I was not going to allow myself to hit the depths. I was not going to become a drunken bum. I had some pride in myself, enough to say to myself, *Come on, you can lick this thing, but you need help to do it.* I pitched ball games where I needed help, and now I needed more help than ever.

When word got out that I was no longer missing, there was a headline on the front page of one of the papers: "Waite Hoyt Was Found" or something like that. You'd think reporters were looking for the Holy Grail or something! Ellen, assuming I was on a bender, was trying to cover for me and made up a story for the newspapers that I had once been hit in the head by a baseball. At any rate, the newspaper report was that I had amnesia. So, I got a wire from Babe Ruth at the time saying, "I heard you had a case of amnesia. I never heard of that brand!"

I was in Good Sam Hospital for a few days when a man appeared, very quietly, unobtrusively, and gently. He stood at the foot of my bed and said, "I hear you have a problem."

I said, "Yes, I guess I do."

He said, "Lots of us have problems."

I asked, "The same kind of problems?"

He said, "Yes, the same kind. My name is Herb Heeken."

I said, "How do you do, Mr. Heeken?"

He said, "I've heard of you."

And I asked, "Just what did you hear?"

He said, "I've heard both sides of the story." He didn't say very much more, except, "You know there are ways of being helped and restoring yourself to mental balance."

I thought, *I'm not crazy—yet!*

He said, "I'm going to ask a favor of you." He was going to ask a favor of *me*.

I said, "Yes, sir, what is it?"

He said, "Do you mind if I call on you occasionally, perhaps two or three times a week, and talk this over with you? You wouldn't mind if Sister Andrew also came in and talked with you, would you?"

I said, "Well, I'm not too familiar with the interdenominational rigamarole. To tell you the truth, I'm a Protestant and Episcopalian, and I don't know what a sister would be doing talking to me—or for that matter me talking to her!"

He said, "I'm sure that you would enjoy talking with her if she comes in."

I said, "That's fine."

Sister Andrew, who was only about 4 feet 11, used to take me out in the garden of Good Sam Hospital where the Stations of the Cross were situated. I didn't know anything about the Stations of the Cross or what I was supposed to say or do when I arrived there. But the philosophy she taught me and the manner in which she spoke to me has stayed with me always.

She said, "Just what do you believe life is?"

I said, "I don't know, Sister. I believe my life is over. I just don't see myself as going anywhere. I feel I have nothing ahead of me. I see no progress, I see nothing productive, nothing to be accomplished."

"Waite," she said, "You are so mistaken, you are *so* mistaken. There's plenty you can do *for* people and *with* people," she said. "There's *so* much you don't understand about life, and there's *so* much that you don't understand about *character*." She said, "You should *not* judge yourself." "There's one side of you that would like to quit drinking," she added.

She was right. I said, "Sister, I've wanted to quit drinking for so long, but I don't know how. Something just compels me to continue."

She talked to me for hours on end, and I finally came around—not to her way of thinking exactly, but at least the doors opened. One door began to open, and another began to open. That old bromide we hear so often became an actual fact: "I began to smell the roses."

That was the initial appearance of Herb Heeken and Sister Andrew, which started perhaps the happiest period of my entire life. I had never heard of Alcoholics Anonymous. Nobody had ever told me about alcoholism. I didn't know what an alcoholic *was*. I suspected that I might be something of that nature. I knew that I could *not* handle alcohol. I knew damn well I couldn't handle it. That wasn't news to me. I just didn't know what to *do* about it.

Herb didn't say a word to me about Alcoholics Anonymous, not a darn word. He just visited with me, sat down alongside the bed, and talked to me. Then finally, one day, after I'd been there about two weeks, he said, would you go to a meeting with me? I didn't know if he was talking about the Elks or something like that.

I said, "I'm not an organization man, Herb. I don't go to meetings." In my business it wasn't too wise or tactful to join too many organizations. I asked him what sort of a meeting it was.

He said, "It may do you some good. It may help you to make an adjustment to restore yourself to some type of mental balance. I think you could use this."

Herb Heeken was one of the greatest men I have ever known. I owe so much to that man. I owe everything I've ever been since 1945 to him, but I must also acknowledge the important role Miller Huggins played in my eventual reconciliation with myself. When it came to alcoholism and I was advised to take a personal inventory of myself, I had some experience along those lines, thanks to Hug.

The winter after the Yankees lost the last game of the 1926 World Series to Pete Alexander and the Cardinals, I fell into thinking about my situation. The Yankees were training in Saint Petersburg. In Tampa Bay there was a stone pier that jutted out about an eighth of a mile. In and about the surrounding basin, handsome—even palatial—yachts drifted lazily at their moorings.

On a particularly lovely evening, I walked on the pier alone and felt the lassitude of the tropics and a complete sense of well-being. I stood looking down at the reflection of riding lights in the water—the almost soft slap of the water washing against the wooden pilings.

The railings were of iron pipe, and I remember leaning my elbow on top of that railing and looking down into what seemed to be black water. I could see the water running beneath me. The mooring lights of the boats were shining very brightly, and the moon was gorgeous. The stars were so wonderful in the sky.

I was acutely conscious of the magnitude of creation—the forces and powers beyond and above us. I contemplated the breadth and scope of life, the deeper shades and nuances beyond the superficialities of satisfaction of the senses.

I thought about myself, very desperately, very deeply. I began to feel as if I were in the midst of a great infinity, and I guess I was. It was as if some human or physical being had tapped me on the shoulder. I felt the presence of some greater power.

I stood there, by myself, thinking, *Waite, what a simple ass you are, thinking you know so much, but you don't know anything at all. Miller Huggins tried to lecture you, your dad tried to help you, and you just turned a deaf ear to them and everybody else. Isn't it about time you listened?* It was almost as if someone was standing next to me saying, "Why not prove, if only to yourself, Huggins, and your dad, that you can organize your character to the point of top success? Why not reach for the ultimate?"

I looked up at the sky, the stars, and the moon—forces far too powerful and mysterious for my understanding—and felt small. Perhaps for a moment, I felt insufficient. Yet there was an inner satisfaction, the feeling I could lead the league, or at least that I had given myself the chance without interruption by forces alien to success.

I left the pier believing in myself, but it was the type of belief that carries with it caution and respect for all opponents. I decided on a program of deliberation. I would invest every thought, every action to the project. I would weigh every situation on and off the mound in relation to its bearing upon my goal.

I decided that I would go to Miller Huggins and tell him about my epiphany. The next day I went to him and said, "Hug, I learned for myself last night the things that you have been trying to tell me for years."

Hug said to me, "Waite, I was wondering if you would ever come to me and admit what you just did, take yourself seriously, and get down to business."

I determined I would do certain things when I stepped foot on the ballfield. I walked to the mound unhurried, and as I crossed the foul lines, I repeated to myself what amounted to a catechism of pitching: *Get the first ball over. Work on the batter as if he were the one and only man to get out the whole afternoon. After him, work on the next man the same way.*

There were no names, no reputations. There was no Ty Cobb, Harry Heilmann, Al Simmons, Goose Goslin, Bibb Falk, Johnny Bassler, or George Burns. There were just batters. The .220 hitter was just as dangerous as Cobb. Each man was a project in himself. *Watch the bunt, the drive through the box, cover first base. Forget the batter, pitch to the catcher, and bear down.*

The formula seemed to work. The more I repeated it, the more I believe it sharpened my reflexes and made me mentally alert. Moreover, I had help—good help from my catchers, Pat Collins and Benny Bengough.

Collins was not the greatest catcher ever to pull on a glove and pads, but he was good for me. He knew my methods and subscribed to my ideas as though he had originated the program. Bengough was one of the greatest receivers I had ever seen. But Benny, because of a lame arm, never realized his potential. Between the two they concentrated targets over the spot I sought to pitch to. We disregarded the possibility of the batter catching a peek at our objective points. We figured it would only make him overeager. I followed Pennock's system. I hooked the first ball (on most batters) over the plate. From then on, the catcher and I were in command.

And, by George, with the help of Miller Huggins, with, I believe, the help of God and my own observations of myself, I led the league the next two years, 1927 and 1928, and the New York Yankees were world champions. To me, that was the greatest victory. It was a man's victory over himself, I believe.

Because of that experience in 1926, I was able to put myself on trial and determine my own guilt when it came to my alcoholism in 1945. I could discover just what my weaknesses were. Those weaknesses are still there—I'm just *that far away* from being a drunkard again. I do not hesitate to admit it. I *cannot* handle alcohol, and if it were up to me, there wouldn't be twelve steps but twenty-four, because the first step, admitting I am powerless over alcohol, would be repeated after every other step again. That's the thing I really needed to admit. Once I did, I was on my way.

I am not an institutional Christian; I do not go to church. Some people say, "Well, how can he be a Christian and not go to church?" It is my belief, and Ellen's, that you could stand in a closet and pray to God and He would listen to you just as effectively as if you prayed in church. To those who do go to church, God bless you and more power to you. I believe that you are doing the correct thing because it is right for you, after a study of yourself. I do believe in God. I do say my prayers deeply and believe that He is the director of our destiny. That, to me, will always be true.

I did not have to struggle to give up drinking. I never slipped. I determined that I was not going to. What I did do was sit down and write reams and reams and reams of notes about alcoholism until it drove Ellen nuts. I used to write pages several inches thick and distribute them to all the alcoholics I could locate. I worked at this for seven years.

I cannot say I helped everyone. I probably *didn't* help 40 percent of them. But I *tried* to. In doing so, I was talking to myself. Every time I told them something, I was telling myself that something. Every time I mentioned alcoholism, I was reminding myself of what I was and to be careful. That helped me a great deal.

You'll *never* know how grateful you will be until after years and years of working at it. I remember saying to Herb, "Gee, do you think I can make two years? God grant that I make it."

And Herb said, "Don't worry, Waite, you'll make it. Just keep going the way you're going."

It was not a sudden awakening. I can best describe it as gaining moral and spiritual weight. When you gain physical poundage, you do not go to bed one night and wake up the next morning five pounds heavier. It comes slowly and without notice. The day arrives when some relative, or friend, says, "Say, you're looking better—gained weight, haven't you?" As that has been your objective you are inwardly pleased, and so you climb on the scale and discover the pleasant truth. Then you look in the mirror and find your face has filled out a bit. You find your entire countenance reflects the healthy rewards of time, attention, and careful diet.

So it is with alcoholism. One day, when you're not thinking too much about it, someone will remark, "Say, I can't get over the change in your disposition. You aren't crabby the way you used to be. You're a different person than you were last spring." You find that although tough problems have arisen, you haven't paid as much attention to them, except to meet them squarely and without confusion or anxiety. You look in the mirror of your consciousness to discover your spiritual and character profile has filled out.

In the beginning, I had a fairly large quota of fears concerning the stigma that would be attached to my name. I felt a bit scared—turning over in my mind what the public, and my friends, would think when they learned I was classified as an alcoholic. I felt that membership in Alcoholics Anonymous might be considered as segregation, that I would be tagged as a man who was partly missing.

However, I washed this angle through my mind and discovered my whole fear of being stigmatized was, in a sense, a hangover from my drinking days. It had its conception there. I distinctly recall saying to myself, *While I hate the idea of drinking, its aftermath, and complement of misery, what good would it do me to quit now? Why, even if I were to go on the wagon, wouldn't people still say, "Oh, he's a drinker, unreliable, unwanted when he's drunk."* Then comes the usual alibi, preparing a justifiable argument for the next binge: *Nobody gives a damn, so I may as well have the game as well as the name.*

I was afraid of being pointed out as something oddly distinctive— weirdly individual, weak of mind and heart—to be treated as a social outcast. Nothing could be further from the truth. In fact, just the opposite is true. First of all, why should there be a stigma? Thousands of people cannot do certain things. Stigma, if it is that, is born of ignorance and disappears when the facts are known.

I don't know what happens to make a person feel compelled or impulsively inclined toward taking a drink. I wish somebody could diagnose it. Do you think it is through the genes in any way? I had a grandfather who disappeared. He, in our family, was the first one who drank the "amnesia brand." He disappeared, but he never came back.

There is something within you that you should try to resist. You cannot physically attack it. You wish sometimes for God's sake that it was a human being, that you could stand it up in front of you and strangle it. You arrive at a state of confusion, helplessness, and of self-condemnation. Then it develops into self-pity; you drink because you think the world is against you.

Realizing and accepting all of this was doubly difficult for me given the nature of my livelihood at the time. My radio sponsor was the Burger Beer Company. When tavern owners heard that I was in AA, they took a dim view of that because I recommended against consuming alcohol. Meanwhile, I was on the air saying, "Now, if you want a good glass of beer—"

My alcoholism became known around the trade. The tavern owners were also known as permit holders: they permitted their customers to get sloppy! Nevertheless, they were estimable gentlemen. Someone from Burger Beer Company said, "Waite, we admire you for everything you've done, but that Alcoholics Anonymous is not quite as anonymous as you believe it is!"

It's true. I'm about as anonymous as a kick in the ass. What they were telling me was that I was giving Alcoholics Anonymous a bad name!

I had only been in Cincinnati a few years and didn't even know the names of the streets yet. I wasn't that well acquainted in Cincinnati and was about to be fired by the Burger Beer Company, my sponsors at WKRC for the Cincinnati Reds games. Herb Heeken helped me by going to my bosses and asking them to bring about an adjustment that allowed me to continue.

The truth is refreshing. For some fortunate reason, people are most willing to help someone making a comeback. That's true in business, sport, and the case of an alcoholic. The public really goes nuts when a boxer who is about to be knocked out, taking a terrible beating, suddenly rallies to come off the floor and wins. So it is that the alcoholic wins respect and assistance in making his own comeback to business and society.

Oh, I know that one class of individuals will always give an extra kick to a fellow who's down, but such people are few and far between and not doing so well themselves. You'll discover to your delight that most people are there with outstretched hands. It may be they like to think of themselves as Good Samaritans, philanthropists, generously tolerant, or all wise, but whatever their prompting impulses they are certainly understanding, definitely interested, tolerant, and kind.

I have come to see that managing my life is something far beyond the ability to make money. Managing my life means getting the best out of my soul, bringing forth the most pleasing of my traits, so that my self-presentation brings something of value to my family and others around me.

My admission that alcoholism had me floored automatically made alcohol my number one problem. It's not like a crack in the ceiling, something to repair in your spare time. It is a full-time job and always will be. Alcoholism transcends the wife, husband, children, business, bank account, or whatever is considered most important. I had to make my inability to handle alcohol the paramount issue of my life, as must every alcoholic.

While you will always be conscious of your inability to drink, you will before long shed that burden. You will find happiness when the load is no longer placed on your shoulders because it is no longer necessary to be a beast of burden. Over time, you will discover the gradual elimination of the causes of your conflicts, anxieties, and frustrations. Your motives will align with common sense, and your emotional scale will balance.

I want to say this *emphatically* to all alcoholics: It is true that if we practice sobriety that we will begin to notice the good things around us, the nice things that happen to us. We start to recognize the wonderful characteristics of the people with whom we associate. We come to understand the motives of others, which in the past we considered only as offensive to our twisted natures.

I believe everyone has singular characteristics. None of us is patterned after the other. We accept AA as we find it. We accept God as we find Him. It does not make a difference if you are a Muslim, Jewish, Buddhist, or a Christian. What matters is that you recognize a power greater than yourself that can bring benefits for which you so often and intensely pray.

Alcoholics Anonymous is a philosophy divided into two parts: the spiritual and the temporal. The spiritual half we accept and apply in the privacy of our meditations, displaying its beneficial effects mostly when the situation calls for that type of treatment. In our privacy we commune with a power greater than ourselves, accepting its will and attempting to carry out its plans.

The temporal half is more a concentration on action beneficial to ourselves, activities to reestablish ourselves in daily life as useful, helpful, trustworthy, and valuable in the pattern of the world. We adjust the spiritual half to our spiritual needs and pursue the temporal activities, performing tasks requiring physical and mental effort, thereby taking ourselves out of ourselves. The fusion of both sides welds the character we eventually possess, after the period of awakening.

I believe we arrive at our destination through the persuasion of a higher power. There's good in every one of us if we allow it to appear. Don't stifle it, don't keep it submerged, and *don't* drown it in *goddamn alcohol!* Forgive me for swearing, but that is the truth.

Our physical perspective changes too. I'll give you an example. Ellen and I had been making some alterations in our home, requiring new furniture. We became "furniture-minded." I was up in Dayton recently, without Ellen, in a car along Dayton's main street. On the nearest corner to my approach there was a brilliantly lighted, attractive tavern. On the other corner, immediately opposite, was a store with furniture displayed in the window.

For some reason, I was most conscious of the fact that I looked beyond the tavern to the furniture store. The thought struck me: *Two years ago, I wouldn't have noticed that store. I'd have thought that tavern looks like a cozy place to snatch a couple quick ones.* My thinking had changed, and my interests now centered on things with more constructive value in my life.

I do not consider myself cured. There is no such thing for an alcoholic. I have no way of knowing whether I will ever wander so far off the emotional beam as to start drinking again. I am most sure that should I have just one drink I would be off on another tangent. The grasp of my program means work, work, work. It has become as much a part of my daily life as walking, eating, and dressing. I find that I put on good habits as I put on clothes, as easily and with as much pride and satisfaction as when I find myself garbed in some particular outfit I like. It's only when I become sloppy in thought in action, as I would in careless dress, that I would be in danger of slipping.

I have one final point to make to those yet to recognize that they cannot win against alcohol. Perhaps through some inner urge they are still drawn irresistibly to its deceptive promise of release.

It's difficult to admit defeat to something that once gave you pleasure, to which even at times has been a friend. But now that friend has turned on you. It's your worst enemy. As we used to say when we were kids, "It's no sin to run when you're afraid." That's sort of facetious, I know. But would you, as an eight-year-old, keep battling a twelve-year-old day in and day out? What if the other kid outweighed you by thirty pounds, had too much power for you, and gave you a terrible beating every time you fought him?

I don't think an eight-year-old would be that dumb, but alcoholics keep battling. They even go out to find the guy. And it's always the same beating.

Why not quit that uneven battle? Surrender. That's not a mark of weakness. It is a mark of strength to be able to say that alcohol, or any enemy, is just too strong for you. Might is not right, and the might in alcohol certainly is not.

24

Then and Now

ONLY AFTER GIVING UP ALCOHOL DID it fully dawn on me that moving to Cincinnati was the luckiest decision I had ever made. I slowly discovered that it was possible to let my other self, that creature of sentiment and sensitivity, that somewhat idealistic young man, to reconcile with the glib and worldly-wise fellow who had been my public self.

Gradually, I realized that far to the west of the Hudson River the real world existed after all, that life could ride on an even keel yet not be dull, that I could be accepted for who I was and not just for what I did. Best of all, I found it was possible to establish a communion with the world such as the public life of a ballplayer had never offered me.

When I was in baseball, the public hardly seemed alive. It was a distant and faceless crowd that made noise but with which I felt no immediate identity or even communication. In Washington, it is true, the fans often gave me special attention, whistling in unison that ancient hippety-hop tune ("There she goes! There she goes! All dressed up in her Sunday clothes!"). The fans made fun of my metronome windup, with the intent of unsettling me, but eventually I welcomed this as an acknowledgement that some real, live people out there were conscious of my existence.

Game broadcasting, by comparison, put me in direct touch with the fans as a group and as individuals. Over time, it came to me that not only was the public accepting me as a performer, but they were also ready to acknowledge me as a person. The trained-seal aspect of my life diminished. I found security in the feeling that I belonged to the community and would hold a place in it even if I could not burn a fastball over the plate for them to watch.

It was this discovery that finally quenched the deep-seated anxiety that had been at the root of my lifelong restlessness. Nervous energy that I had expended in coping with this inner turmoil—hidden and unacknowledged as it often was—could be conserved now, and I could afford to let my guard down. I could love my family frankly and whole-heartedly and respond without embarrassment to the affection of the fans and my associates.

My relationship with the fans remade my life and perhaps even improved me as a person. They provided satisfaction to me that I could not measure and also enabled me to find new and quiet satisfactions in pursuits for which I never previously had any taste—listening to good music, for instance, or touring quietly with Ellen along the back country roads, savoring the unspoiled countryside that, to quote a country friend, "God had not let go of yet." I even developed talents I had lacked the energy to cultivate in earlier years, as I did by becoming a Sunday painter.

I had new opportunities to meet and know the men and women who had been listening to me and relished every opportunity to talk to them in small groups, face-to-face. I was mature enough by this time to understand that it was not my "manly beauty" or my baseball reputation (some fans didn't even know about that) or even my dulcet baritone that won over the fans.

It was simply that I represented to them the Cincinnati ballclub—the darling of their hearts. They could see in me the embodiment of their team, or their pipeline to it, not merely as its voice but as its ears too, into which they could pour their appreciation and criticisms.

I smiled when fans would earnestly require me to carry to Manager Fred Hutchinson bits of sage advice on how to handle a pitcher or strengthen the batting order. I was always flattered by requests that assumed I stood in the role of elder statesman to the ballclub. I was never quite so lost to good sense as to try to give the manager the "word" on how the club should be operated, of course. I stuck to my job of reporting and commenting, telling stories and occasionally philosophizing about the game.

My advice would be of minimal value for many reasons, not least of which was that the game of baseball as it was played during my broadcasting days was not quite the game I used to play. It was rather far removed from my game—not a direct descendant but sort of a cousin. While basically the ends sought were the same, the methods were altogether new. It is not that I am a devotee of the old days or the old ways in baseball, but many others were better equipped than me to offer their wisdom.

As an incurable fan myself, as well as a veteran ballplayer, I will say I had a different attitude from some other broadcasters, and perhaps even a slight advantage. Sometimes I could thrill to a performance simply because I knew, from having been there, just what the man I was watching was going through and how mighty an effort he was really making.

I was also lucky in Cincinnati to have watched a historic effort in 1961 as well as come to know some of the game's greatest: Joe Morgan, Johnny Bench, and Pete Rose. During my tenure, the Cincinnati Reds had nine different managers: Bill McKechnie, Bucky Walters, Luke Sewell, Johnny Neun, Mayo Smith, Birdie Tebbetts, Jimmy Dykes, Fred Hutchinson, and Rogers Hornsby. Their ability as managers varied widely. All of them—save one—were good friends and pleasant companions.

The one exception was Rogers Hornsby.

As I've said many times, Rogers was unquestionably one of the game's greatest batters, a man who could hit almost any ball pitched and who studied batting as a priest studies religion. However, Hornsby seemed a cold man to me, and I often wondered if he had a single friend except himself. I ran into Rogers first in 1921, when I was training with the Yankees in New Orleans. I encountered him last in 1953 at an old-timers celebration in Cincinnati.

Johnny Murdough of the Cincinnati Reds decided that it might make an interesting spectacle to reenact the famous game in the 1926 World Series when Alexander came in to strike out Lazzeri with the bases full. Before Alexander appeared, the St. Louis shortstop, Tommy Thevenow, had made the hit—off me—that put the Cards ahead to stay. Jess Haines had been the St. Louis starting pitcher, and a number of other men were available who had been in one lineup or the other.

The Reds brought in Old Pop Haines from his home in Dayton and Tommy Thevenow from Indiana. Earle Combs, who had been the Yankees center fielder that day, arrived from Richmond, Kentucky. My old battery mate, Benny Bengough—now a coach for the Phillies—also was on hand to help set the stage. Naturally, Hornsby, who had been the St. Louis manager in 1926, was to be there to add some luster. Rogers had been giving batting exhibitions around the National League. His sharp eyes, which he had always babied, had never failed him, and he could still hit a baseball hard and far.

Haines and I were to open the proceedings by pitching to some of the men who had faced us that day. He was to throw to Combs and Bengough and the other old Yanks, and I had to pitch to Thevenow and, of course, Hornsby. Neither Jess nor I had thrown a ball seriously in years. More than that, I had been fitted with trifocals and would likely see two of any fast-moving objects tossed my way. So, before the exhibition began, I went into the dressing room and found Hornsby.

"Rog," I said, "I don't see too well these days. So, try to avoid hitting any through the box. I won't see them coming, and you may wreck me."

Rogers nodded and went about the business of putting on his uniform. As I left the clubhouse, the caretaker motioned me to one side and muttered, "You see what Hornsby uses for baseballs? Ninety-nines!"

Ninety-nines were a hopped-up imitation of the regulation Major League ball. They had almost double the bounce and would fly from a bat like a golf ball. These were what had helped Rogers make his exhibitions so spectacular. The clubhouse man brought Rogers' baseball bag out to the field before Hornsby appeared so I quickly switched the balls in the bag to regulation.

A good thing I did too.

Rogers came up, Benny Bengough spoke to him, Rogers muttered a reply, and I began to pitch. I threw them down the middle because I knew the crowd wanted to see him hit. Rogers must have let ten or twelve pitches go by, waiting for one that would be perfect. When he did find one, he swung hard and drove the ball back in my direction. But it did not have the life he was looking for and merely bounced back through the infield.

Later, I learned that Benny had said to Hornsby, not knowing I had already spoken to him, "Waite can't see a damn thing without those cheaters. Pull the ball to the left if you can."

"Oh yeah?" replied the gallant Rogers. "Let that SOB take care of himself." Fortunately, I had.

Rogers had always let the other guy take care of himself. He coddled no one's feelings and gave no quarter. When he wanted to change pitchers, he would not walk out to offer the man he was removing a word of sympathy. He would stand on the dugout steps and whistle the new pitcher in and the old one out. He made little effort to conceal his scorn for the modern ballplayer. "Just a bunch of Humpty Dumpties," he would say.

There was no question that ball players of the succeeding era were different from those with whom Rogers and I had played. Naturally, I was inclined to favor the ones I knew, the men who made baseball their whole life and tried to develop all their skills equally. I do recognize that ballplayers who came later were playing a different game and had different ends in view, so no fair comparison can be made.

It is futile to argue, for instance, whether Willie Mays could hit a ball as solidly as Ty Cobb, Harry Heilmann, Bill Terry, Lefty O'Doul, Honus Wagner, or Al Simmons. Mays was not trying to do the same thing that they were and was not using the same equipment. His emphasis was on the long ball—the mighty wallop that could fetch three or four runs at a time.

The ball became far livelier than it had ever been so that it would travel farther. The bat was lighter, whip-handle style, so it could be swung quickly in an enormous arc for maximum distance. In the old days, the long-distance hitters used monstrous war clubs that a boy could not hold level. A broken bat, shattered by hitting a ball, so common in later times, was a comparative rarity and cause for comment. The high-average hitters of my time were slapping and poking the ball to get it past the fielders. They were followed by power hitters who tried to pull every pitch and did not fret about their batting average.

Fielding styles, too, became altogether different, chiefly because of changes in the size and shape of the glove. The old-time outfielder used to cut a hole in the palm of his glove to help him grip a ball and counteract its spin. Later outfielders snagged the ball in a big scoop that did not involve the palm of his hand at all. Even the catcher used a glove that required only the fingertips to take the impact of the pitch.

Comparative records on this account mean very little to me. I think any of the great old-timers would be great today too, but they would have to play today's game. I also believe the current heroes are the equal of those I knew, even if the averages do not always say so. I never, for instance, saw a better shortstop than Roy McMillan.

Pitching changed because of the lively ball—and because there was such a generous supply of baseballs. In the early days, club managers, like Hartford's Jim Clarkin, would fight to get foul balls back. A pitcher often worked with a scuffed and soiled baseball that would sail. A ball sails or takes off when it deviates suddenly, free from its straight course—not in a curve away from the batter but usually in a sharp shot toward the batter.

When the spitball was banned, it put an end to far more than just a ball loaded with slippery elm, tobacco juice, or saliva. The rule prevented the raising of both hands to the mouth where, hidden by the glove, the ball could be doctored in a dozen different ways. Pitchers were roughing the ball with teeth or fingernail pressure, embedding bits of dirt into the seams, or applying a high shine to one side of the ball—all strategies designed to make the ball sail. A ball that had been roughed up on one side with a serrated fingernail (prepared for the purpose) and shined on the other side would sail as much as six inches.

The pitcher operated under different rules in the old days too. In 1927 and '28, the American League pitchers were not allowed to use resin bags, touch the ground with their hands, nor wipe their hands across their mouths. In the National League, the pitcher could use the quick pitch, and the batter was not permitted to leave the batter's box while the pitcher was on the mound. This rule, of course, gave the pitcher an edge over the baserunner as well as the batter, for the runner after a pick-off throw really had to scramble to get back and take his lead before the pitcher could start his motion.

Pitchers in the days of Cobb and Carey could use a number of tricks to deceive the runner—to feint him back to the bag or make him believe the pitching motion had begun. A wiggle of the elbow, a twitch of the hip, a distant compression of the knees—any such move might keep the runner off balance.

Never in my day did a foul ball hit the concrete floor of the grandstand and bounce back into the upper deck as I have seen balls do in more recent days. We never used to see foul bunts fly into the seats either. Even half-hit balls can carry into the deep outfield in the more modern era. In 1962, in Los Angeles, I saw a long drive hit the turf and bounce over a ten-foot wall into the seats.

I do not mean to say that such a baseball makes the game any easier to play. In many ways it makes it more difficult and in every way different, so the comparisons make little sense. I like change. Just like any fan, I thrill to the home run and find no fault with games that feature six or seven four-baggers. Suddenly turning the game upside down with a blow that scores four runs is just as dramatic to me as a game full of tight pitching.

In my years at the microphone, I was fortunate enough to sit in on some of baseball's choicest spectacles. Most satisfying to me and most packed with emotion was the roller-coaster ride the Cincinnati Reds took to the 1961 pennant, when they dipped from the heights to the very depths from week to week and then roared back to the top again with the vigor of champions.

Some people perhaps have forgotten how dismally that season began. Before the hot weather set in, the Reds lost nine in a row. Then they won ten straight. That's how the season went: runs of losses and then long stretches when almost no one could beat them. They played four games in Chicago against the Cubs in which the home team took all four games and scored a total of 46 runs, spreading them almost evenly through the innings of each game. Then, immediately after that disaster, the Reds went to Milwaukee and swept a series, flew to San Francisco to beat the Giants two of three, and arrived in Los Angeles not much more than a game out of first place.

It almost seemed as if the Reds were trying to confuse the opposition by playing possum for a game or two, then leaping to life like a tiger. They used the same tactics occasionally in a game, playing like patsies for the first few innings, and then turning into champions in time to carry home the victory. In Los Angeles, in the first game of a twi-night doubleheader, Manager Hutchinson, a confirmed gambler—as all great managers must be—started Ken Hunt, a rangy right-hander who was frighteningly short of experience.

The mighty Dodgers, in the first five innings, scored three runs off Hunt on a passed ball, four walks, a hit batter, and a scattering of hits. The Reds looked sloppy in the field too, yet when the five innings were over, Cincinnati was leading, 8–3. This doubleheader was described as starting at sunset and ending at sunrise, and the Reds took both ends of the marathon. This was the series that gave us all the pennant bug and prompted us to put pressure on the fans to "Root the Reds Home." Of course, the fans responded. There were bumper stickers carrying the slogan, window signs, and buttons, even on ceramic goods and jewelry in the exclusive shops on Fourth Street. There were songs and banners.

On the surge of this support, the Reds rode on to the pennant. The day they brought it all home, thirty thousand fans swarmed into Fountain Square to greet them in a wild celebration such as the city had not seen since the original Red Stockings had come home from their national tour undefeated, more than ninety years earlier.

It is too bad the World Series that year did not go to nine games, as it had when I first pitched in one. For the Reds, after rolling over and playing dead (almost) in the first five games, I am sure they would have conformed to the season's pattern by blazing to life and taking the next four in a row. However, four games are all it takes these days to carry home the winner's share, and the Reds simply ran out of room.

Sitting in on Jackie Robinson's first appearances in Cincinnati was another thrill I shall not soon forget. It is difficult to re-create the feeling among fans, players, writers, broadcasters, and even club owners when the odious color line was broken in baseball. Men like big Dan Parker of the *New York Daily Mirror* had been urging and predicting for a long time that baseball, if it meant to remain a national game, would have to follow the lead of other sports, notably football and track.

But prejudice, like an iceberg, is something hard to measure until you run into it; Jackie's joining the Dodgers had been accompanied by all sorts of threats. When he came to Cincinnati, he had already been accepted as a player, but there was a hint of tension all the same. The sight of Robinson in action, however, was enough to lift the heart of any fan—big, alert, daring, fast, a fierce competitor who could give any pitcher the shakes.

Like a true champion, Jackie Robinson did his best when the pressure was on. He was not merely good; he was great. He made such an enormous impression on the game that it is hard to believe his career was as short as it was. I have a feeling Robinson could have hung on a good deal longer had he wanted to, but he wisely decided to lay the groundwork for his lifetime security while he still had his fame to bargain with. Some writers seem to begrudge him that right, but having been along that road myself, I could only admire him for making his decision and sticking with it.

A number of players have had their stories muffled in "if onlys"—if only he had not quit so soon or if only his arm had not gone bad or if only he had not eaten himself out of the league or if only his legs had held up or if only he had not been sick. Mickey Mantle is someone whose weak legs and other ailments never allowed him to set the records he seemed capable of. At his best he was without a doubt one of the most dangerous hitters of all time, but he was not long at his best. So, I have to rate him in my book below Joe DiMaggio and not even on the same page with Babe Ruth, who did everything so well for so long.

Yes, here I go, making comparisons of the old and the new when I promised myself I would not. Baseball changed in nearly every way from the game of my era. It became different even in the way it was set up, with armies of front office and farm personnel, so that a player might actually find a lifetime career in the game when he could no longer perform on the diamond.

In the Yankees' front office I used to know, a ballplayer could peek in through the glass and see if Ed Barrow had shaved and watch all the business being transacted on two desks and a table. The realization that there was no postbaseball career awaiting was bound to affect a ballplayer as he felt the juice going out of his joints.

On his best days, a player never thought about his condition, weariness, or ability to perform. All these were taken for granted, just as he took for granted his ability to eat and drink what was set before him. As the distance from base to base grew longer, however, and the pitching arm felt heavier, he had to face the fact that the game itself could not use him much longer. He could not hope for a coaching or managing job somewhere on the farm, or a scouting assignment, or even a public-relations spot in the same organization.

The whole atmosphere of the game became different too. A ballplayer is no longer usually an object of opprobrium as he was in my day. He is welcomed into the best hotels and in good restaurants. Even on the road he lives in relative comfort. I do not believe, however, that the ensuing generations of ballplayers became softer or less devoted to the game. Many people I know have held that the old "hungry" ballplayer was a better competitor. This I don't agree with. It has become far easier for ballplayers to see how much success can mean to them in terms of security and status. In the old days, a hungry player could often see very little ahead worth struggling for when the game started to become a grind.

Perhaps one difference is that the old-time player had to make baseball his whole life—his work, his play, his social life too—so he involved himself in it more thoroughly. However, no one can tell me that Willie Mays, Joe Nuxhall, Roger Maris, or Joey Jay were given to loafing on the diamond or holding back even an ounce of their strength when victory was in the balance.

Joey Jay won a permanent place in my private Hall of Fame for pitching, fielding, and courage. My private Hall of Fame! It is filled with faces and names that most fans might find as strange as the street signs in a foreign city: Muddy Ruel. That suave and soft-spoken, almost regally mannered young man was once one of the best catchers in baseball. He's dead now, and who even recalls his wonderful skills? Or, Johnny Griffin, that lively and ribald soul, majordomo of the Dodgers clubhouse, who used to wear almost anything on his head, from a babushka to an old-fashioned army cockade, just to keep a victory streak going. He was another link with my youth, a Christmas card that brought a voice from the past each year, and now silenced.

Sometimes I think it is best not to dwell on how the idols of my boyhood have faded, gone where no one recalls them anymore. What matters is that I can still savor the immense satisfaction that probably only those in the September of their years know—the feeling of having accomplished the major goals in my life through urgent self-discipline. Despite my occasional backward glances, I still find today's baseball and ballplayers a vital part of my life.

In 1944 an incident brought me back to my own boyhood days. On Opening Day of that season, a youngster of fifteen tender years reported to the Cincinnati Reds directly from a high school in Hamilton, Ohio. He was big, blessed with early strength, a left-handed pitcher. He decorated the Reds' bench as sort of an extra, pitching batting practice and hoping someday to get a break, relieving a faltering pitcher when a game was lost. The war years gave youngsters opportunities, and it might be said they provided the first real openings for youngsters in almost any venue.

This young southpaw, one day, was sitting idly on the Cincinnati bench when the Reds were losing to the Cardinals, 13–0, in the ninth inning. Suddenly, the kindly Deacon Bill McKechnie, the Reds' manager, said, "Say, young fella, trot down and warm up, will ya?"

The astonished youngster, Joe Nuxhall, literally fell off the bench and stumbled up the dugout steps, his knees wavering like saplings in a stiff breeze. However, he warmed up dutifully before making his debut as the youngest player at that time to play in a Major League game.

It would be nice to report Joe's invincibility, but he had a rough go, giving up five walks, two hits, one wild pitch, and five runs for a final score of 18–0. I sat in the broadcaster's booth, undergoing the agony along with Joe Nuxhall, because, of course, in 1915, I had been the "boy wonder."

Baseball keeps me alive and young and close to the sounds and sights that still spell youth to me. I suppose somewhere in the wide expanse of these United States, a young boy waits with longing heart and anxious eyes for the next baseball season. There must be, because there always has been, and I imagine always will be.

I know I am not the man I was, but it is good to look back and think of what I once could accomplish. Being a different man now, who knows but that I may be a better one? My lately discovered satisfaction in being a part of a community, and not just a bit of baseball bric-a-brac, of a continuing and exciting and kindred relationship with a whole small nation of fans—this more than makes up to me for the lost suppleness and strength of the pitching arm that, in a sense, first opened this pathway for me.

At least I don't have to hustle out every spring now and win a baker's dozen ball games to maintain my status. Finally, I have learned to accept that I won't ever get out and mow the batters down again or improve my lifetime batting average by so much as a single point.

This was brought home to me a few years ago by my son Christopher, whom I took with me to a baseball game one night. The game was won by a mighty home run, far over the fence, by someone whose name I am ashamed to say I do not recall. In the car on the way home in the lovely night, I was musing about my own career, and about Christopher's.

"Well, Christopher," I said, "do you suppose you could ever drive a baseball over the fence like that?"

Christopher was silent for a time.

"No," he said at last. "And neither could you."

Epilogue

Christopher's Question

IT'S BEEN SAID THAT YOUR VALUES, or your personality, change every seven years. It seems to me it's about every ten years, as you begin to look through different lenses at what's taking place around you. You have different opinions than you had ten years prior. Sometimes, for instance, I'm inclined to indict the youth of today. Then I look back and think, *How can I say that about them? I did the same thing, or something similar to it, when I was their age.*

The one thing that puzzles me the most, and I would like to give force to, concerns my son Christopher and a conversation I had with him about mistakes that are made by youth of today as compared to fellows like myself.

Christopher graduated summa cum laude, with two diplomas, from Princeton. Once, I was invited to his home in Connecticut and to stay with him through the night. He and his wife had two friends over for dinner, so five of us were there. We entered a discussion about the behavior patterns of the youth of today as against when I was a young fellow.

I made an offhand statement, with which I think most people would agree.

I said, "I cannot understand, Christopher, why the youth of every generation cannot profit from the mistakes of their elders."

He didn't miss a beat: "What could we possibly learn from *you?*" he retorted.

I was taken aback. I wasn't speaking about *his* youth; I was speaking about the youth of *every* generation. It seems that every generation must have a complement of its own errors and live and die and profit and lose by their own mannerisms, characteristics, investments in life, and behavior patterns.

Yet, I have pondered Christopher's question ever since.

I've also thought a lot about myself, which enabled me in later years to regain balance and restore my sense of fitness. The story of my life and my choices was in some respects comical and exciting, combined with sadness, grief, and remorse. I experienced every emotion a human being could have. In parallel fashion, I attempted to rectify everything that had gone amiss along the way. With that, I had my hands full.

When I was playing ball with the New York Yankees, Detroit Tigers, Philadelphia Athletics, New York Giants, Pittsburgh Pirates, and Brooklyn Dodgers, I certainly surrendered to impulse many, many times and to situations that were wrong. I freely admit it. I don't look back on those days with any degree of satisfaction. I can't say that I was ever really a bad person, but I certainly was rebellious or counteracting.

As I sit here and look back, I do not know how to evaluate those days. How, on a scale of ten, would I grade whether any transgressions I may have been guilty of were above the midway point of five, or below that, or how far below? I was never vicious nor in any entanglements really. I never harmed anyone, to my knowledge, except in disagreements domestically. I did cause personal hurt to my first wife and our family when I was younger. But I was never involved in any scandal or muck of any description.

I look upon my life—or the thread of it—as a boy born of good, attentive, middle-class parents who were guided by the moral codes of the day. Their big mistake was allowing me to venture into a world while still innocent, uninformed—naive—with a character and personality susceptible to temptation that was exercised after association with the more uncivil, rugged, abrasively sophisticated men with whom I was thrown in my younger years of professional baseball.

I basically was, by fact of birth and nature, good, and refinement was a native virtue. I was not ready for the world as it was at that time and by the age of twenty was inoculated by the wrong philosophies and practices. Then, throughout my career, I experienced waves of good and bad, highs and lows.

I misbehaved but still had traits of good, basic character. As a matter of fact, I was rather idealistic. I don't know what prompted me to do some of the things I did when I knew damn well they were wrong. It was my inner man against my own conscience. I guess that happens a great deal in life; people are at cross-purposes with their consciences and don't realize until after they have committed a transgression that they wish they hadn't.

I just wasn't Jack Armstrong, the All-American boy. I was a long way from that. I was adventurous and took advantage of every opportunity to explore. I've been to Japan, China, and Honolulu. I have been to Europe. I've been pretty much all over the United States, in most of the cities, playing ball here and there. I've been on the stage in many different cities. I've had quite an experience in peregrination, you might say, if you want to use a word.

I had a one-man art show in Cincinnati and sold many of my paintings at substantial prices. I received commissions to paint a couple pieces for the Cincinnati club to present to what they called the "Man of the Year." I've done a lot of public speaking. I'm not saying all of this to boast. I'm just reciting the fact that I have experimented in so many areas of life.

Yet, in the past I also had what I call "character cavities," which are like so many empty electric light sockets—the filling of which could have illuminated my life with bright, glowing beams of contentment, happiness, and productive effort. Instead, I seemed to prefer the darker corners, dull and drab, an atmosphere wholly conducive to resentment, intolerance, selfishness, and egocentrism. I attempted to play host in this atmosphere and wondered why people despised my twisted nightmare of weird design, elucidated only by the exploding lights of illusion sparked by alcohol.

As my attitudes changed, I stirred myself to fill those empty sockets, those cavities, with gleams of generosity in thought, action, and warmth of personality; the glow of happiness was present and people wanted to share that with me. With the arrival of character change comes a rebirth of ambition, new outlets for emotions, for nervous energies. I found myself seeking different channels through which to release these energies of work and play, which profited not only me but also others.

Life, in my estimation, is a series of challenges that must be met. If you survive the challenges or overcome them, you're that much better off. Failure is yours many times, however. My philosophy may be faulty, but it pertains to me. I go from one project to another, and it seems I am never quiet. My nervous energy keeps me on the run and doing things, some of them good and some not so good. I think back to the things that were not so good, stories that are not so wonderful to tell, and I regret those things. Yet, when I look back upon them, they do form the structure that is me.

I played baseball for so long that it is hard for me to depart from that consciousness and enter into a world where social aspects are entirely different. Deep within my soul, my psyche, or whatever you care to call it, is the elation, the willingness to participate in the very high ideals that are presented, the fullness of generosity to other people, or the very loveliness I feel when talking to fans in hotel lobbies and other places. I have found many glorious blessings when you get down to it.

I think about my years with the Yankees, from 1921 through 1930, with delight and satisfaction. I proved myself to the point, in baseball, where I eventually wound up in the Hall of Fame. I don't think you do that without some virtue and some talent. In some ways my work with the Yankees, especially in the early years, justified the entry. But I would have had a more solid claim had I not allowed things to go astray for a while.

I have a thorough belief that, in the depth of your psyche, you have this storehouse of sentiments, emotions, and reactions. Occasionally, they arise at the most opportune time—and sometimes at an inopportune time—to teach you, penalize you, or cause certain feelings, reactions, trauma, or delights. I had tried, in a very limited way, to study myself and approximate the expectations other people had of me. Very often I failed, and frankly I admit that. I become very confused at times in trying to assert the proper procedures and to administer my personality, my talent, or whatever the occasion called for, to the proper proportion.

Shortly before I was released from baseball for the last time, I published the essay "Why the American League Wins," in the *Saturday Evening Post*. In it, I condemned the National League—my employer—as inferior to the American. I wrote that National League teams lacked pitching strategy, didn't understand that a strong offense is what wins games, and exerted too much oversight over the personal lives of players off the field. (Ellen joked that it sounded like I was just cranky because the Dodgers made me go to bed on time!) I also opined that American League players, because they tended to come from cities, were better businessmen and had a stronger will to win.

Newspaper reports of my release from the Dodgers speculated that my commentary was not coincidental to my dismissal. It is hard to argue otherwise—my advancing age notwithstanding—but I was never one to hold back, and it wasn't the first time I got myself in trouble for speaking my mind in public.

In my day, ballplayers weren't interviewed or allowed a voice. They were written about, but they didn't write and were not permitted to speak for themselves. When I held out one year, I put out a public statement that a pitcher would never make $20,000 a year. This was what I was holding out for. I was called up to the Yankees office and told that they would handle the public statements, not me. We were not at liberty to give expression to our innermost desires or thoughts. Perhaps it was better that way, but at that point I had almost nothing to lose.

At age thirty-eight, when I cried outside Ebbets Field on that beautiful afternoon, May 16, 1938, I knew my day was done. I no longer possessed the physical capacity to carry on as the big league baseball star I had been destined to become as a fifteen-year-old schoolboy.

At age eighty-three, my sorrow comes from introspection, a consciousness long delayed (known in substance, perhaps, but not admitted nor clearly seen) that all my life I have been a performer—a good one, doubtlessly—but never a leader.

I am without the stability of the truly successful man, without the substantial structure of one on whom another can depend; without the cleverness to convert time, effort, and money into security; without the stature, the early development of character, to recognize the needs, encourage the virtues, and turn aside the injurious.

I was born with talent of varied sorts—and on high planes of accomplishment—but also with a definite weakness: the unstable foundation that constantly undermines and negates the solidification of success.

The weakness I experienced in 1945, and the few years leading up to that, was of proper decision, or indecision. The knowledge of this is always present. Yet it is my insufficiency to mold, build, and become a truly fine—if not big—man, at least in measure to the opportunity provided. I feel insufficient now because I have lived crippled by this insufficiency that I realize—only too late—is exacting a punishing toll.

I wonder why some of us are chosen as receptacles for certain combinations of strengths and weakness and why, as in this case, the person is introspective enough to understand that after all these years and all the success in many fields, the weakness remains as a blight, too ingrown for elimination.

Now I understand more clearly what was meant in 1945 when it was pointed out to me that "man is very often suffering from conflict with himself." Thus, it is so!

I feel I have failed—failed in life. I am of the opinion that I have had many gifts from the Divine Providence but have not put them to the proper uses. I foresee just a form of tragedy, leaving behind very little, much unfulfilled—much started, never finished.

Much disappointment in myself.

So, when Christopher said to me, "What could I learn from you?" I can only hope that he might have learned a whole lot about my life's choices, good, bad, and indifferent, just as I could have learned more than I did from other people who had made mistakes. I really don't know what Christopher was thinking. He is a brilliant man in his own right and accomplished things I dreamed of but never achieved.

I used to say, "Christopher, listen to me and listen closely please. Being a businessman, a philosopher, or a schoolteacher is very doubtless much more to be desired than to be a baseball player. A baseball player gets his picture in the newspapers. He's written about; he's talked about. Christopher, you can go further and produce more for society; you can give more to your fellow man than a baseball player ever can. You can become greater than any baseball player who ever played, or any football player or athlete, if you can produce something from which the world can profit."

Christopher should ask questions. A young baseball player should ask questions. An older fellow who has been in the league for a good many years should also ask questions. When I was broadcasting the Reds, Pete Rose used to come and sit with me. We talked about Ty Cobb and some of the older ball players. Regardless of whether Pete had any education—which he didn't have too much of, as he was always sort of a street guy—he has a very shrewd mind. I think if he had been well-educated, his IQ would have been around 140. Pete is a guy who asks questions. God, he used to sit with me and ask me questions.

It comes down to this: Who are we and what are we? We are human beings; we are people. Not one of us is *better* than another, not a *damn* one of us better than the other. I just wish I had the command of semantics and phraseology with which I could set down my thoughts and feelings today in such an orderly fashion and with wisdom, tact, and explanations so that you would know that what boils down and foments in my heart is actually purposeful, clean, good, and appreciative of other people.

I am so deeply thankful for the way others have helped me build my life and how they came to my assistance when I needed it the most: my mother and father, Miller Huggins, Ed Barrow, Babe Ruth, Lou Gehrig, Sister Andrew, Herb Heeken, the people of Cincinnati, Ellen, Christopher, and so many others.

I have embedded their love into the very depths of my soul—brick by brick.

Acknowledgments

CURATING THIS BOOK WAS THE MOST fun I've had with any project, ever. For that, I first and foremost thank my dear friend Christopher Waite Hoyt for entrusting me with his dad's legacy, and his gracious cousin, Ellen Frell Levy, for making it all possible. The eight boxes of files Ellen shipped to my doorstep appeared hopelessly disjointed until I arrived upon the plastic binder of her interview transcripts with her uncle Waite, which are the narrative heart, soul, and voice of his untold memoir.

After a year or so of living, breathing, walking, and talking *Schoolboy*, and with the loving encouragement and deft editorial eye of my brilliant and beautiful wife, Beth, we had a book. What then? I knew finding a literary agent was a long shot for an unknown writer like me. Anyone who has ventured into that email abyss knows the odds.

Well, along came Henry Thayer of Brandt & Hochman, one of America's most venerable literary agencies, who shot back a quick "I love this project!" Henry and I spoke by phone; he read the entire manuscript, advised me how to improve my proposal, did whatever it is he does, and led me directly to Rob Taylor of University of Nebraska Press. Do you think Chris Hoyt was thrilled? It was a dream come true for us both. Rob, Courtney Ochsner, Haley Mendlik, Rosemary Sekora, and Sarah Kee are a championship team. Joseph Webb is a master of checking facts, clarifying thoughts, and applying the rules.

Several others helped along the way. Jeff McElnea, a former client and longtime friend, introduced me to best-selling baseball-book author David Fisher, who gave me invaluable advice on my pitch to agents.

David, in turn, introduced me to Yankees historian and author Marty Appel, who also helped sharpen my book proposal.

Sarah Staples and Arabeth Balasko of the Cincinnati Historical Society, along with Rachel Wells, Cassidy Lent, and Rachel Jacobe of the National Baseball Hall of Fame, arranged for access to files Waite had donated to them. Nancy Swift contributed her uncanny ability to decipher Waite's sometimes inscrutable handwriting; Spencer Manners added his astute baseball and storytelling insights; and Holly and Alex Reustle celebrated every step of this remarkable journey with me.

David B. Jacobs and Don Schneider helped me reach the unreachable. Louise Akillian, Carol Schneider, Anita Marshall, Jon Manners, Connie Halpern, Jane Manners, Peter F. Eder, Al Wittemen, Ed Dzubak, Sharon Epstein, Alison Bricken, Keith Stein, Brett Aronow, Elspeth Roake, Jaki and Brian Suter, Jan and John Corey, and Sharon and Leigh Behar bestowed their unconditional enthusiasm. I am also indebted to Michael Chait for enshrining me in my own private Cooperstown and to Julie Manners and Jeff Seaver for donating their artistic intelligence, both artificial and natural.

My parents, Ruth Ann and David, were authors both, and their DNA is evident in everything I write, edit, or imagine.

How do I begin to thank the man, himself, Waite Charles Hoyt? I can't, really, and never could have. He passed away a few months before I met Chris, although now I certainly feel like I knew him. One of my biggest kicks was how much Waite and Chris spoke alike.

I can only say that, ever since my uncle William Manners authored *TR & Will: The Friendship That Split the Republican Party* in 1969, it's been my goal to publish a biography of some sort. I was well past the point where I could reasonably hope this would happen when eight boxes of paper landed on my front porch.

Thanks, Schoolboy.